Bringing the Common Core Math Standards to Life

As high school math teachers shift to the Common Core State Standards, the question remains: What do the standards actually look like in the classroom? This book answers that question by taking you inside of real Common Core classrooms across the country. You'll see how exemplary teachers are meeting the new requirements and engaging students in math. Through these detailed examples of effective instruction, you will uncover how to bring the standards to life in your own classroom!

Special features:

◆ A clear explanation of the big shifts happening in the classroom as a result of the Common Core State Standards
◆ Real examples of how exemplary teachers are using engaging strategies and tasks to teach algebra, geometry, trigonometry, statistics, mathematics across the curriculum, and more
◆ A detailed analysis of each example to help you understand why it is effective and how you can try it with your own students
◆ Practical, ready-to-use tools you can take back to your classroom, including unit plans and classroom handouts

Yvelyne Germain-McCarthy is Professor Emerita of mathematics education at the University of New Orleans. She is a frequent speaker at conferences and a consultant to school districts.

Ivan P. Gill is Associate Professor and Science Education Coordinator at the University of New Orleans, where he has taught elementary and secondary science methods courses.

T0274934

Bringing the Common Core Math Standards to Life

Exemplary Practices from High Schools

Yvelyne Germain-McCarthy and Ivan P. Gill

Routledge
Taylor & Francis Group

NEW YORK AND LONDON

Second edition published 2015
by Routledge
711 Third Avenue, New York, NY 10017

and by Routledge
2 Park Square, Milton Park, Abingdon, Oxon OX14 4RN

Routledge is an imprint of the Taylor & Francis Group, an informa business

First edition published by Eye On Education (as *Bringing the NCTM Standards to Life: Exemplary Practices for High Schools*) 2001

Library of Congress Cataloging-in-Publication Data

Germain-McCarthy, Yvelyne, 1948– author.
Bringing the common core math standards to life : exemplary practices
  from high schools / Yvelyne Germain-McCarthy and Ivan Gill.
    pages cm
  1. Mathematics—Study and teaching (Secondary)—Standards—Evaluation.
I. Gill, Ivan, author.   II. Title.
  Q181.G36 2015
  510.71'273—dc23
  2014015068

ISBN: 978-0-415-73474-5 (hbk)
ISBN: 978-0-415-73342-7 (pbk)
ISBN: 978-1-315-81976-1 (ebk)

Typeset in Palatino
by Apex CoVantage, LLC

Contents

Acknowledgments

The authors would like to express sincere appreciation to the teachers profiled in this book for their hard work and for their commitment to improving the teaching and learning of our children. In particular, we wish to thank them for sharing their ideas and for responding to our many communications. We also wish to express gratitude to the countless teachers, too numerous to mention by name, with whom we have worked, for sharing their passion for learning, their expertise in teaching, and their belief in their students' success.

Yvelyne acknowledges Robert Sickles and Lauren Davis for suggestions that sparked improvements in this second edition of the book. She also wants to thank Kerry Davidson, Bryan Jones, and Noreen Lackett for their expert leadership of the Louisiana State Systemic Initiative Program; codirecting grants from this program have challenged her to grow in the areas of developing effective professional development experiences for teachers. She also thanks Craig Jensen, Dongming Wei, Kenneth Holladay, Ivan Gill, and Norma Felton, who worked with her on the grants and helped to form the University of New Orleans Mathematics and Science Collaborative for Teaching and Learning, which sparked collaborative enterprises between local schools and the mathematics and education departments.

She extends special appreciation to her family: her loving Heavenly Father; her parents, Georges and Eugenie Germain; her brothers, Gerard, Serge, and Claude Germain; her nieces, Georgine and Hermiaune Germain; her sister-in-law, Sara Germain, her nephew, Claude Germain; and friend, Lina Botavara for providing a wonderful retreat away from home when deadlines were approaching. Most important, she expresses loving gratitude to her husband, Henry McCarthy; her sons, Julian and Germain McCarthy; and her nephew, Carlos Germain, for their love, patience, and unfailing support.

Ivan gratefully acknowledges his friends, family, and colleagues who have supported this effort and taken the load off other aspects of his work, most especially his wife, Jeanette, as well as Pat Austin and Abram Himelstein. His friend and dog Moose provided expert commentary.

Finally, we wish to dedicate this book to children in impoverished sections of the world where freedom or the means to participate in the types of learning environments described in this book are but a dream. We donate the proceeds from this book to promoting the best education available to children from Rivière Froide, a small town in Yvelyne's homeland, Haiti.

Foreword

Bringing the Common Core Math Standards to Life: Exemplary Practices from High Schools has an important and relevant message for the mathematics education community. The initial overview of reform efforts in mathematics education is a valuable resource, with descriptions of central features of major documents since 1989 and how these are connected. These documents include not only policy documents such as standards but also summaries of classroom practices that research suggests may hold promise for enhancing the learning experience for all students. The discussion can help educators understand the impact of these documents on teaching and learning mathematics and provides a foundation for thinking about the evolving landscape of education reform. An important perspective that permeates the text emphasizes the shift over the years from mastering procedures to developing understanding of mathematical concepts and connections. Of particular importance is the attention paid to the distinction between classroom practices that on the surface seem to be reform based but that, in fact, pertain to the letter but not the spirit of the changes suggested by the research and in the reform documents. With claims from so many sources that particular resources or practices are "Common Core" or "Standards" aligned, teachers and educators need to develop the discriminating lens described in several different situations as they make choices for their own classrooms.

Embedded in this broader context of reform is a focus on teaching and learning high school mathematics, providing a vision and examples of what that vision can look like in classrooms at that level, something often lacking in the literature. The classroom examples span a wide variety of content from functions to statistics and include lesson descriptions, innovative assessment practices, and strategies for organizing and managing class work, giving teachers a comprehensive view of teaching and learning mathematics that has developing understanding at its core. The professional development illustrations add a useful dimension that suggests ways to build the capacity of teachers to reflect on how their teaching can make a difference for students. Collectively, the chapters present a valuable resource for engaging the field in productive and thoughtful discussions about what it means to teach and learn high school mathematics in an era of reform.

Gail Burrill

Mathematics Specialist in the Program in Mathematics
Education at Michigan State University; formerly
President of the National Council of Teachers of
Mathematics (1996–1998) and Director of the
Mathematical Sciences Education Board at the
National Research Council (2000–2001)

About the Authors

 **Yvelyne Germain-McCarthy** is Professor Emerita of mathematics education at the University of New Orleans, where she has directed and taught the elementary and secondary mathematics methods courses for graduate and undergraduate students. She received her B.S. in mathematics and M.Ed. in mathematics education from Brooklyn College. She earned her Ph.D. in mathematics education from Teachers College at Columbia University. She taught high school and middle grades mathematics for 17 years.

As a consultant to schools and school districts, she continues to lead efforts to implement reformed-based instruction in classes of in-service mathematics and science teachers. These have provided many opportunities for her to work with teachers and students to support student learning. She has written books **on best practices for teaching and learning,** is a frequent speaker at professional conferences, and has also written articles for the National Council of Teachers of Mathematics (NCTM) and other professional organizations. One of her articles was selected by NCTM for CD and online reproduction because of its significant contribution to particular areas of mathematics education.

Her work in education and the community has earned her recognition that includes the Brooklyn College School of Education's Dorothy Geddes Mathematics Education Award for dedication and excellence as a teacher of mathematics and teacher educator and the Milton Ferguson Faculty Award from the College of Education and Human Development of the University of New Orleans for her contributions and commitment to education. In 2010, She was one of 50 Woman of the Year Honorees recognized by *New Orleans City Business* for having made notable contributions to both the local business community and society at large.

Her teaching and research interests continue to focus on helping teachers and students develop a solid conceptual understanding of mathematics as well as an appreciation for engaging in a collaborative and reflective process for teaching and learning.

Ivan Gill is Associate Professor and Science Education Coordinator at the University of New Orleans, where he has taught the elementary and secondary science methods courses for graduate and undergraduate students. His master's and bachelor's in geology are from the University of Rochester, with fieldwork at the West Indies Laboratory. He completed his doctoral degree in geology at Louisiana State University on an Alumni Federation Fellowship. He has spent more than 14 years teaching earth science at Tulane University, the University of New Orleans, and the University of Puerto Rico and 6 years teaching high school science in the New Orleans Public Schools.

He has been the co-principal investigator with Yvelyne Germain-McCarthy and others on systemic initiative grants in Louisiana dealing with mathematics- and science-teacher training. He is the author of numerous articles on science education as well as sedimentology and geology. He maintains a strong interest in science teaching and public education, as well as in coral reefs, paleoclimate, geochemistry, and sedimentology.

Preface

This book is a revision of the book *Bringing the NCTM Standards to Life: Exemplary Practices for High Schools*. Because the chapters of the first edition are of teachers implementing the NCTM Standards, they all also reflect best practices for the Common Core State Standards for Mathematics (CCSSM). For this second edition, four chapters were replaced with four new ones to update the content, and other chapters were updated to integrate CCSSM and recent research on the content or pedagogy.

The teacher case studies are descriptions constructed from classroom visits, written statements, interviews, or videos of how the teachers implement standards-based lessons in their classrooms. These profiles of educators across the nation who have gone beyond mere awareness of the CCSSM to conceptualizing and implementing them with students in the high schools are brought to life through classroom scenarios and discussions with each teacher.

Chapter 1 presents overviews of the National Council of Teachers of Mathematics (NCTM) and CCSSM documents and some of the research providing the rationale for their development. Chapter 2 describes key elements of exemplary practices, and chapters 3–13 are profiles of educators who are successfully implementing CCSSM with high school students or classroom teachers. Three of the chapters profile the work of teachers participating in professional development opportunities. Chapter 7 shows how university mathematicians and mathematic/science education professors can engage classroom teachers in challenging tasks to promote appreciation for classroom discourse so that, after reflection, classroom teachers may similarly engage their students. Chapter 10 is a research lesson resulting from teachers participating in the lesson study process and focuses on the important elements that have made lesson study a valued form of professional development in the United States. It also includes the details of its lesson study open house, which is an event to which the community is invited to serve as observers for helping to improve the lesson. Chapter 12 shows strategies teachers apply to transform low-level tasks into high-level engaging tasks to better prepare students for critical thinking and perseverance when solving unfamiliar problems.

In each chapter, there is a Discussion between Colleagues section that clarifies or expands ideas from the profile. A Commentary section highlights the specific standards, issues, or research that informs the strategies used by the teachers. The Unit Overview summarizes key ideas in the form of a lesson plan to help teachers implement or modify the lessons. Resources specific to the content of each chapter are also listed at the end of each chapter's overview. Although the lessons list specific content domains, readers will find that they can be readily modified; ideas for extensions of the curricula will emerge not only because of the richness of the activities but also because the activities flow from concrete to higher-level abstract concepts. Thus, this reform-based approach provides ways to vary the emphasis of the concepts presented by having coherent connections of the content across grade levels.

While the profiles incorporate a number of different content standards, they *all* reflect the NCTM Principles for Equity and Access, Teaching, Curriculum, Learning, Tools and Technology, Assessment, and Professionalism. All profiles demonstrate many classroom applications of the NCTM process standards now embodied in the CCSSM Mathematical Practices. The content in all of the profiles also exemplifies the three major shifts in the CCSSM in that they *focus* on the important CCSSM content; they are *coherent* in making connections to other grade levels and in linking to major topics within grades; they are *rigorous* in requiring a balance of conceptual understanding, procedural skill and fluency, and application of skills in solving problems that include real-world situations.

This Book's Purpose

The audience for this book is anyone interested in gaining insight into how the reform movement in mathematics, as advocated by NCTM and CCSSM, is being implemented by teachers in the United States. Classroom teachers, teacher educators, and mathematicians will find the book useful for its examples of reformed-based strategies that pose challenges for classroom teachers as they strive to teach more rigorous content and apply alternative means of assessments. For administrators in schools and districts, it will help bring to the forefront the quality of professional development support teachers need to implement the CCSSM. Professional development leaders can use the case studies as tools to guide their participants' discussion on the shifts important for implementing the CCSSM through questions such as: "In this chapter, which questions or activities would you keep, delete or change? Why? What classroom evidence or research support your decisions?" Parents and other members of the community will find the profiles of interest in helping them understand and appreciate the differences between traditional and standards-based teaching as well as the structures that need to be in place to get all students prepared for the demands of the twenty-first century.

The profiles will give all readers ideas on how to implement CCSSM as well as an opportunity to learn strategies for presenting or using a mathematical concept or tool. The companion book, *Bringing the Common Core State Standards to Life: Exemplary Practices from Middle Schools*, provides similar insights.

Table 0.1 summarizes the CCSSM content, mathematical practices, and NCTM principles addressed in each profile. A specific practice or principle is listed for those profiles that have such a focus.

TABLE 0.1 Principles, Standards, and Practices in the Profiles

Chapter: Teacher(s)	NCTM Principles	Content	CCSSM Math Practices
3: Michael Lehman	Equity Assessment	Algebra, Algebra 2	Problem Solving: SMP1–3 Model with Math Use of Tools Attend to Precision
4: Mark Lonergan	Equity Professionalism	Geometry	Problem Solving: SMP1–3 Model with Math Use of Tools Attend to Precision Look for Structure
5: Henry Kranendonk	Curriculum	Statistics	Problem Solving: SMP1–3 Model with Math Use of Tools Attend to Precision
6: Virginia Highstone	Technology	Algebra 2	Problem Solving Reasoning Model with Math Look for Structure
7: Craig Jensen	Teaching	Algebra 2	Problem Solving: SMP1–3 Model with Math Use of Tools Attend to Precision Look for Structure
8: Ben Preddy	Equity Professionalism	Algebra, Geometry	Problem Solving: SMP1–3 Model with Math Use of Tools Attend to Precision
9: Murray Siegel	Technology	Statistics	Problem Solving: SMP1–3 Model with Math Use of Tools Repeated Reasoning
10: Susan Morere & Lesson Study Team	Learning Professionalism	Algebra 2, Trigonometry	Problem Solving Reasoning Representation Use of Tools Model with Math Attend to Precision
11: Claudia Carter	Professionalism Technology	Algebra 2, Precalculus, Calculus	Problem Solving Reasoning Model with Math Attend to Precision
12: Adapted Tasks	Teaching	Algebra, Algebra 2, Geometry	Problem Solving Reasoning Model with Math Attend to Precision Representation
13: Don Crossfield	Learning	Algebra/Algebra 2/Trigonometry, Precalculus	Problem Solving: SMP1–3 Model with Math Attend to Precision Look for Structure Repeated Reasoning

1

Trends and Issues Leading to the Common Core State Standards

In April 2000, NCTM unveiled a political document, Principles and Standards for School Mathematics. . . . Most in attendance came to hear about the mathematics content and professional development updates of Curriculum and Evaluation Standards for School Mathematics, released in 1989. Few regarded Principles and Standards for School Mathematics as a political statement about school mathematics and school change. Few recognized the need for NCTM to deepen its political initiatives to better promote the ideals of the Standards.

The original 1989 Standards document was a political document. It talked about the content of mathematics, the pedagogy of mathematics classrooms, and the evaluation of mathematics curricula. The Standards suggested ways to improve the status of countless underserved students and changed the status quo in all classrooms across the United States and Canada. Because of this Standards document, we continue to question what we believe about ourselves and about others. It has forced us to make educational and political decisions about what we are willing to do to turn the vision of a high quality mathematics education for every child into a practical set of behaviors. It has reached far beyond the schools into the universities, industry and business, and political institutions.

Lee V. Stiff, Past President, National Council of Teachers of
Mathematics (2001)

In this quote from the "President's Message" column of the December 2001 *News Bulletin* of NCTM, Stiff summarized the major thrust of NCTM's reform efforts. As he predicted, the *NCTM Standards* continues to impact education decision makers, and its political influence has now extended to recommendations for the statewide adoption of its basic tenets. In her final NCTM President's Message, Linda Gojak summarizes what has happened since the 1989 *Standards*:

> Twenty-five years ago NCTM released *Curriculum and Evaluation Standards for Teaching Mathematics*, which presented a comprehensive vision for mathematics teaching, learning, and assessment in grades K–12. Other significant publications, including *Principles and Standards for School Mathematics* and the Common Core State Standards for Mathematics continue to identify what we believe students should know and be able to do throughout their school mathematics experience.
>
> (Gojak, 2014)

The Common Core State Standards for Mathematics (CCSSM) can be considered an updated version of the *NCTM Standards* that has very strong political support since CCSSM is a state-led effort. A review of the major standards documents produced or motivated by NCTM will support an understanding of the CCSSM.

Curriculum and Evaluation Standards

In 1989, NCTM's *Curriculum and Evaluation Standards for School Mathematics* recommended that we teach and assess students in very nontraditional ways. It called for less attention to procedural manipulation without understanding and a greater focus on conceptual understanding and connecting mathematics across its content areas and to other disciplines. Noting that mathematics education needs to continually address societal needs, it also included recommendations to add certain topics such as probability, statistics, and technology when appropriate.

Professional Standards for Teaching Mathematics

In addition to the shift in curriculum, NCTM recommends three other major shifts in learning, teaching, and assessment. In learning, the shift supports actively involving students in problems that are authentic and giving students access to a variety of mathematical tools to support mathematical reasoning. In teaching, the shift supports a variety of approaches to reach all students. In assessment practices, the shift supports integrating teaching with multiple types of assessments.

What are some strategies for preparing teachers to reach all students? NCTM's *Professional Standards for Teaching Mathematics* document (1991) suggests principles for the professional development of mathematics teachers and for the evaluation of mathematics teaching. It also provides guidelines for helping teachers create a rich mathematical environment in which all students are engaged in the challenging mathematics to make them *mathematically powerful*. Students with such power can demonstrate application of the standards by their ability to explore, conjecture, reason logically, and successfully apply a number of different strategies to solve non-routine problems. These standards are now updated in the NCTM document *Principles to Actions: Ensuring Mathematical Success for All* (2014), hereafter called *Principles to Actions*.

Assessing students' acquisition of these skills requires tools that must extend beyond the traditional paper-and-pencil tests to include alternative means of assessments. These are highlighted in the NCTM *Assessment Standards*.

The Assessment Standards

The *Assessment Standards* document (1991) addresses the principles educators should use to build assessments that support the development of mathematical power for all students. It recommends that teachers derive information from multiple sources during instruction and that, in addition to pencil-and-paper tests, evidence to support student learning be collected from sources that include close observation, one-on-one discussions, projects, homework, and classroom discourse. A key difference between the *NCTM Standards* and traditional methods is the use of assessment tools as a process for stimulating growth and interest in mathematics rather than as a way for separating and ranking students. Assessment recommendations are updated in NCTM's *Principles to Actions* (2014).

Recognizing that information is changing and increasing at a rapid pace, the writing group for the *Curriculum Standards* wisely planned to revisit and revise the *Curriculum Standards* in the future. NCTM past president Gail Burrill posed the following questions to illustrate the need for a future edition.

> Do history textbooks stop at the end of World War I? How does a map of Africa today compare to one from 20 years ago? What happened to science textbooks when DNA was discovered? Mathematics is no different—changes around us make changes in how we think about mathematics. Changes in what we know about how students learn affect the way we think about teaching.
>
> (Burrill, 1996, 3)

To alleviate concerns about yet another set of major changes, Burrill clarified that the *Principles and Standards for School Mathematics* will build on and extend the foundations of the original standards publications. If we substitute CCSSM for the *Curriculum Standards*, we find words of wisdom in her statement below for the implementation of the CCSSM today:

> Teachers should continue aligning teaching with the *Curriculum Standards*, and should also: Think seriously about the meaning of the present standards and their implications for your classroom. Developing an understanding of what the *Curriculum Standards* are about is a continuous process whose growth should be consonant with the *Curriculum Standards*, both old and new.
>
> (Burrill, 1996, 3)

The Third International Mathematics and Science Study

Ironically, the results of international tests that included Third International Mathematics and Science Study (TIMSS) showed that, while Japanese teaching and learning methods adhered to NCTM recommendations, they were not prevalent in the United States. In 1995, TIMSS gathered data on a half-million students from 41 countries, focusing on student achievement, curricula, and teaching. The fact that Japan's students scored highest while U.S. students scored below the international average motivated a huge call to look carefully at the U.S. education system to determine where improvements could be implemented. In the report *A Splintered Vision* (Schmidt, McKnight, and Raizen, 1996), an examination of the curriculum and teacher data of TIMSS revealed that the U.S. curriculum was redundant and less challenging than those of many other countries. This report was a major catalyst for generating interest in developing a coherent and *national* vision on curriculum.

Soon after the TIMSS report, the National Research Council published the book, *Adding It Up: Helping Children Learn Mathematics* (2001), which included recommendations supporting NCTM's recommendations for improving teaching, curricula, and teacher education for grades Pre-K–8. The Council identified five interdependent components of mathematical proficiency:

1. *Conceptual understanding* refers to the "integrated and functional grasp of mathematical ideas," which "enables them [students] to learn new ideas by connecting those ideas to what they already know."
2. *Procedural fluency* is defined as the skill in carrying out procedures flexibly, accurately, efficiently, and appropriately.
3. *Strategic competence* is the ability to formulate, represent, and solve mathematical problems.
4. *Adaptive reasoning* is the capacity for logical thought, reflection, explanation, and justification.
5. *Productive disposition* is the inclination to see mathematics as sensible, useful, and worthwhile, coupled with a belief in diligence and one's own efficacy.

(NRC, 2001, 116)

Although much has been written about the content results, it is important to note that TIMSS 1999 also videotaped classrooms. The videos show seventh- and eighth-grade math and science lessons in Australia, the Czech Republic, Hong Kong SAR, Japan, the Netherlands, Switzerland, and the United States. Each lesson includes transcripts, comments, and reflection by the teacher. The analysis of the videotapes of eighth-grade mathematics teaching in typical classrooms of the six countries show that while 54 percent of the mathematics lessons in Japanese classrooms challenged students to work on nonroutine problems, 0 to 52 percent in the U.S. eighth-grade mathematics lessons did so (Hiebert, Gallimore, et al., 2003). These videos can be viewed at http://timssvideo.com/videos/Mathematics.

Trends in International Mathematics and Science Study

TIMSS, administered every four years, is now called *Trends in International Mathematics and Science Study*. It continues to compare the mathematics and science knowledge and skills of fourth- and eighth-graders, and its reports have the goal of helping countries make informed decisions about how to improve teaching and learning in mathematics. The reports include trends in mathematics achievement over time for participants in previous TIMSS assessments in 1995, 1999, 2003, and 2007, as well as student performance at the TIMSS International Benchmarks.

Since TIMSS 1999, U.S. students have exceeded the international average. TIMSS 2011 had 63 participating countries and 14 regional benchmarking jurisdictions. While the United States exceeded the international average, a *significant* margin existed only in fourth-grade math. In addition, U.S. students are still lagging behind the Asian countries (Mullis, Martin, et al., 2012).

Program for International Student Assessment

Beginning in 2000 and every three years thereafter, an international assessment of 15-year-old students called the Program for International Student Assessment (PISA) has been administered by the Organization for Economic Cooperation and Development. The information that follows is a highlight of the PISA data reported by Kelly, Xie, et al. (2013). PISA defines and assesses mathematics literacy as,

> An individual's capacity to formulate, employ, and interpret mathematics in a variety of contexts. It includes reasoning mathematically and using mathematical concepts, procedures, facts, and tools to describe, explain, and predict phenomena. It assists individuals to recognize the role that mathematics plays in the world and to make the well-founded judgments and decisions needed by constructive, engaged, and reflective citizens.
>
> (Kelly, Xie, et al., 2013, 1)

Like NCTM's *Reasoning and Sense Making* document (NCTM, 2009), PISA places a focus on major mathematical content and process categories. The mathematical process categories are:

> *Formulate:* Can 15-year-olds recognize and identify opportunities to use mathematics and then provide mathematical structure to a problem presented in some contextualized form in order to formulate situations mathematically?
>
> *Employ:* Are students able to employ mathematical concepts, facts, procedures, and reasoning to solve mathematically formulated problems and obtain mathematical conclusions?
>
> *Interpret:* Can students interpret, apply, and evaluate mathematical outcomes in order to determine whether results are reasonable and make sense in the context of the problem?
>
> (Kelly, Xie, et al., 2013, 2)

The content categories are:

Change and relationship: Can students model change and relationships with the appropriate functions and equations?

Space and shape: Can students understand perspective, create and read maps, and manipulate 3D objects?

Quantity: Are 15-year-olds able to comprehend multiple representations of numbers, engage in mental calculation, employ estimation, and assess the reasonableness of results?

Uncertainty and data: Can students use probability and statistics and other techniques of data representation and description to mathematically describe, model, and interpret uncertainty?

(Kelly, Xie, et al., 2013, 2)

Kelly, Xie, et al. (2013) show the PISA rubric applied to categorize the proficiency levels of mathematics literacy, which are reported in terms of proficiency levels and a scale score from 0–1,000 (see Table 1.1).

In PISA 2012, there were 65 participating education systems that included the U.S. states Connecticut, Florida, and Massachusetts. The scores in mathematics literacy from Kelly, Xie, et al. (2013) show:

* The U.S. score of 9% was below the OECD average of 13% for top-performing 15-year-old students. *Top performing* is defined as those students scoring at Level 5 or above in mathematics literacy (55% in Shanghai-China). Top-performing students averaged 16% in Connecticut, 6% in Florida and 19% in Massachusetts.

(9)

* The U.S. had 26% of 15-year-old students scoring below the baseline proficiency of Level 2. This score was higher than the OECD average of 23% (4% in Shanghai-China). Low performers (Level 2 or lower) averaged 21% in Connecticut, 30% in Florida, and 18% Massachusetts.

(Kelly, Xie, et al., 2013, 9)

* The U.S. score in mathematics literacy was lower than the OECD average of 494 (613 in Shanghai-China). The mathematics literacy average for Florida was 467, but Connecticut scored higher than the OECD average (506), as did Massachusetts with its score of 514.

(Kelly, Xie, et al., 2013, 9)

The PISA 2012 report on the U.S. students' poor performance on nonroutine tasks requiring high cognitive demands states, "An alignment study between the Common Core State Standards for Mathematics and PISA suggests that a successful

TABLE 1.1 2012 Description of PISA Proficiency Levels on Mathematics Literacy Scale

Proficiency level and lower cut score	Task descriptions
Level 6 669	At level 6, students can conceptualize, generalize, and utilize information based on their investigations and modeling of complex problem situations, and can use their knowledge in relatively non-standard contexts. They can link different information sources and representations and flexibly translate among them. Students at this level are capable of advanced mathematical thinking and reasoning. These students can apply this insight and understanding, along with a mastery of symbolic and formal mathematical operations and relationships, to develop new approaches and strategies for attacking novel situations. Students at this level can reflect on their actions, and can formulate and precisely communicate their actions and reflections regarding their findings, interpretations, arguments and the appropriateness of these to the original situations.
Level 5 607	At level 5, students can develop and work with models for complex situations, identifying constraints and specifying assumptions. They can select, compare, and evaluate appropriate problem-solving strategies for dealing with complex problems related to these models. Students at this level can work strategically using broad, well-developed thinking and reasoning skills, appropriate linked representations, symbolic and formal characterizations, and insight pertaining to these situations. They begin to reflect on their work and can formulate and communicate their interpretations and reasoning.
Level 4 545	At level 4, students can work effectively with explicit models for complex concrete situations that may involve constraints or call for making assumptions. They can select and integrate different representations, including symbolic, linking them directly to aspects of real-world situations. Students at this level can utilize their limited range of skills and can reason with some insight, in straightforward contexts. They can construct and communicate explanations and arguments based on their interpretations, arguments, and actions.
Level 3 482	At level 3, students can execute clearly described procedures, including those that require sequential decisions. Their interpretations are sufficiently sound to be a base for building a simple model or for selecting and applying simple problem-solving strategies. Students at this level can interpret and use representations based on different information sources and reason directly from them. They typically show some ability to handle percentages, fractions and decimal numbers, and to work with proportional relationships. Their solutions reflect that they have engaged in basic interpretation and reasoning.
Level 2 420	At level 2, students can interpret and recognize situations in contexts that require no more than direct inference. They can extract relevant information from a single source and make use of a single representational mode. Students at this level can employ basic algorithms, formulae, procedures, or conventions to solve problems involving whole numbers. They are capable of making literal interpretations of the results.
Level 1 358	At level 1, students can answer questions involving familiar contexts where all relevant information is present and the questions are clearly defined. They are able to identify information and to carry out routine procedures according to direct instructions in explicit situations. They can perform actions that are almost always obvious and follow immediately from the given stimuli.

Source: Retrieved March 20, 2014, from nces.ed.gov/surveys/pisa/pisa2012/pisa2012highlights_2a.asp

implementation of the Common Core Standards would yield significant performance gains also in PISA" (Kelly, Xie, et al., 2013, 1).

Constructivism

Because constructivism is applied or experienced in an environment where learners are trying to make sense of a problematic situation by constructing their own knowledge about the world around them, it is a framework for the CCSSM. Jean Piaget (1973) wrote:

> To understand is to discover . . . a student who achieves a certain knowledge through free investigation and spontaneous effort will later be able to retain it: he will have acquired a methodology that can serve him for the rest of his life, which will stimulate his curiosity without the risk of exhausting it. At the very least, instead of his having his memory take priority over his reasoning power . . . he will learn to make his reason function by himself and will build his ideas freely. . . . The goal of intellectual education is not to know how to repeat or retain ready-made truths. It is in learning to master the truth by oneself at the risk of losing a lot of time and of going through all the roundabout ways that are inherent in real activity.
>
> (106)

Thus, learning is not simply the acquisition of information and skills; it also includes the acquisition of a deep understanding. This requires time but enables the learner to better construct meaning from a problem. Learning occurs when a novel situation contradicts the learner's beliefs and therefore requires new constructs to make sense of and interpret the situation (Confrey, 1990).

Simon (1995) notes that constructivism does not define a specific way to teach mathematics. Rather, it "describes knowledge development whether or not there is a teacher present or teaching is going on" (117). Attention to the misconceptions of students provides teachers with a rich source of information that allows them to detect and understand the areas in which students need guidance. The teacher's task is to help students learn to find tools that are useful for solving problems—problems that students have identified from their own work should be included.

Some constructivists view the small-group process—by which students work together on mathematical tasks that require a high level of communication about a problem —a critical component to the development of conceptual understanding. Social interaction as an essential factor in a learner's organization of experiences underlies the theory of social constructivism. According to Vygotsky (1978), "Any function in the child's cultural development appears twice on two planes. First it appears on the social plane, and then on the psychological plane" (57).

Thus, the constructivist approach begins with what the student already believes regarding a particular idea: student attempts to verify these ideas, which then serves as a catalyst for the learning process.

Skills for Citizens of the Twenty-first Century

Rather than a classroom based on constructivist application of teaching and learning, some teachers still practice a traditional approach based on giving students the rules to memorize, without understanding why the rules make sense. This is contrary to brain-based researchers who view the mind's design as that of a "pattern detector." Learners continually search for meaning by creating patterns.

Lectures or rote memorization produce a type of learning that is classified as surface knowledge. Although this is important, success in the twenty-first century will require *meaningful knowledge,* or knowledge that makes sense to the learner. Hiebert's (2003) research shows that making connections between previous knowledge and new learning facilitates a student's understanding and retention of new material. Thus, teaching that strives to maximize the way that the brain processes information not only enhances and increases the likelihood of meaningful knowledge but also helps citizens develop the attributes they need to thrive in the twenty-first century.

Productive Struggle

NCTM has advocated changes toward a more focused, rigorous curriculum as well as an integrated approach to teaching and assessment practices for helping students develop the understanding and ways of thinking necessary to address the challenges of the twenty-first century. These ways are reflected in what Dewey (1929) calls a "disciplined mind":

> A disciplined mind takes delight in the problematic . . . The scientific attitude may almost be defined as that which is capable of enjoying the doubtful.
>
> (228)

Many students who shy away from a problem with no quick solution soon become frustrated and abandon problems for which they have no clear method of approach. They therefore stop learning. According to Wheatley (1991):

> If you look at any of the work on creativity and learning, or if you look at your own creative process, it is not a nice orderly step-by-step process that moves you towards a great idea. You get incredibly frustrated, you feel you'll never solve it, you walk away from it, and then Eureka!—an idea comes forth. You can't get truly transforming ideas anywhere in life unless you walk through that period of chaos.
>
> (3)

Duckworth, in her National Public Radio interview with Smith (2014), used the word "grit" in this context and defined it as "This quality of being able to sustain your passions, and also work really hard at them, over really disappointingly long periods of time." It is likely that students who are not encouraged to pursue experiences that require grit will have little desire to continue the study of mathematics and may be incorrectly perceived by some parents or teachers as not having a "math brain." Grit is what the mathematics community refers to as "productive struggle." Hiebert and Grouws (2007) define it as students exerting effort

> . . . to make sense of mathematics, to figure something out that is not immediately apparent. We do not use struggle to mean needless frustration or extreme levels of challenge created by nonsensical or overly difficult problems. We do not mean the feelings of despair that some students can experience when little of the material makes sense. The struggle we have in mind comes from solving problems that are within reach and grappling with key mathematical ideas that are comprehendible but not yet well formed.
>
> (387)

The focus of the productive struggle is on the *process of thinking* and is therefore an overarching habit of mind that students need to practice and attain in order to be successful. Cuoco, Goldenberg, and Mark (2010) describe the qualities of tasks that can engage students in this process. Such tasks:

◆ Promote sound and significant mathematical content;
◆ Reflect students' understandings, interests, and experiences;
◆ Support the range of ways that diverse students learn mathematics;
◆ Engage students' intellect by requiring reasoning and problem solving;
◆ Help students build connections; and
◆ Promote communication.

(102)

Principles and Standards for School Mathematics

In 2000, NCTM integrated and updated its recommendations about curriculum, teaching, and assessment into one document, called the *Principles and Standards For School Mathematics (Principles and Standards)*. *Principles and Standards* consists of 6 principles, 5 processes, and 10 standards that describe characteristics of quality instructional programs and goals for students' mathematical knowledge. Together they form the basis for developing effective mathematics instruction within four grade-band chapters: Prekindergarten through grade 2, grades 3–5, grades 6–8, and grades 9–12.

At the high school level, "All students are expected to study mathematics each of the four years that they are enrolled in high school, whether they plan to pursue the further study of mathematics, to enter the work force, or to pursue other postsecondary education" (288). The principles are updated in NCTM's *Principles to Actions* (2014) and are discussed at the end of this chapter.

NCTM'S Quest for a Coherent Curriculum

Curriculum Focal Points

In response to the TIMSS (1999) report that the U.S. curriculum is unfocused and covers too many topics, NCTM released *Curriculum Focal Points for Prekindergarten through Grade 8 Mathematics: A Quest for Coherence* to identify the most important mathematical topics for each grade level pre-K–8 to guide the development of mathematics curriculum and instruction (NCTM, 2006, henceforth called *Focal Points*). *Focal Points* specifies the mathematical content that a student needs to not just know but also understand deeply, guided by the principles and processes described by *Principles and Standards*. At each grade level for pre-K–8, it clusters the most important concepts and skills and adds a focus on reasoning and skill to arithmetic, geometry, and algebra, which are foundations for the further study of math and science. To clarify that a balance between skill and concept is necessary, the need for good understanding of basic facts is stated explicitly.

Focus in High School Mathematics

For high schools, NCTM published the book *Focus in High School Mathematics: Reasoning and Sense Making* (2009). It describes and provides models of the type of reasoning processes that cut across the high school curriculum and should be expected of our high school students. *Reasoning* is defined as "the process of drawing conclusions on the basis of evidence or stated assumptions," and *sense making* is "developing understanding of a situation, context, or concept by connecting it with existing knowledge" (4). Each process or *reasoning habit* is a "productive way of thinking that becomes common in the processes of mathematical inquiry and sense making" (9). Thus they should not be taught as isolated skills but should instead be applied daily across all grade levels, especially in the high schools. The following broad list of reasoning habits illustrates the types of thinking that should become routine:

- ◆ Analyzing a problem
- ◆ Implementing a strategy
- ◆ Seeking and using connections
- ◆ Reflecting on a solution.

(9–10)

The Common Core State Standards

The *Common Core State Standards* (CCSS) for mathematics and English language arts arose from state-led efforts to better prepare U.S. students for college and career. The CCSS is an attempt at defining the knowledge and skills students should have within their K–12 education no matter where they live in the United States. The Council of Chief State School Officers (CCSSO) and the National Governor's Association Center formed several working groups to ensure that input was received from teachers, parents, administrators, community organizers, and national education experts. These groups attempted to make the standards clear and realistic, while building upon the strengths and lessons of current state standards as well as the standards of top-performing nations.

Through a CCSS initiative, adopting states and territories collaborate to create and share tools for common assessments, curricula, and instructional materials. Thus, the role of local education leaders is to decide how the standards are to be implemented and to make decisions about the curriculum. Because this is a state-led initiative, the federal government is not involved in the development of the standards.

The Common Core State Standards for Mathematics (CCSSM)

Just before the release of the *Principles and Standards,* past president Gail Burrill, feeling the need to alleviate concerns about yet another set of major changes, clarified that the *Principles and Standards* would build on and extend the foundations of the original *Curriculum Standards* publications. Thus, teachers should continue aligning teaching with the *Curriculum Standards* and should also "think seriously about the meaning of the present standards and their implications for your classroom. Developing an understanding of what the *Curriculum Standards* are about is a continuous process consonant with the *Curriculum Standards,* both old and new" (Burrill, 1996, 3).

We need to heed those thoughts today as we implement the CCSSM. Those teachers proficient in applying the *Principles and Standards* are already teaching to the CCSSM and should continue doing so as they integrate the updates. Other teachers should be mindful that CCSSM sets forth rigorous and critical standards for teaching and assessing competencies. It consists of the *content standards* that delineate which content areas are to be taught and the *mathematical practices* that suggest the "how" to teach the content.

Content Standards

The K–8 standards are organized within six domains that define what students should know and be able to do at each grade level. The domains are groups of the following related standards: ratios and proportional relationships, the number system, expressions and equations, functions, geometry, and statistics and probability. As Table 1.2 shows, the standards overlap within and across grade levels because of the connections existing within mathematics itself. In high school, the domains *algebra, functions, geometry,* and *statistics* overlap through an emphasis on modeling taught by means of the Standards for Mathematical Practice.

TABLE 1.2 CCSSM Content Overlap across Grade Levels

GRADES		
6	**7**	**8**
Ratio and Proportional Relationships		Functions
Expressions and Equations		
The Number System		
Geometry		
Statistics and Probability		

Instructional Shifts

Three major shifts from traditional teaching to the CCSSM are:

◆ A greater *focus* to help students learn the important mathematics and engage in discussions; that reflect the mathematical practices;
◆ *Coherence* to make connections within and across grade levels so that math is viewed as a discipline where connections at one level provide deeper understanding for another;
◆ *Rigor* in major topics to provide for a balance between concept understanding, procedural skills and fluency, and application.

Table 1.3 shows the fluency expectations for grades K–8 summarized by the Tennessee Department of Education (2013). While the high school standards for mathematics do not list fluencies, the PARCC Model Content Frameworks for Mathematics

TABLE 1.3 Fluency Recommendations: K–8

Grade	Required Fluency
K	Add/subtract within 5
1	Add/subtract within 10
2	Add/subtract within 20, add/subtract within 100 (pencil and paper)
3	Multiply/divide within 100, add/subtract within 1,000
4	Add/subtract within 1,000,000
5	Multi-digit multiplication
6	Multi-digit division, multi-digit decimal operations
7	Solve $px + q = r$, $p(x + q) = r$
8	Solve one-variable linear equations, problems involving volumes of cones, cylinders, and spheres, 2x2 systems of equations

Fluency Recommendations: High School

Course	Standard	Recommended Fluency
Algebra 1	A/G	Solving characteristic problems involving the analytic geometry of lines
	A-APR.A.1	Fluency in adding, subtracting, and multiplying polynomials
	A-SSE.A.1b	Fluency in transforming expressions and seeing parts of an expression as a single object
Geometry	G-SRT.B.5	Fluency with the triangle congruence and similarity criteria
	G-GPE.B.4, 5, 7	Fluency with the use of coordinates
	C-CO.D.12	Fluency with the use of construction tools
Algebra 2	A-APR.D.6	Divide polynomials with remainder by inspection in simple cases
	A-SSE.A.2	See structure in expressions and use this structure to rewrite expressions
	F.IF.A.3	Fluency in translating between recursive definitions and closed forms

Source: http://tncore.org/sites/www/Uploads/2.25.13Additions/fluency%20documents%20final.pdf

Grades 3–11 suggest fluencies for Algebra 1, Geometry, and Algebra 2 that are also summarized in Table 1.3.

The Standards for Mathematical Practice

The *Standards for Mathematical Practice* (SMP) describe the attributes of mathematically proficient students and are the same from elementary school through high school. What differs are the tasks used to increase the depth of understanding as students master new and more advanced mathematical ideas. A close look at the SMP shows that they are founded on the NCTM process standards (problem solving, reasoning and proof, communication, representation, and connections) and the strands for mathematical proficiency from the National Research Council's report *Adding It Up* (adaptive reasoning, strategic competence, conceptual understanding, procedural fluency and productive disposition). Following are descriptions for the SMP that include the related NCTM process standards in parentheses. The practices recommend that students be provided tasks that help them to:

1. Make sense of problems and persevere in solving them. (Problem Solving, Reasoning and Proof, Connections, Communication, Representation)

Mathematically proficient students start by explaining to themselves the meaning of a problem and looking for entry points to its solution. They analyze givens, constraints, relationships, and goals. They make conjectures about the form and meaning of the solution and plan a solution pathway rather than simply jumping into a solution attempt. They consider analogous problems and try special cases and simpler forms of the original problem in order to gain insight into its solution. They monitor and evaluate their progress and change course if necessary. —CCSSM

2. Reason abstractly and quantitatively. (Problem Solving, Reasoning and Proof, Connections, Communication)

Mathematically proficient students make sense of quantities and their relationships in problem situations. They bring two complementary abilities to bear on problems involving quantitative relationships:
- ◆ the ability to *decontextualize*—to abstract a given situation and represent it symbolically. In addition, to manipulate the representing symbols as if they have a life of their own, without necessarily attending to their referents;
- ◆ and the ability to *contextualize*—to pause as needed during the manipulation process in order to probe into the referents for the symbols involved.

Quantitative reasoning entails habits of creating a coherent representation of the problem at hand; considering the units involved; attending to the meaning of quantities, not just how to compute them; and knowing and flexibly using different properties of operations and objects. —CCSSM

3. Construct viable arguments and critique the reasoning of others. (Communication; Reasoning and Proof)

Mathematically proficient students . . . justify their conclusions, communicate them to others, and respond to the arguments of others. They . . . distinguish correct logic or reasoning from that which is flawed, and—if there is a flaw in an argument—explain what it is. . . . Elementary students can construct arguments using concrete referents such as objects, drawings, diagrams, and actions. Such arguments can make sense and be correct, even though they are not generalized or made formal until later grades. . . . Students at all grades can listen or read the arguments of others, decide whether they make sense, and ask useful questions to clarify or improve the arguments. —CCSSM

4. Model with mathematics. (Problem solving, Representation, Connections)

Mathematically proficient students can apply the mathematics they know to solve problems arising in everyday life. . . . In early grades, this might be as simple as writing an addition equation to describe a situation. . . . Mathematically proficient students who can apply what they know are comfortable making assumptions and approximations to simplify a complicated situation. . . . They are able to identify important quantities in a practical situation and map their relationships using such tools as diagrams, two-way tables, graphs. . . .They . . . reflect on whether the results make sense. —CCSSM

5. Use appropriate tools strategically. (Problem Solving, Representation)

Mathematically proficient students consider the available tools when solving a mathematical problem. These tools might include pencil and paper, concrete models, a ruler, a protractor, a calculator, a spreadsheet. . . . Proficient students are sufficiently familiar with tools appropriate for their grade or course to make sound decisions about when each of these tools might be helpful, recognizing both the insight to be gained and their limitations. —CCSSM

6. Attend to precision. (Representation, Communication)

Mathematically proficient students try to communicate precisely to others. They try to use clear definitions in discussion with others and in their own reasoning. They state the meaning of the symbols they choose, including using the equal sign consistently and appropriately. They are careful about specifying units of measure and labeling axes to clarify the correspondence with quantities in a problem. They calculate accurately and efficiently. . . . In the elementary grades, students give carefully formulated explanations to each other. —CCSSM

7. Look for and make use of structure. (Connections, Representation)

Mathematically proficient students look closely to discern a pattern or structure. Young students, for example, might notice that three and seven more is the same amount as seven and three more, or they may sort a collection of shapes according to how many sides the shapes have. Later, students will see 7×8 equals the well-remembered $7 \times 5 + 7 \times 3$, in preparation for learning about the distributive property. . . . They also can step back for an overview and shift perspective. They can see complicated things, such as some algebraic expressions as single objects or as being composed of several objects. —CCSSM

8. Look for and express regularity in repeated reasoning. (Connections, Reasoning and Proof)

Mathematically proficient students notice if calculations are repeated and look both for general methods and for shortcuts. Upper elementary students might notice when dividing 25 by 11 that they are repeating the same calculations over and over again and conclude they have a repeating decimal. . . . As they work to solve a problem, mathematically proficient students maintain oversight of the process, while attending to the details. They continually evaluate the reasonableness of their intermediate results. —CCSSM

Mathematical Practices 1–3 and 5 are about students developing the ability to engage in problems that are new to them and for which they have no immediate algorithm. This requires that they have a positive disposition towards mathematics, and are willing to persist toward a solution by trying different strategies or conceptual pathways. Persistent students are willing to engage in challenging tasks because they accept false starts and struggles as a by-product of learning. They also take time to reflect on their process so that they can redirect or justify their thinking. They attend to precision in their computations and in communicating their understanding of the problem in writing and verbally.

Mathematical Practices 4 and 5 for modeling and using tools strategically focus on students' ability to use tools to model situations in the world and mathematics. Students are able to use appropriate tools that include diagrams, tables, graphs, algebraic representations, manipulatives, and estimations. It is important that students also view mathematics as a problem-solving tool for making sense of problems. For students to use tools *strategically* requires that several tools be available and that the students, not the teacher, decide which to use for a given problem. If students have engaged in SMP1–6, they are better able to apply practices 7 and 8. For some students, teachers may need to guide them to the mathematical representations through questions such as:

◆ Can you represent what you wrote in words, mathematically?
◆ Can you rewrite these expression in ways that show how they connect to each other?
◆ You have a two-column table for input and output. Insert a column in between the two to show your calculations. Now, if you input the variable, n, can you represent its output from the calculation in the middle column?

Bill McCallum, one of the lead writers of CCSSM, created a structural diagram to cluster the SMP (see an adaptation in Figure 1.1). It shows how SMP1 and 6 are overarching practices if mathematics is to be taught within a problem-solving framework.

Content standards that set an expectation of *understanding* are areas for integrating the content standards with the SMP—even across content areas. For example, in CCSS English Language Arts, problems can be posed that require students engage in reading or writing logical arguments based on substantive claims, sound reasoning, and relevant evidence. In both areas, if we launch the content with an engaging problem that motivates students to think deeply and we allow them to do so, then we have a situation

Figure. 1.1 Organizational Structure of the CCSSM Mathematical Practices

Overarching habits of mind of a productive mathematical thinker
1. Make sense of problems and persevere in solving them.
6. Attend to precision.

Reasoning and explaining	**Modeling and using tools**	**Seeing structure and generalizing**
2. Reason abstractly and quantitatively. 3. Construct viable arguments and critique the reasoning of others.	4. Model with mathematics. 5. Use appropriate tools strategically.	7. Look for and make use of structure. 8. Look for and express regularity in repeated reasoning.

Adapted from Bill McCallum: http://commoncoretools.me/wp-content/uploads/2011/03/practices.pdf

that meets the conditions for productive struggle, the math shifts, and some, if not all, of the mathematical practices. "The single most important principle for improving the teaching of mathematics is to allow the subject of mathematics to be problematic for students" (Hiebert et al., 1996). Such problems invite students to engage in the productive struggle process. We should note that in order for the problem to be challenging or "problematic" for the student, the student must first be interested in solving it.

Special Student Populations

The question of best practices for teachers to meaningfully engage students with special needs (struggling students, students who perform above grade levels, English-learning students) is addressed in The Council of Chief State School Officers' document *InTASC: Model Core Teaching Standards and Learning Progressions for Teachers 1.0* (CCSSO, 2011, 2013). Its Interstate Teacher Assessment and Support Consortium (InTASC) developed standards of teacher practices grouped into four domains of teaching: (A) The Learner and Learning, (B) Content, (C) Instructional Practice, and (D) Professional Responsibilities. Applicable across grades K–12 to improve student achievement and guided by the collaborative work of practicing teachers, teacher educators, school leaders, state agency officials, and CCSSO, the document states:

Teachers need to recognize that all learners bring to their learning varying experiences, abilities, talents, and prior learning, as well as language, culture, and family and community values that are assets that can be used to promote their learning. To do this effectively, teachers must have a deeper understanding of their own frames of reference (e.g., culture, gender, language, abilities, ways of knowing), the potential biases in these frames, and their impact on expectations for and relationships with learners and their families. Finally, teachers need to provide multiple approaches to learning for each student. One aspect of the power of technology is that it has made learners both more independent and more collaborative.

(4)

Assessment

To achieve student mastery of the skills and concepts, both the practices and content must interact in such a way that the practices guide probing class discourse for the acquisition of the skills and concepts. At the same time, the content is set within an engaging context that is best learned through the practices. Creating state assessments to measure this complex interaction is the work of two state-led consortiums charged with developing a system of valid and reliable CCSS assessments: Smarter Balanced Assessment Consortium (SBAC, www.smarterbalanced.org) and the Partnership for Assessment of Readiness for College and Careers (PARCC, www.parcconline.org).

States adopting the CCSS will administer new tests given on computers rather than on paper, and they will replace the current state assessments. The types of questions targeted for such measures include:

◆ Selected-response items;
◆ Technology-enhanced items to assess a deeper understanding of content and skills;
◆ Constructed-response items; and
◆ Performance tasks.

Sample test items are on the websites already mentioned. To help teachers decide where to place emphasis when teaching the content, PARCC's Model Content Frameworks for Mathematics (2014) designates clusters as *Major*, *Additional*, and *Supporting* for each grade and course:

◆ *Major Clusters* will be a majority of the assessment.
◆ *Supporting Clusters* will be assessed through their success at supporting the Major Clusters.
◆ *Additional Clusters* will be assessed as well.
◆ However, PARCC clarifies that the demarcation should not imply that some content in the standards should be excluded since that will leave students underprepared for the content in later grades, which may cause gaps in students' skills and understanding. Supporting and Additional clusters should therefore not be omitted.

High-Stakes Assessments

Tests whose results are used to make important decisions such as student promotion or teacher retention are called high-stakes tests by Wilson (2007). CCSS assessments that contribute to our understanding of the academic strengths and weaknesses of our students will serve as tools to help states allocate resources for improvements in professional development and student support. However, if the assessments have to be high stakes, then time should be allotted for programs to be put in place to help with the implementation of CCSSM so that teachers and students have the support necessary to succeed. Otherwise, history shows that the negative consequences of the testing contribute to fear and dissention in the communities. What Darling-Hammond (2014) cites as the most important consequence of evaluations that rank and sort teachers is the negative impact it has on teachers collaborating to improve practice. She writes, "Research shows that student gains are most pronounced where teachers have greater longevity and work as a team. . . . At the end of the day, collaborative learning among teachers will do more to support student achievement than dozens of the most elaborate ranking schemes ever could" (5).

NCTM president Linda Gojak (2013a) reminds assessment-makers and teachers that:

If we are to realize the potential of the Common Core, we must begin to think about assessment differently. We must assess students daily through the questions we ask and the tasks we present. We must use the information that we gather from listening to our students to decide our next instructional moves. We cannot wait for end-of-the-year high-stakes assessments to determine whether students have learned the mathematics. We cannot spend hours of valuable instructional time on formal assessments.

In her November 2013 message, she adds her concern about the United States becoming a test-driven society:

With the advent of high-stakes testing, the number of assessments we give students has greatly increased and their purpose has changed. Test preparation takes place in some classrooms every day, often consuming as much as one-quarter of instructional time. We teach to the test because we are told to. We have regular, building-wide testing days throughout the year. Often conducted in the name of "Common Formative Assessments," these exercises can take the form of multiple-choice tests that are prepared by someone in the district. They may align with the pacing chart but often have little teacher input and provide teachers with little information about their students' deep understanding of a concept. We give students tests to take home to practice for the "real" test. We have become a test-driven society!

(Gojak, 2013b)

It would be best, in the authors' opinion, if the assessments were for informing instruction only. If so, will teachers and students then not take the assessments seriously? We think they will. The negative pressures are still huge because the principals, teachers, parents, and community all have access to the results regardless of whether or not they come from explicitly high-stakes tests. Most teachers and students with scores below the national average will be motivated to do better because they care.

Principles to Actions: Ensuring Mathematical Success for All

The NCTM publication *Principles to Actions: Ensuring Mathematical Success for All* (2014) provides recommendations and guidelines to help the education sector, parents, and the community all work together and take action so that our students receive high-quality mathematics instruction regardless of state standards. This document updates the six principles from the Principles and Standards document and adds a seventh. Its revised set of principles includes Equity and Access, Teaching, Learning, Curriculum, Tools and Technology, Assessment, and Professionalism. Professional educators are those who "hold themselves and their colleagues accountable for the mathematical success of all students and for their personal and collective professional growth in meeting this goal" (NCTM, 2014, 5). For each of the principles, NCTM discusses the barriers, productive practices, and policies for eliminating the barriers, as well as recommendations for widespread implementation of NCTM's vision of students who are capable of working productively to solve worthwhile mathematical problems in an environment that includes effective teachers, an inviting workspace, and the materials and tools for thinking critically. See NCTM's website for more information (www.nctm.org).

A list of Web resources for implementing the CCSSM is in Table 1.4.

TABLE 1.4 Web-Based CCSS Resources

CCSS Documents for:	
Math	**www.corestandards.org/Math**
Special Ed	**www.ode.state.or.us/search/page/?id=3741**
Informative Videos about the CCSS	**www.youtube.com/user/TheHuntInstitute#p/u/0/9IGD9oLofks**
NCTM	**www.nctm.org.** Online NCTM provides information and publishes math events, books and journals. Its Illumination site (illumination.nctm.org) offers free access to lesson plans, resources, and reflections that are provoked by classroom video vignettes of teaching and learning; NCTM also offers institutes for professional development on the CCSSM throughout the United States.
NCTM: Core Math Tools	**www.nctm.org/resources/content.aspx?id=32702**. Downloadable interactive software tools for algebra and functions, geometry and trigonometry, and statistics and probability for high school.
National Council of Supervisors of Mathematics (CSSM)	**www.ncsm.org**. At NCSM, Web tools that allow mathematics education leaders to connect, share and collaborate with one another are available. They are part of the Internet's social networking landscape and provide a means for people to build and maintain communities of practice.
The Charles A. Dana Center	The Charles A. Dana Center at The University of Texas at Austin and the education company Agile Mind, Inc., with support from the Bill and Melinda Gates Foundation, have launched an online CCSSM toolbox, available at **www.CCSSMtoolbox.org** or **www.CCSSMtoolbox.com**. The toolbox is freely available to support educators and learners as they implement the mathematics standards.
CCSS Blogs	Dr. William McCallum, head of the mathematics department at the University of Arizona and one of the lead authors of the Common Core State Standards for Mathematics, maintains a blog about resources related to CCSSM implementation at **http://commoncoretools.me**.
Illustrative Mathematics	**http://illustrativemathematics.org**. Illustrative Mathematics provides guidance and develops resources to support the implementation of the standards. The Illustrative Mathematics project has developed hundreds of tasks that illustrate the meaning of each standard and provide instructional best practices for teachers.

Inside Mathematics	**www.insidemathematics.org**. This professional resource for educators features classroom examples of innovative teaching methods, insights into student learning, and tools for mathematics instruction that are being aligned to the Common Core.
Implementing the Mathematical Practice Standards	**http://mathpractices.edc.org**. A site with illustrations of student dialogues to help explore how to connect the mathematical practices to the content standards.
PBS Learning Media	**http://lpb.pbslearningmedia.org**. Site has lessons and videos on important topics in most subjects and at all grade levels.
Supporting ELLs in Mathematics	**http://ell.stanford.edu**. The goal of these materials is to illustrate how Common Core aligned math tasks can be used to support math instruction and language development for ELLs at three grade spans (elementary, middle, and high school) using adapted tasks from two publicly accessible curriculum projects.
TODOS: Mathematics for All	**www.todos-math.org**. The mission of TODOS: Mathematics for All is to advocate for equity and high-quality mathematics education for all students—in particular, Latina/o students.
LearnZillion	**www.learnzillion.com/topics#topic-10**. Site has YouTube videos on important math topics. Lessons/Tasks/Tests are aligned to CCSS & Practices and grouped by level of difficulty.
North Carolina Common Core Instructional Support Tools—Unpacking the Standards–Math	**www.ncpublicschools.org/acre/standards/common-core-tools/#unpacking**. For each grade level and CCSS area, this document provides explanations and examples for each Standard for Math and ELA and what each looks like by grade level.
New York State Education Department	http://www.google.com/search?client=safari&rls=en&q=http://www.p12.nysed.gov/apda/common-core-sample-questions&spell=1&sa=X&ei=1vvM U4OgEYaHyASY8oKYBQ&ved=0CBwQBSgA">**www.p12.nysed.gov/apda/common-core-sample-questions**. This site includes sample 3–8 math and ELA questions to help students, parents, and educators better understand the instructional shifts demanded by the Common Core and the rigor required to ensure that all students are on track to college and career readiness.
Engage New York	**http://engageny.org**. This is another Common Core site for New York State. You'll find videos, lessons, and general resources here. New York will be adding curriculum units to this site.
Ohio Department of Education	**www.education.ohio.gov/GD/Templates/Pages/ODE/ODEDetail. aspx?page=3&**. Each grade-level document unpacks the standards and provides instructional strategies, sample items, common misconceptions, and connection to diverse learners and links to other resources aligning to the standard.
Progressions for the Common Core in Mathematics	**http://ime.math.arizona.edu/progressions**. The authors of the Common Core State Standards in Mathematics release draft papers that provide in-depth discussion of the domain progressions across grades, highlight connections across domains, elaborate on the learning expectations for students, and provide instructional suggestions.
Student Achievement Partners	**www.achievethecore.org**. Student Achievement Partners offer a variety of practical resources and examples for working with the Common Core Standards in both E/LA and Mathematics.

(Continued)

TABLE 1.4 (Continued)

CCS Documents for:	
Teaching Channel	**www.teachingchannel.org**. This site includes videos of classroom vignettes with teacher voice-overs relating to CCSS. (most about 10 minutes long).
Think Math has ideas for lessons	**http://thinkmath.edc.org.**
Hands-on: Online Resources for Mathematics	
National Library of Virtual *Manipulatives*	**www.nlvm.usu.edu/en/:** A digital library containing Java applets and activities for K–12 mathematics. Just download the free trial version and you can use as often as necessary.
Set the Manipulatives Free	**http://jimmiescollage.com/2009/08/set-the-manipulatives-free**. This site has many resources for using manipulatives. These are samples from the site: Hand Made Manipulative Instructions: **http://mason.gmu.edu/~mmankus/Handson/manipulatives.htm** Printable manipulatives: **http://olc.spsd.sk.ca/de/math1-3/p-printables.html** Printable math game boards (pdf & doc): **http://olc.spsd.sk.ca/de/math1-3/mathgameboards.html**
Kentucky Center for Mathematics–Math Manipulatives	**www.kentuckymathematics.org/resources/mathmanipulatives.asp**. Websites for games, printing *free manipulatives*, virtual manipulatives, finding *online manipulatives* for fractions, decimals, functions, and more.
Electronic worksheets for grades K–High School Geometry	**www.ixl.com/promo?partner=google&phrase=Search%20-%20math%20worksheets&gclid=CLDistTImbgCFWRp7AodjBIATA**
Interactive White Boards	
Promethean Planet for	**www.prometheanplanet.com/en-us/resources/subjects/math/**
SMART EXCHANGE:	**http://exchange.smarttech.com/#tab=0**
Math Websites for Interactive Whiteboard	**www.theteachersguide.com/InteractiveSitesMathSmartBoard.htm**. Most, if not all, of the whiteboards are free.
Free Interactive Whiteboard Teacher tools	**www.dreambox.com/teachertools**
Mathematical Modeling Lesson Plans—Indiana University	**www.indiana.edu/~iucme/mathmodeling/lessons.htm**. These lesson plans were developed by IMI mathematics teachers and tested in their classrooms. The lessons cover a wide range of topics and grade levels ranging from seventh grade through twelfth grade. These are all Word document files that can be saved to your computer.
Assessments	
Mathematics Assessment Project	Funded by the Gates Foundation, this site provides units, lessons, assessment, and professional development on the Common Core for middle and high school grades: **http://map.mathshell.org/materials/background.php**

Partnership for Assessment of Readiness for College and Careers (PARCC)	**www.parcconline.org/ for information about PARCC** . For sample items in mathematics see **www.parcconline.org/samples/item-task-prototypes**. Click on the grade level on the left side (under SAMPLES-MATHEMATICS), and then scroll down to view sample test items by clicking under SAMPLE TASKS. *To take a sample test* for grades 3–5, 6–8, or High School, go to **http://practice.parcc.testnav.com/#** and then click on Practice Tests at the top, then look down and see Sample Items Tab on the right, and click on it. NOTE: You can stay informed about PARCC by entering your e-mail address in the upper right corner of the website and then providing some contact information. You will receive a confirming note.
Smarter Balanced Assessment Consortium	**www.smarterbalanced.org**. Smarter Balanced Assessment Consortium is a state-led consortium developing assessments for 25 states that are aligned to the Common Core State Standards in English language arts/literacy and mathematics. The assessments are designed to help prepare all students to graduate from high school ready for college or career. You can view their released sample items for math and ELA—all done on the computer. Math items are at **http://sampleitems.smarterbalanced.org/itempreview/sbac/index.htm**. ELA items are at **http://sampleitems.smarterbalanced.org/itempreview/sbac/ELA.htm**.
National Assessment of Educational Progress	Released items
Additional Videos	
Dan Meyer's Table of list of Three-Act Math Tasks	**https://docs.google.com/spreadsheet/ccc?key=0AjIqyKM9d7ZYdEhtR3BJMmdBWnM2YWxWYVM1UWowTEE#gid=0**
Dan Myer's GRAPHING STORIES in three acts	**http://graphingstories.com/**
Andrew Stadel 3-Act Math Tasks list	**https://docs.google.com/spreadsheet/ccc?key=0AkLk45wwjYBudG9LeXRad0lHM0E0VFRyOEtRckVvM1E#gid=0**
More Video Links	
Graphing Linear Equations—Full Body Style (Eighth Grade)	**www.teachingchannel.org/videos/graphing-linear-equations-full-body-style?fd=1**
Statistical Analysis to Rank Baseball Players (High School)	**www.teachingchannel.org/videos/statistical-analysis-to-rank-baseball-players**
YUMMY MATH	**www.yummymath.com**. Provides real-life activities organized by content and grade levels.
Finally, for up-to-date information on educational issues, subscribe to Jerry Becker: **jbecker@SIU.EDU**.	

2

Exemplary Practice:
What Does It Look Like?

While I was helping my daughter Lisa with her math homework, I asked her to explain why she chose the operation she used to solve a problem. Not only did she not know, but also she did not care. She was more interested in getting the right answer by plugging in the proper formula. This is how she was taught math, and she doesn't seem to want to change the way she learned it. I can only generalize that this is how many students are responding to attempts by teachers to create conceptual understanding. This age group is where so many students lose interest in math—just when they should be finding the beauty of it. Perhaps I shouldn't worry too much; Lisa's passion lies in social studies and literature. She is not a "math-brained" child, I guess. Are these children born, and not made that way?

Eugenie, preservice teacher

We can surmise that Lisa has procedural fluency but that, because she lacks conceptual understanding, she is not able to apply the strategic and adaptive competencies necessary to solve real-life problems, which in turn contributes to her unproductive disposition toward mathematics. Many students perceive mathematics to be a bunch of numbers that go into formulas to solve problems. More often than not, the problems they are asked to solve are not *their* problems, nor do the problems come close to something they are interested in pursuing. Lisa's experiences with mathematics are similar to those that Yvelyne had as a mathematics student—the mathematics that she learned focused on finding the teacher's or the book's answer to a problem. But when she studied mathematics methods at Brooklyn College, she and her classmates explored a different kind of teaching and learning. Rather than offering lectures about what they needed to know, Professor Dorothy Geddes invited them to experience mathematics as a dynamic discipline that sometimes required tools such as toothpicks, geoboards, or mirrors to resolve thought-provoking problems. Dr. Geddes's definition of mathematical competence clearly went beyond numbers and computations; she included the ability to test a hypothesis, find patterns, and communicate understanding—all of which are recommended by CCSSM as essential elements for both teaching and learning mathematics.

In her reflection, the preservice teacher Eugenie writes about her concern about getting Lisa to understand and appreciate mathematics. Unfortunately, Eugenie's acceptance of Lisa's dislike of mathematics as a natural outcome also contributes to the problem. Another problem is that teachers bypass conceptual understanding and substitute a "fast forward" to rules. In her article on teaching to the CCSS, Crowley (2013) writes about what she learned from one mathematics educator, Ann Shannon. Shannon would describe this fast-forwarding process as teachers' tendency to "GPS" students by giving them step-by-step directions for solving problems followed by worksheets to practice the steps. If those steps bypass concept understanding, then students will likely not be able to apply the concept to real-world situations and the concept will not serve as a simpler problem whose process helps to solve more difficult problems:

> What Ann Shannon would say is that in this particular situation, the students have been "GPS-ed" from problem to solution. Just as when I drive in a new city using my global positioning system, I can follow the directions and get to where I need to go. But I can't replicate the journey on my own. I don't have a real understanding of the layout of the city. If a road were blocked because of a parade, for example, I would be in trouble because I have no real understanding of the city's geography.
>
> (1)

We need to shift away from GPS-ing students, which is the traditional way of teaching mathematics. We also need to shift away from believing that only "math-brained students" should be expected to understand math.

What happens to Lisa's mathematics learning when her mom or her teacher believes that she does not have a math brain? The answer depends on their response. If they think that it is acceptable for Lisa not to succeed in mathematics because she's smart in other areas—just not in mathematics—and that there is no reason to work to enhance her mathematical understanding, then Lisa may never change her own attitude about mathematics. On the other hand, if the belief that Lisa is not "math-brained" encourages her mother and her teacher to work toward connecting the mathematics to her strong areas of interest—by thinking about how math is integrated in literature, art, science, the movies, music, politics, sports, puzzles, or some other interest of Lisa's—then she has a chance to understand and appreciate mathematics. In her National Public Radio interview with Smith (2014), described in Chapter 1, Duckworth agrees that the responsibility for helping kids develop a positive disposition toward mathematics lies with schools, teachers, and parents. Duckworth says, "I don't think people can become truly gritty and great at things they don't love . . . so when we try to develop grit in kids, we also need to find and help them cultivate their passions. That's as much a part of the equation here as the hard work and the persistence."

The PISA 2012 in Focus Newsletter (OECD, March 2014/03) summarizes this discussion:

> The bottom line: practice and hard work go a long way towards developing each student's potential; but students can only achieve at the highest levels when they believe that they are in control of their success and that they are capable of achieving at high levels. The fact that large proportions of students in most countries consistently believe that student achievement is mainly a product of hard work, rather than inherited intelligence, suggests that education and its social context can make a difference in instilling values that foster success in education.
>
> (4)

The reality is that every student has a unique and complex brain. Our classrooms are composed of many Lisas, with varying interests and aptitudes, but they can all learn to do and to appreciate mathematics.

Envisioning a Reform-based Classroom Environment

The information in Chapter 1 on NCTM/CCSSM recommendations for reforming curriculum, teaching, and assessment provides ideas on what a classroom informed by reform principles should look like to reach students. Not surprisingly, creating coherent lessons that promote such reform is not easy, partly because acquiring a clear vision of the Standards for Mathematical Practices (SMP) and how they interrelate and connect to the content requires different ways of thinking, as well as practice, guidance, and time to evolve.

Teachers or curriculum writers must exercise caution against a limited vision of the CCSSM that might lead to superficial or misguided applications. As an example, consider the following lesson in an algebra class, and ask, "How different are the teaching, instructional activities, and student participation from those of a traditional classroom?"

Example One: Reformed-based Instruction?

The bell rings, and Nancy's students enter class. They quickly sit in their assigned groups of four and take out their calculators. Nancy's goal for the students is to have them model binomial multiplication with algebra tiles. She begins with a review of the properties of algebra tiles and their relationships to addition and multiplication of binomials and then gives each student a set of algebra tiles and a worksheet on

Figure 2.1 Using the distributive law to show the use of algebra tiles

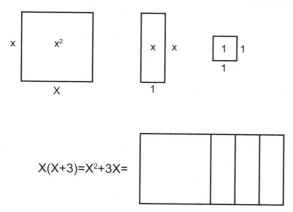

$X(X+3)=X^2+3X=$

multiplying binomials. Students decide who will tackle which problem, and the groups set to work. Nancy visits each group to monitor its progress.

This description includes many of the concepts that we associate with reform: the students are working in groups with manipulatives that include calculators, and the teacher monitors progress. How could the lesson not be reform based? Let us take a closer look.

In her discussion of the tiles, Nancy first defines the tiles: the length of the sides of the small square is 1 unit and its area is 1 square unit; the larger square has sides of length x units so its area is x^2 square units. The rectangle has a length x units by a width of 1 unit, so its area is x square units (see Figure 2.1). She then shows how the tiles can be used to combine like terms in expressions such as $3x^2 + 1 + 2x + 2x^2 + 2x + 6$ by just collecting like terms represented by the tiles–collect 5 big squares, 4 rectangles, and 7 unit squares to get $5x^2 + 4x + 7$. Next she reviews how to multiply $x (x + 3)$ by applying the distributive property and then representing each term by the corresponding tile. Hence, because $x (x + 3) = x^2 + 3x$, the product is represented by one large square and three rectangles.

A student asks, "Why do we have to use the tiles if we can get the answer by using the distributive property first anyway?" Nancy responds that this is just another way to do such problems. As she hands each student a sheet with exercises on binomial multiplication, Nancy instructs students to use the distributive property and then the algebra tiles to show the results of the distributive property. Students decide who will do which problem and begin working. Some use calculators to check their answers, and when most are finished, they wait for other students to finish working. Nancy visits each group, correcting any student errors and then assigning different students to put problems on the board.

Closer scrutiny shows that what looks like reformed teaching lacks key ingredients of reform. Let's look at some of her strategies.

Small-Group Work

Consider students sitting in pairs, which may be conducive to small-group processing of ideas. In Nancy's groups, students worked individually applying her rules. Therefore, there was little motivation for group members to share ideas even though the small group size would have made that easy to achieve. Furthermore, it was Nancy, not group members, who judged the correctness of answers. Wheatley (1991) succinctly describes key elements for facilitating small groups. He writes that in preparing for classroom instruction,

> a teacher selects tasks which have a high probability of being problematical for students—tasks which may cause students to find a problem. Secondly, the students work on these tasks in small groups. During this time the teacher attempts to convey collaborative work as a goal. Finally, the class is convened as a whole for a time of sharing. Groups present their solutions to the class, not to the teacher, for discussion. The role of the teacher in these discussions is that of facilitator, and every effort is made to be nonjudgmental and encouraging.
>
> (15–16)

If Nancy has English-language learners, then students with the same first language could be paired in small groups to allow them to brainstorm before having to worry about the translation for sharing with the whole class. Small-group strategies for helping English-language learners meet the standards are in the *High School Publishers' Criteria for the Common Core State Standards for Mathematics* (National Governors Association, 2013).

Manipulatives

Manipulatives are alternative, concrete representations that are conducive to the discovery of more abstract concepts or algorithms. They are valuable when they are introduced as an integral part of a lesson to challenge student thinking. Nancy's use of the algebra tiles could have pushed students thinking, but she presented the tiles in the same algorithmic manner as the distributive property. Yet an application of this tool is in helping students see or discover the algorithm for multiplying binomials and the distributive property.

Questioning

Nancy asked few if any questions of her students because her focus was on directing students on how to use the tiles. However, she could have used questioning to engage students in the SMP. Suppose she has base-10 blocks and algebra tiles available for the students. Consider the following questions with possible student answers or comments below each question:

* *How can we represent the product of (5)(3) geometrically?*
   Use blocks to make a rectangle with length 5 units and width 3 units. Its area has 15 unit squares = 15sq. units.

Do similarly for (12)(13).

Some students will use repeated addition to show 13, twelve times. Applaud the process and then ask them to try it with the *fewest* number of blocks. This results in a 12 by 13 rectangle or array that looks like Figure 2.2 where x = 10. Its area is 100 + 30 + 20 + 6 or 156 square units.

Can we always represent the product of two natural numbers as the area of a rectangle? Why?

Yes. Because multiplication is repeated addition, it can be represented as an array or rectangle.

How can we represent the product of (10 + 2)(10 + 3) geometrically?

This is the same configuration for using the fewest blocks for 12x13.

What properties for numbers are illustrated in (10 + 2)(10 + 3)?

Distributive property.

How can we show the product of (x + 2)(x + 3) geometrically?

This is the same configuration for using the fewest blocks for 12x13.

What is the product?

In Figure 2.2, the dimensions of the rectangle are shown, and its area, $(x + 2)(x + 3)$ square units, is what students must understand to be that which they are seeking. Once students place tiles in the space to fill the entire area of the rectangle (Figure 2.3), they will have determined its area to be $x^2 + 3x + 2x + 6$, or, $x^2 + 5x + 6$.

Figure 2.2 Area model for multiplication using algebra tiles

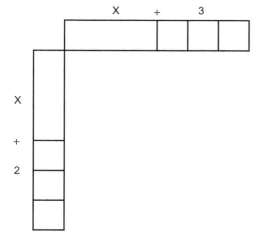

Figure 2.3 Preparing to multiply binomials with algebra tiles using the area model for multiplication

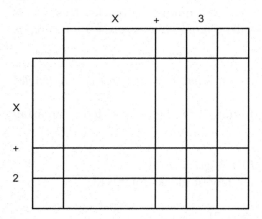

* How does that illustrate the distributive property?

Connections to the distributive property are fundamental to this process and should be reinforced at this point so that students see how it connects to the area model. It is also important to see the abstraction that justifies why we can add like terms: $2x + 3x = (2 + 3)x = 5x$. (SMP7).

Students are now prepared to use distributive property to multiply binomials with the tiles (SMP2, SMP4) and to look for patterns to explain a process for multiplying binomials (SMP3, SMP8).

Technology

Now, what about the use of the graphing calculator? If students are using it for simple computations, it might help a student who is weak in the basics to continue processing the algebra, but otherwise, this is not the best use of the graphing calculator for students at that level. However, if the graphing calculator can multiply binomials or if Nancy allows students to go to the Web and access one of the sites that does that, then students who are using the technology to check their actions, to generate numerous binomial products to verify patterns, or to find new patterns are engaging the full power of the technology to promote higher thinking. Unfortunately, most of the calculator websites for multiplying binomials also provide rules, so the teacher needs to find one having the least guidance or be prepared to make the best use of it. See http://easycalculation.com/algebra/polynomial-multiplication.php.

Alternatively, the calculator or a website with a calculator for multiplying binomials could be used as the manipulative for helping students *initially* see the process and derive a rule. To do so, Nancy could ask students to:

1. Use the calculator to complete the worksheet on multiplying binomials;
2. Look for a pattern to guess the calculator's rule;

3. Create three problems to verify your rule;
4. Compute the answers to your problems using your rule;
5. Have a partner check the answers to your problems;
6. Use the calculator to check your rule;
7. If your rule fails, discuss with your partner and go back to step 2;
8. Share and justify your rule;
9. If the website already gives a rule, then justify why that works and how it connects to yours;
10. Think of real-life situations to model some of your problems and, in your journal, explain how to solve them.

Assessment

In addition to the informal assessment Nancy gathers as she monitors the groups, she can collect the journal from Step 10 for information on individual student's conceptual understanding of the lesson to decide who needs help and how to assist.

Example Two: Traditional Instruction?

Now let's consider a typical classroom of 30 students who are sitting in straight rows and busily working individually on a worksheet. Claudette, the teacher, stands at the front of the room or occasionally circulates about and looks over their shoulders. Is she teaching from a reform perspective? Maybe. It depends on what the worksheet requires and whether students have opportunities to learn in other ways on other days. Suppose Claudette's goal is for students to apply the heuristic "think of a simpler problem" to problems that are not routine. Here are examples from the worksheet:

1. Find the last two digits of $11^{20} - 1$.
2. Determine a rule for finding the following sum:

$$1^2 - 2^2 + 3^2 - 4^2 + 5^2 \ldots + 1999^2$$

3. Be prepared to explain your strategies for getting your answers to the class.

The sheet is not of the "drill-and-kill" variety. It requires students to apply sound problem-solving heuristics to problems that are suitable for individual work. Further, the third question promotes the sharing of students' ideas and discourse. If she occasionally varies her teaching style, she may be teaching from a reform-based perspective.

Transitioning to CCSSM

Was Nancy's approach bad? No. There might have been some educational gains for some students. Learners construct their own knowledge at all times and in all types of situations, but different instructional approaches may influence the quality and content accuracy of the construction. The fact that students faced each other in small groups rather than sitting in rows looking at each other's backs may have promoted some worthwhile discussion among students. Although the tiles were not applied in the best way to enhance the students' ability to make connections between multiple representations, they still provided an alternative representation for algebraic terms and for the distributive property, so they may have helped some students better understand the mathematics. Nancy also had students present their answers, thus opening an opportunity for students to share their thinking and summarize ideas.

We surmise that Nancy's perception of teaching mathematics is one that relies on teacher control or is conceptually rule driven. She probably has had little experience using various tools, such as manipulatives, to guide exploratory activities. However, the fact that she has elements that are conducive to reform activities in her class indicates that she is trying to embrace different approaches to teaching. Her instruction and choice of activities are those of a teacher in transition to a reform-based teaching approach supported by CCSS. What is lacking is implementation of the SMP together with the mathematics content in her instruction. A clearer vision of what the SMP entails is key to her success in moving forward with the transition.

These two examples show that labeling an activity or class as reform-based or not requires close scrutiny of the tasks students are doing, how they are instructed to do them, and whether a single teaching method is used exclusively. Let's consider the revisions made to Nancy's lesson and ask one final question: Is it now aligned to the CCSS? Some would say yes, somewhat, but ask: "What about a real-life challenging application for which the need to multiply binomials arises? (SMP1). Why not have students do individual explorations first, before going into groups?"

Our point is that many of us are teachers in transition, with various levels of understanding what the CCSS imply. Furthermore, we all come to the table with different experiences, expertise, and expectations. "Opportunities to reflect on and refine instructional practice—during class and outside of class, alone and with others" will be instrumental to helping us move closer to a common vision for teaching and learning" (NCTM, 2000, 19).

Exemplary Practices

There are exemplary practices that clearly demonstrate best practices for teaching and learning for understanding. For example, the teachers profiled in this book:

◆ Engage students in challenging, mathematically appropriate tasks that align with the CCSSM and make sense to students;
◆ Apply the mathematical practices within a classroom atmosphere conducive to discourse that encourages students' alternative conjectures, approaches, and explanations;
◆ Use appropriate tools, cooperative group work, and individual instruction to accommodate students with different learning styles;
◆ Use alternative assessment methods to assess students and inform their instruction;

◆ Collaborate with colleagues and pursue other professional development activities to stimulate reflections for improving practice.

Do any of the teachers lecture at times? Sure. Many of us learned from lectures (of course, how well we understood what we learned is subject to debate). Past NCTM president Gail Burrill (personal communication, updated March 2014) elaborates on perceptions to avoid when attempting to implement reform:

> We must avoid misinterpretations such as: everything must be done in cooperative groups; decreased emphasis means none at all; every answer to every problem has to be explained in writing; the teacher is only a guide; every problem has to involve the real world; computational algorithms are not allowed; students should never practice; manipulatives are the basis for all learning, and the latest educational buzzword will really make a difference. The challenge is to make choices about content and teaching based on what we can do to enable students to learn.

As mathematics leaders, we know very well to be wary of universal statements such as "For all x, y is true." We must be mindful that its negation, "There is an x for which y is false," is often true when x represents students in our class and y represents a statement about the effectiveness of a specific activity or method. Keeping our focus on all of our students' learning highlights the fact that our students are too diverse to be neatly served by instructional methods labeled "Use me all the time!" The key reflective question that should guide whatever approach we take is, *"How can we best facilitate students' understanding of the mathematical content in a meaningful way that contributes to their success in the twenty-first century?"* Suggestions to answer this question may be found in the Council of Chief State School Officers' document *InTASC: Model Core Teaching Standards and Learning Progressions for Teachers 1.0* (CCSSO, 2011, 2013). Within each of its four domains of teaching are progression indicators, specific teacher performances, and knowledge needed to improve instruction. The progression indicators include:

(A) The Learner and Learning

Standard #1: Learner Development
The teacher understands how learners grow and develop, recognizing that patterns of learning and development vary individually within and across the cognitive, linguistic, social, emotional, and physical areas, and designs and implements developmentally appropriate and challenging learning experiences.

(16)

Standard #2: Learning Differences
The teacher uses understanding of individual differences and diverse cultures and communities to ensure inclusive learning environments that enable each learner to meet high standards.

(17)

Standard #3: Learning Environments

The teacher works with others to create environments that support individual and collaborative learning, and that encourage positive social interaction, active engagement in learning, and self-motivation.

(19)

(B) Content

Standard #4: Content Knowledge

The teacher understands the central concepts, tools of inquiry, and structures of the discipline(s) he or she teaches and creates learning experiences that make these aspects of the discipline accessible and meaningful for learners to assure mastery of the content.

(24)

Standard #5: Application of Content

The teacher understands how to connect concepts and use differing perspectives to engage learners in critical thinking, creativity, and collaborative problem-solving related to authentic local and global issues.

(27)

(C) Instructional Practice

Standard #6: Assessment

The teacher understands and uses multiple methods of assessment to engage learners in their own growth, to monitor learner progress, and to guide the teacher's and learner's decision making.

(28)

Standard #7: Planning for Instruction

The teacher plans instruction that supports every student in meeting rigorous learning goals by drawing upon knowledge of content areas, curriculum, cross-disciplinary skills, and pedagogy, as well as knowledge of learners and the community context.

(32)

Standard #8: Instructional Strategies

The teacher understands and uses a variety of instructional strategies to encourage learners to develop deep understanding of content areas and their connections, and to build skills to apply knowledge in meaningful ways.

(38)

(D) Professional Responsibility

Standard #9: Professional Learning and Ethical Practice

The teacher engages in ongoing professional learning and uses evidence to continually evaluate his/her practice, particularly the effects of his/her choices and actions on others (learners, families, other professionals, and the community), and adapts practice to meet the needs of each learner.

(41)

Standard #10: Leadership and Collaboration

The teacher seeks appropriate leadership roles and opportunities to take responsibility for student learning, to collaborate with learners, families, colleagues, other school professionals, and community members to ensure learner growth, and to advance the profession.

(43).

Best Societal Practices for CCSS Implementation

The following reflection from Mary, a preservice teacher, is a catalyst for the following discussion on additional support teachers and students need to embrace the CCSS:

Writing this final journal brings me back to last semester in my first math methods course. I was a wreck. I was not sure if I knew anything, learned anything, or was doing anything right. I am in a much better position at the end of this second and final math methods semester. I am confident that I know a great deal of math content, I know that I have learned a vast amount of information, and I am secure in my work and accomplishments. Having said that, I think that I am ready to concretely state my mathematical teaching philosophy, which I have yet to do solidly since last semester.

I believe that every student is capable of learning and doing math. Some students come with an aptitude for math that allows them to absorb ideas and concepts relatively easily. Some students take time to figure things out. By tapping in to a student's interests, a link may be found to connect what they are most interested in to the math content. By doing so, the student will be able to find their interests within mathematical content and thrive. It is my job as their teacher to help them find that connection.

I also believe that there are many types of learners. There are visual, kinesthetic, and auditory learners. Each of those students should be reached in every lesson that I create. It is my duty to allow students to learn the way they naturally do by fostering their needs in my lessons. I will not leave any student behind. Regardless of whatever hectic schedule I may be handling, there is always time to help a student that is struggling. I think that is it, for now. I am sure as I move along in my teaching career things will be added, changed, or revisited. For now, I am confident in my statement of my teaching philosophy.

Some veteran teachers may read this reflection and think, "Good luck! She has a *lot* to learn about the reality of teaching kids." It is true that Mary has very high ideals (e.g., *every* lesson should include *all* learning styles) but, ideally, we believe that that is where teachers should start because she has the teaching and learning philosophy that connect directly to the CCSSO's Standards 1–8. If she is not discouraged in pursuit of her goals, she will likely advance to Standards 9 and 10 to seek help in addressing difficulties she will encounter.

Research from the U.S. Department of Education on Post Secondary Education (2014), show that for the 2014–2015 school years, the areas of greatest need in education-related disciplines include teachers and related service personnel in special education, mathematics, and science. Since Mary is open to adjusting her thinking when necessary, an important question is: What is needed to sustain Mary's enthusiasm for teaching mathematics so that she is still teaching after three years? In one of Jerry Becker's list-serve e-mails is a cartoon by Signe Wilkinson of a teacher being blamed by "drive-by education experts" for the failure of her students. (What are you doing Wrong? Posted March 18, 2013, 3:37 P.M.) The poor teacher says nothing, but on the desks of her students are labels that read *homeless, teen mom, abused, drugs, no books, no discipline, TV on 24/7 and . . . hungry*. On her desk are a pile of paperwork, test schedules, and a small box labeled "my own $ for supplies." While Mary has the necessary preparation, knowledge, skills, and values to be an excellent teacher, the cartoon makes clear the conditions under which it would be difficult for Mary to achieve her goals for students. Darling-Hammond (2014) cites additional conditions under which Mary may well be unsuccessful: "An excellent teacher might be unsuccessful if asked to work with a flawed curriculum, substandard materials, a crumbling facility, inadequate support for struggling students, overly large classes, or if asked to work outside his or her area of expertise. Conversely, a less skilled teacher might be successful if provided with excellent professional working conditions and collegial support" (7).

In her reflection, Mary writes, "I will not leave any student behind. Regardless of whatever hectic schedule I may be handling, there is always time to help a student that is struggling." If Mary teaches in a school having students primarily from low socioeconomic backgrounds, can her determination help her students to perform well on the CCSS assessments? One would expect that CCSS test scores of poor students will be much lower than those of the rich because the latter can afford to go to schools that have more experienced teachers and better resources and because they can also get extra support after school if needed. In his article summarizing his research on the widening of the academic gap, "No Rich Child Left Behind," Reardon (2013) reports that, while differences in quality between schools serving low- and high-income students are contributing factors, there is another factor that has a larger impact:

> It may seem counterintuitive, but schools don't seem to produce much of the disparity in test scores between high- and low-income students. We know this because children from rich and poor families score very differently on school readiness tests when they enter kindergarten, and this gap grows by less than 10 percent between kindergarten and high school. . . . That isn't to say that there aren't important differences in quality between schools serving low- and high-income students—there certainly are—but they appear to do less to reinforce the trends than conventional wisdom would have us believe.

Reardon (2013) cites preparation for kindergarten as a major factor influencing performance. Rich students are increasingly entering kindergarten much better prepared to succeed in school than middle-class students, and so his suggestions for breaking the link between educational success and family background include investing in developing high-quality child care that is open to all students. Reardon also recommends professional development for preschool teachers and child care providers. But much more is needed, he writes:

> There is a lot of discussion these days about investing in teachers and "improving teacher quality", but improving the quality of our parenting and of our children's earliest environments may be even more important. Let's invest in parents so they can better invest in their children. . . . These are not new ideas, but we have to stop talking about how expensive and difficult they are to implement and just get on with it.

Reardon (2013) concludes with a statement that speaks to the success of the implementation of CCSS:

> The more we do to ensure that all children have similar cognitively stimulating early childhood experiences, the less we will have to worry about failing schools. This in turn will enable us to let our schools focus on teaching the skills–how to solve complex problems, how to think critically and how to collaborate–essential to a growing economy and a lively democracy.

The PISA 2012 data (OECD, 2013) support Reardon's conclusion. They show that, in most of the participating countries, after accounting for students' socioeconomic status, 15-year-olds who had attended preschool outperformed those who had not.

For implementation of CCSS to be successful, it is crucial to provide teachers and students with the support they need to transition to the demands of the new curriculum and assessment system. The support should include not only a nurturing environment that blends theory with the realities of teaching kids from different socioeconomic backgrounds and culture, but also professional development to help teachers implement the curriculum. While the CCSS is state led, the help of the federal government is needed to address the societal needs cited by Reardon (2013) so that the future will show students' performances on the CCSS assessments unaffected by their socioeconomic level. Without this confluence of support, the CCSS may become a wonderful reform movement that positively affects a select group of students.

Finally, we end the discussion with a reminder from past NCTM president Cathy Seeley's book (2014), *Smarter Than We Think:*

> Students come in all different kinds of packages, not just *college bound* and *everyone else*. Some will complete a four-year college degree, some may complete a graduate degree, some may complete a two-year degree, some may complete a technical certificate, some may get partway through any of the above, and some may

enter the workforce directly. Few students are likely to know as they begin high school where they are likely to be headed a few years later; many who think they know their direction end up someplace else altogether. We have a responsibility to all students to prepare them for a fulfilling future so that every one of them can become a productive, happy, fulfilled adult.

(68)

The teachers described in this book demonstrate how educators can try to move toward the CCSSM goals by teaching the CCSSM content through the mathematical practices and with support from colleagues.

3

Michael Lehman: Group Performance Assessments

I realized that for some students, this was their first chance to be successful on a mathematics exam. Whenever I put a traditional paper-and-pencil test in front of them, they would freeze and not do very well. During class I thought they knew what they were doing but on the test they performed poorly. On the performance assessment final exam, however, they were able to communicate what they understood. The judges could help them relax, ask a few questions to get them started, and soon they would take over and do a good job of explaining what they knew.

Michael Lehman, Roscommon, Michigan

Michael Lehman taught at Holt High School, in Holt, Michigan, for 33 years and is now working with teacher development. Some years ago he became dissatisfied with his standard paper-and-pencil approach to assessing students at Holt High School. He wanted students to do more than simply show how well they had memorized mathematical concepts—he wanted them to apply these concepts to a wide range of situations. However, "I was not sure what this type of student understanding looked like. I did not know if I could recognize it if I saw it, much less devise an assessment to measure it."

As a result of his school's close involvement with the Education Department at Michigan State University (MSU), he began to change his teaching practices to align more closely with the *NCTM Standards*. He decided to begin with cooperative groups but quickly discovered that putting students in groups was just the first step. "I had a lot of group work going on, but nothing I would call cooperative learning—unless you count one student doing the first four or five problems and then cooperatively giving them to the rest of the group in exchange for the rest of the problems."

His affiliation with MSU led to a cooperative learning study group composed of faculty from MSU and his school. The group read the research, discussed the theory, and shared ideas about practice. Michael eventually learned to devise activities that engaged students in high-level discussions and were conducive to a good understanding of the mathematics.

After he changed the focus of his teaching from traditional skills-based instruction methods to an emphasis on conceptual understanding, Michael faced a new challenge—how to assess this type of student understanding. He decided a performance-based final exam would serve the purpose. He knew that designing and implementing such an assessment would take time and effort, but, with support from colleagues, Michael took the plunge.

The first step was to require students to write in his class. Many students prefer not to answer questions with more than a word or a sentence in math class; predictably, Michael's students resisted. They complained to counselors that he didn't know how to teach, and some parents came to school to express their concerns. Because Michael believed he was right and had the administration's support, he decided to hold his ground.

Having students write their ideas and explain their reasons proved to be a valuable tool. "I might ask them to state whether a graph was a function, and to explain how they knew their answer was correct. If they said they used the vertical line test, I asked them to explain why this test worked. This type of writing gave me a better idea of what my students did or did not understand—and as time went on, I found it also helped them. As they chose their words, they had to really think through the concept."

Michael carefully read and commented on their responses, and students appreciated the comments. But with 150 students, he found the task laborious and time consuming. Rather than giving up, he tried requiring fewer writing tasks or asking for shorter explanations. This worked, but "as time went on, I realized that I was reading my own words. The students had learned to ask me specific questions they thought I might ask and then took detailed notes of my answers. If they picked the right question, they would have a good answer without much thinking on their part."

Again, rather than retreating, Michael forged ahead. Turning his attention to the final exam, he designed a performance-based assessment that would require his students to explain mathematical concepts orally to a panel of three judges.

In his algebra classes, students were given six problems in advance, and they worked together in class to prepare their answers. During the exam, each student was asked to explain one of these problems, chosen at random. In addition, during the last half-hour of the 90-minute exam period, students as a group were given a new problem to solve and explain cooperatively. (Figures 3.1 and 3.2 show the instructions to students and a typical algebra exam.) Judges evaluated students on the clarity of their individual presentations and on their contribution to the group's solution of the new problem and explanation of the concepts.

Figure 3.1 Instructions for algebra students

In this packet are six problems. You should work on these problems as a group as well as on your own time. During the exam period, you will be asked to explain your results before a panel of judges. Each member of the group needs to be able to explain each of the problems. Other members will be present but will not be able to offer ideas about an individual's problem. *You will not know which problem you will be asked*, so be sure to study all the problems. In your explanations, include samples of graphs you may have used, calculations you may have done, charts that you made up and any other information that you feel will help the judges understand what you know. *Do not* write a script to read—that would only prove that you can read. Suggestions for exam day:

1. Wear nice-looking clothes.
2. Look the judges in the eye.
3. Say "Please" and "Thank You" when you ask for a question to be repeated.
4. Don't say, **"I don't know."**
5. If you don't understand a question, ask the judges to clarify or to ask the question another way.
6. If you still don't know, answer another question! By going on, you may be able to figure out the answer to the original question.

Figure 3.2 Algebra 1 final exam

Name_____ Hour_____

Below are six (6) problems. Answer each of them as completely as possible. As you work through these problems, be sure to keep careful records that will be useful to you during the exam.

1. Using the rule $-5x + 2$, make a table of values with inputs that range from -5 to 5, sketch a graph, and write everything you can about the graph and chart.
2. Write two stories. One story should illustrate the concept of "average" and the other story should illustrate the concept of "average rate of change."
3. Given the situation that you want to get a good grade in this class, list the independent and dependent variables. Write a sentence to illustrate the relationship between each pair.
4. Write a story that corresponds to the following graph.
5. Given the situation below, make a chart and graph. Be prepared to explain the key components of the chart and the graph in relationship to the situation.
   Tom has $1,600.00 in his savings account. He is going to withdraw $200.00 per month for rent.
6. Decide whether the following statements are **sometimes, always,** or **never** true. If you state that the statement is **always** or **never** true, give three (3) examples to support your opinion. If you state that it is **sometimes** true, give one (1) example for which it is true and one (1) example for which it is false. Be prepared to support your opinion.
   a. A straight line will pass through two quadrants.
   b. A straight line that is increasing will have a positive y-intercept if it has a positive x-intercept.
   c. A straight line that is decreasing will pass through only the first and fourth quadrants.

Michael's precalculus students were given a series of related questions about a particular concept or situation (see Figure 3.3). After answering the questions, they wrote a paper that explained and connected their answers and showed why each part of the mathematical model worked for the given situation. The papers had to include figures and graphs to support their results. During the exam period, they presented their papers to a panel of judges. According to Michael, "For precalculus

Figure 3.3 Precalculus exam

Recall the Ferris wheel problem: The top of the wheel is 45 feet from the ground, the wheel is 40 feet in diameter, and it is traveling at a uniform speed of 2 revolutions per minute. After one first boards the wheel it takes 10 seconds to reach the top. An equation for the height f(t) off the ground of a person t seconds after boarding is:

f(t) = 25 + 20cos((π/15) (t − 10))

   This project is intended to show you how the function was derived. The method used is based on the one in Lesson 6–4.

a. You don't know the height from the ground of the boarding point. In other words, you don't know f(0). You do know what f(t) is when t = 10: f(10) = 45 feet. Build the function relative to t = 10 or t − 10 = 0. The wheel is turning at a rate of 2 revolutions per minute or 4π radians/60 seconds = π/15 radians per second. At this rate, the wheel turns (π/15)(t − 10) radians in t − 10 seconds. This expression allows you to determine where the boarding point was when it is measured in radians from the top of the wheel. Find this measure and explain why using t − 10 = 0 makes sense. Include in this explanation why it is appropriate to use the cosine function for this type of situation.
b. By design in **part a**, (π/15)(t − 10) = 0 when t = 10. At this time, the value of the function should be a maximum. The circular function that has a maximum at 0 is y = cos x, so cos((π/15)(t − 10)) has a maximum at 10. Sketch f(t) = cos((π/15)(t − 10)) on an automatic grapher to verify this. (Use graph paper to copy the graph from the automatic grapher.) Find the next value for t at which this function has a maximum. Give your answer to the nearest tenth of a second.
c. The center of the wheel is 25 feet above the ground, and a person's position relative to that point varies between 20 feet above the center and 20 feet below the center. Explain how this leads to the final form of the function:

   f(t) = 25 + 20cos((π/15)(t − 10)).

d. Check the results for **part c** by verifying that 25 seconds after boarding, a person is at the bottom of the wheel. Explain why you know that after 25 seconds the person is at the bottom of the wheel.
e. How high is the boarding point from the ground? Explain how you found your answer.
f. After you board and ride for 2 minutes and 43 seconds, the wheel breaks down. The operator has a 26-foot ladder. Will you be able to get off the wheel? Explain your answer.
g. Alter the given function for the Ferris wheel to describe a wheel that rotates in the opposite direction.
h. Write a paper that will explain your answers to all the above questions. Please be sure that the paper flows well and connects all of your answers. This paper should explain to the reader why each part of the function works to model this situation as an example of how mathematics can be used to model real-life situations. Include drawings and graphs that support your results. Please type your paper. If you need access to a computer, I can arrange it for you after school. Be sure to see me before the due date.

This project is adapted from the University of Chicago mathematics program's text *Functions, Statistics, and Trigonometry*.

students, these projects make more sense than isolated problems to prepare. The problems are geared toward the major concepts of the course, they are broader and more interesting, and they give the students and judges much more to discuss."

   Finding appropriate problems and projects was a challenge. Michael's sources included other mathematics teachers and professors, NCTM publications and other professional literature, and reform-based mathematics textbooks. He looked for problems that illustrated the major concepts students had studied that semester and then extended and adapted them to fit his exam format.

Perhaps surprisingly, recruiting volunteer judges was less of a challenge because Michael's colleagues were supportive. He also sent a letter to parents and to local businesses asking for support. Each semester, he assembled 24 judges who worked in teams of three to evaluate three or four students at a time. (He carefully avoided assigning parents to judge a class that included a family member.) Each judge received instructions and a detailed scoring rubric (see Figures 3.4, 3.5, and 3.6).

As they prepared for the exam, Michael's students worked independently as well as cooperatively. They could ask Michael to clarify the problems, but solving them was up to the students—he reminded them that this was their final exam and their opportunity to demonstrate their understanding of what they have learned. Students were allowed to share papers, ask questions, practice explanations of problems, and critique one another.

According to Michael, the learning that occured during the preparation time was more valuable than the final assessment. Students linked concepts they had not linked earlier; they searched their textbooks for ideas; they asked good questions—"Mr. Lehman, I got this far and I see what the result should be, but I'm not sure how to verify it." "Mr. Lehman, if I explain this problem using this approach, do you think the judges will understand? Or should I add more details?" They used to ask, "Will this be on our final? Can we use our notes? We don't need to review—can we get out early today?"

During this phase, Michael's students also began to appreciate the difference between a performance-based assessment and a traditional final exam. Students felt they had more control over how they would do. They knew what would be tested; they also knew that the only factor that determined their grade was how much work

Figure 3.4 Notes to judges

1. The exam periods are 90 minutes each. Third hour is from 7:35 to 9:05 and fourth hour is from 9:15 to 10:45. Please keep track of the time so that all students have a fair chance. Remember that the exam is in two parts. For third hour, students present their prepared problems for one hour. Students discuss one of the problems I will give you during the exam for the last half-hour. For fourth hour, let them use the time they need to discuss the problems. They should discuss all of their problems.
2. For third hour, Algebra 2, be sure you pick the problem for each student. DO NOT let them pick the problem they want to discuss. If some judges allow students to pick and others do not, then it is not a fair assessment for all students. For fourth hour, Algebra 1, we have agreed to let the students pick their problems or to work together, whichever they prefer.
3. If you finish early during third hour, please keep the students at your station or at least nearby until the end of the exam period. Do not send them back to my room, as there are two groups being assessed there. If you finish early during fourth hour, please send them back to room C-2.
4. Before you leave, please be sure I get your evaluation forms. Please remember to write comments on them about what the student was and was not able to do. Your comments are very important to the students.
5. Thank you very much for your time. Your willingness to give of your time makes this type of assessment possible and goes a long way toward helping us improve the education we give our students.

Figure 3.5 Judges' grading rubric

This rubric is designed to help you with assigning a grade, A–F. My hope is to make it easier for you to assess the students and to make the grades accurately reflect the performance. Below are guidelines for each grade and the grading scale.

Performance Indicator: Orally communicates an accurate understanding of the mathematical concepts inherent in a problem situation.

Problem Presentation: (2/3 of exam grade)

A
- Demonstrates a thorough understanding of the problem and its concepts.
- Selects appropriate strategies.
- Accurately interprets the results in relationship to the situation of the problem.
- Effectively communicates results using visual aids and appropriate mathematical terms.

B
- Demonstrates a good understanding of the problem and its concepts.
- Selects appropriate strategies.
- Accurately interprets the results in relationship to the situation of the problem.
- Communicates results.

C
- Demonstrates an adequate understanding of the problem and its concepts.
- Selects appropriate strategies.
- With probing, accurately interprets the results in relationship to the situation of the problem.
- Communicates results.

D
- Lacks an understanding of some key concepts of the problem.
- Is unable to explain and interpret the results in relationship to the situation of the problem.

F
- Lacks an understanding of the concepts contained in the problem.
- Is unable to explain and interpret the results.
- Seems not to have prepared for the assessment.

Grading Scale: A: 45–50;   B: 40–44;   C: 35–39;   D: 30–34;   F: 0–29

Figure 3.6 Group performance assessment

Performance Indicator: Demonstrates mathematical understanding and group processing skills when working on group problem-solving tasks.

Group Problem Solving: (1/3 of exam grade)

A
- Consistently and actively contributes ideas that lead to a solution of the problem.
- Helps the group explain the solution and the mathematical concepts of the problem.
- Demonstrates effective interpersonal skills.

B
- Consistently contributes ideas that lead to a solution of the problem.
- Helps the group explain the solution and the mathematical concepts of the problem.
- Demonstrates effective interpersonal skills.

C
- Contributes ideas to the group and participates during the explanation of the solution sporadically.
- Demonstrates effective interpersonal skills.

D
- Rarely contributes ideas.
- Demonstrates effective interpersonal skills.

F
- Does not collaborate with the group.

Grading Scale: A: 45–50;   B: 40–44;   C: 35–39;   D: 30–34;   F: 0–29

they put into the preparation. Furthermore, they knew that the outcome would be public; students who might shrug off a poor grade that only the teacher and the student know about were not willing to embarrass themselves before three judges and their other group members. As a result, they worked hard to be well prepared.

After the oral exams, each student received an evaluation form from three judges. Both Michael and the students read the reports with interest. "We discussed all the results—both the mathematics and the overall process. I listened to their reactions and learned from them; they also learned from one another's reactions." Although some complaining is to be expected, most students thought the scores were reasonable. Figure 3.7 is a sample of a student's work in Algebra 2, and Figure 3.8 is the corresponding report from a judge.

Many students commented that the oral performance was easier than a written exam. "That's fine with me," said Michael. "I wasn't looking to make my exams harder; my students will tell you that I already knew how to write difficult tests." What is important is that the exam promoted learning. Michael also notes with satisfaction that students who had trouble communicating what they knew during the individual performance often were able to articulate their understanding as they participated in the group problem-solving process. "I firmly believe that if you truly understand mathematics, you will be able to demonstrate this understanding in a novel situation and to explain what you are doing symbolically, in written form, and orally. A good assessment format allowed my students to show me what they knew."

Discussion between Colleagues

Let's start with a few nuts-and-bolts questions. If you have eight groups presenting at the same time, how did you manage the space requirements?

Fortunately, that was not a problem for me. I could easily have four or five groups presenting in the library. My classroom or other classrooms that were used for conferences were also available.

Were panelists concerned about the level of mathematics they would be judging?

Yes, but I had one person on each panel who knew the math very well—a math teacher from my building or other districts, or sometimes an MSU professor. The "math person" could question students in more detail and guide them to use language that the other judges could understand. I also sent all judges complete answer keys to help them prepare.

How did you control for the variability of having several panels of judges?

With as many as 24 people serving as judges, consistency was always a concern. I gave the judges explicit instructions and outlined exactly what they should be assessing, but of course I could not guarantee total consistency. But even when I graded 150 exams myself, I was not totally consistent from start to finish. I think a little variance is to be expected and acceptable.

Figure 3.7 Algebra 2: Performance assessment—sample student work

Name : Mimi

1. Suppose you have a piece of paper 8.5" x 11" which is 0.001 cm thick (about the thickness of notebook paper).

a) Think about what happens to the thickness and the area of the paper as you fold it (after 1 fold, 2 folds, 3 folds...). State and test your conjecture.

$$.001 \times .001 =$$

$.001 (2) = .002$
$.001 (2)^2 = .004$
$.001 (2)^3 = .008$
$.001 (2)^4 = .016$

$.001 (2)^x = T$ ← how many times you fold
T ← thickness
← each time you fold it, it doubles

b) After how many folds would the paper be 1 cm thick?

$$\frac{.001 (2)^x = 1}{.001}$$ $$2^x = 1000 \quad \frac{\log 1}{\log 2} = x$$

$$\frac{.001 (2)^x = 100}{.001}$$ $$\frac{\log 1000}{\log 2} = x = 9.9$$

almost 10 folds

c) After how many folds would the area be 1 square inch?

8.5

11

area
$8.5 (11) = 93.5 (.5)$
to get half

$.0106 = (.5)^x$

$$\frac{\log .0106}{\log .5} = \frac{x \log .5}{\log .5}$$

$6.62 = x$

you would have to fold the paper 6.62 times

$$\frac{\log 8}{\log 3} = x$$
$$8 = 3^x$$

Figure 3.8 Algebra 2: Performance assessment—sample evaluator's comments for student

Part 1: Problem Presentation

1. Understanding of the problem and concepts:

   Mimi, you had a good understanding of how to work through the problem once you got on the right strategy. However, you appeared not to understand why particular strategies were used (ex. logs) and had trouble seeing the relationship between elements of the problem.

2. Strategies selected:

   With probing, you were able to see relationships and what strategy might be used.

3. Results - accuracy and interpretation:

   Mimi, your results were correct. Due to lack of confidence on why a strategy worked best for this problem, you needed probing to pull out your interpretations. At times, you said you didn't know.

4. Communicating - visual aids and terms:

   As a whole, you were fairly confident as you spoke making eye contact + speaking clearly. Having a visual aid to give to panel members would have helped to explain your work and was an element we were to assess you on.

Part 2: Group Problem Solving

1) Contribution of ideas:

   You all did a good job contributing to the solution of the problem.

2) Contribution to explanation of solution and concepts:

   Your explanation to the solution was well done. You spoke up even with one team member taking the leadership from other members of the team.

3) Interpersonal Skills:

   Mimi, you listened well + considered the ideas of others. You should be proud of your ability to hang in when one team member doesn't stop to listen or indicates an idea of a team mate wasn't liked. You were persistant, offered excellent ideas and didn't show any intimidation. Be proud of your mind and don't be afraid to show it! You did a great job in this part of the exercise today.

What did you consider when assigning students to groups?

For my algebra students, because of the amount of writing I required, a balance of reading ability in each group was important. When my school gave the Stanford Achievement Test at the end of eighth or ninth grade, my students' reading scores on that test were helpful as I determined the groups. In precalculus, I assigned students to groups at random because there is usually not too much difference in their ability levels. I made changes only if there were major problems.

How did the students handle working as a group?

For the most part, students had been working together all year and had developed a working relationship with each other. But the exam did add extra pressure. During the year, students may put up with a person who does not contribute, but when 20 percent of their grade is at stake they won't tolerate slacking. I think it's reasonable for the group to put pressure on a student who isn't sharing the load. It was my job to monitor this to be sure the pressure was appropriate, not rude or degrading. Working with others is an important skill to learn; rather than changing groups around if they were not getting along, I mediated, or even took a group to counseling if necessary.

Why were Algebra 1 students allowed to choose their problems?

Holt is a tenth- through twelfth-grade high school, so Algebra 1 is a remedial course. Also, because we mainstreamed all our mathematics students, the class included several with learning disabilities. I considered this to be an appropriate accommodation—but I waited until the day of the exam to tell the students that they had this option.

The instructions to students suggest not to say, "I don't know" to a judge's question. Yet we often remind students that even teachers sometimes may not know the answers and that this is OK. Please comment.

In general, some students are too quick to say, "I don't know." In this situation, they are supposed to know. If they simply tell the judges they don't know, how can the judges find opportunities to give them the grade they deserve? I worked with the students beforehand on how to present themselves—it's like helping a person prepare for a job interview. We talked about asking the judges to repeat or rephrase the question. As a last resort, they could talk about something they did know that was related, and hoped that it partly answered the question.

What did you do for students who missed the exam?

I placed a lot of pressure on the students to be present for the exam. If students were absent—or, more often, needed to take the exam early because they were leaving before school is officially out—I gave a makeup exam, but they were responsible for lining up judges that met with my approval.

How did you get parents to understand and support the assessments?

I had many parents question me about the process. I tried to explain it to them at school conferences, and once I explained it, they were very supportive. For the parents whose child was struggling with mathematics, they saw it as an opportunity for their child to show what he/she knew in a different way. To those parents, it was overly apparent that the traditional methods had not worked. They welcomed someone who was willing to try something new. I had parents come in and helped the students prepare. A few days before the exam, the parents would come in and question the students about their work. This gave the students an idea of how well prepared they were and what they needed to work on. The parents and students usually arranged this on their own, and I only provided the time, place, and materials needed.

This performance-based assessment is an ambitious and an elaborate undertaking. Do you have advice that might make it a less daunting prospect for teachers?

First, let me say that the process was very satisfying to me as a teacher. Think how long it takes to grade 150 tests in detail, only to have students look at the grade and throw away the test! Here, the work was done up front, and the students were learning the whole time—right through reading the judges' comments thoroughly. The process also changed my relationship with the class—I was no longer "judge and jury." They came to me for advice about how to explain an idea; they actually listened to me when I explained a concept or questioned them about their strategy.

My advice to interested readers would be to start out small. Try it for one class for a year, get the kinks out of it, and then expand.

Did you still use traditional assessment?

Yes. I gave traditional tests at the end of each unit (although I questioned this practice, considering all the writing my students did). I still gave quizzes and required homework. Sometimes I gave take-home final as in Figure 3.9, which is designed to push their thinking and understanding of their projects. The performance assessment is yet another source of information about my students' understanding.

Changing our teaching and assessment practices is a lifelong goal. Where do you think the mathematics community still needs to grow in assessing students?

There is always the difficulty of finding or creating a bank of problems for such exams. Teachers need problems that apply the content of the course, yet present a novel situation—problems that are open ended enough that students have to think for themselves, yet not so open ended that they have no idea where to start. This is a challenge that must be addressed to help teachers prepare students to engage in challenging task. There are lots of websites with good ideas on how to start that but teachers will need the time to work collaboratively to match good and appropriate assessments to their curriculum.

Commentary

Evaluation, test and assessment—how are they different? Evaluation that is "built around the root 'value' is more about assigning a worth to something" (Davis 1996, 245). Wood (1987) writes that "assessment is regarded as providing a comprehensive account of an individual's functioning in the widest sense—drawing on a variety of evidence, qualitative as well as quantitative, and therefore going beyond the testing of cognitive skills by pencil and paper techniques" (2). Traditional classroom tests, while typically administered for the purpose of getting a single score to represent a student's knowledge, contributes to an assessment. Some educators think that the primary role of assessment is to guide teaching. Davis (1996) writes, "Assessment, which is drawn from the Latin word *assidere* (to sit beside), is a word that I prefer to use in reference to those teaching actions that are directed toward developing a fuller understanding of both a learner's subjectivity and a learner's collectivity for the purpose of adapting one's teaching approaches" (244). Assessments assigned to help guide instruction are called *formative* assessments, and those used to evaluate students learning at the end of a unit or given as a final exam are called *summative* assessments.

Michael's evaluation of students integrated large-scale evaluation, tests, and performance assessments to gain a fuller representation of his students' understanding and thinking about mathematics. When he decided which group in which to place students, he used the Stanford Achievement test, which is a wide-scale evaluation of students' reading levels. To decide a student's final grade, he used pencil-and-paper tests, written work, and a group performance final exam. Important to the students' ability to learn from the experience of the final exam was Michael's use of class time before the exam to listen and "sit beside" students as well as have class discussions to share developing ideas and to use that information to adjust his teaching.

In their 2009 article on how to orchestrate class discussion to help students engage in high-level tasks, Smith, Hughes, Engle, et al. suggest a model to help teachers facilitate students' participation. They list five practices for teachers:

1. Anticipating student responses to challenging mathematical tasks;
2. Monitoring students' work on and engagement with the tasks;
3. Selecting particular students to present their mathematical work;
4. Sequencing the student responses that will be displayed in a specific order; and
5. Connecting different students' responses and connecting the responses to key mathematical ideas.

(550)

While these practices do serve as a formative assessment for future instruction, Michael's work provides examples of how the practices can also serve as a *summative* assessment so that the instruction eventually becomes the "test." We suggest the following adaptation of the model for such an alignment:

1. (a) Include questions with some multiple choices that anticipate student responses to the tasks. Teachers should thus make students aware of those processes that lead toward solutions, as well as those that may lead them astray (see chapter 12 of this book).
1. (b) Include open-ended questions with multiple solution paths;
2. Monitor students' work on and engagement with the tasks through questions that ask explanations for intermediate steps or that require work be shown so that teacher may assess the process applied;
3. Require *all* students to present their mathematical work;
4. Sequence the student's task so that questions will be displayed in a specific order, without leading the students. This may best be accomplished by having *students* determine the logical sequence of questions to be answered to solve the problem (see Dan Myer's fifth and sixth recommendations in chapter 12).
5. Connect different students' responses and connect the responses to key mathematical ideas after having students discuss all results from the assessment.

While this adaptation of the model to summative assessments may seem daunting to some teachers, Michael not only provides a model of how to do that but also demonstrates how an assessment can play *both* a summative and a formative role that actively engages students.

Having students present their tasks to an audience was exciting for students because they had help developing their ideas (SMP1–SMP6) and they thus expected to do well. Knowing that the judges would be asking additional questions prompted the students to better prepare and thus learn as much as possible. Noteworthy is that struggling students were encouraged and helped to display their knowledge in ways not possible through standard paper-and-pencil tests. The students were also practicing communication in writing and speaking, which are important skills across all content areas in the CCSS. Finally, both the students and Michael were interested in what the judges had to say, which resulted in further learning for student and teacher during and *after* the summative assessment, much like a formative assessment.

In response to my question on any changes he had made since the first edition of this book, he said:

> An important thing that changed was the papers I asked my students to write. They wrote between 10 and 12 major papers a year in Algebra 2 because I went to more of a data-driven or project-based instruction. We would collect some data in class, for example students' heights and arm spans, analyze the data with the appropriate mathematical tools, which we would develop, draw conclusions about our data and then they would write a paper about their results. These papers then became the basis of their performance exams. I am attaching a few examples of some of the situations we used for these projects. (See Figures 3.9–3.14.)

Figure 3.9 Algebra 2: Take-home final exam

This part of your exam will count as 30% of your final exam grade. This is due at the end of the hour on June 5th. **No late papers will be accepted.**

This exam covers material studied during the second semester in your projects. You may use your calculator and projects from this semester during this exam. You may not use any other materials.

For each of your responses include your calculations and show all your work.

1) In the Bean Shaker Project we had to calculate outliers. Explain what an outlier is and how it is calculated.

2) Using the Weight method, we had the 5-number summary given below. Use the method you described in problem #1 to check for outliers in these data. Do the original data contain any outliers?

Min	929.06
1Q	4395.10
Median	4681.54
3Q	4937.83
Max	5454.00

3) In the Bean Shaker Project we also used something called the Standard Deviation. Explain what the Standard Deviation is.

4) Using the data given below, show how you calculate the Population Variance and the Standard Deviation.

   0, 2, 4, 6, 8, 10   Variance = _____   Standard Dev. = _____

5) We found that on average (by combining the estimates from each class) there were 171.67 cups of beans in the bucket. Given this value for the number of cups in the bucket and there are 410.25 beans per cup on average, how many beans were in the bucket?

6) We found that on average each 2-lb bag of beans contained 4879.95 beans. Using your results from problem #5 and the fact that each bag of beans costs $1.73, how much profit could we expect from the sale of the bean shakers?

7) Using the weight method we found that on average 100 beans weighted 18.09 grams and that the bucket weighted 12,500 grams. Using this method, how many 2-lb bags of beans are in the bucket?

8) Given that each bean shaker would contain 100 beans, how much profit could we expect from the sale of the bean shakers if we use the weight method?

9) If we had used a 6-gallon bucket instead of a 5-gallon bucket and we used the volume method, how much profit could we expect from the sale of the bean shakers?

10) If Mr. Lehman's dream GTO costs $17, 650.00, how many 5-gallon buckets of beans would he need in order to afford this car if we used the volume method?

11) For the Fate of Holt High School Project we looked at the ACT data. One thing we looked at was whether the data were normal. Explain the three tests we used to check the data to see whether they were normal (Why did we care whether the data were normal?).

12) Show the test you used to prove the data for the class of 2005 are normal.

13) Explain what a z-score is.

14) Given the mean is 12 and the standard deviation is 2, what is the z-score for 15?

15) If the mean score on a test is 20 and the standard deviation of the test is 3, what is the probability of picking a random score from the test scores that is less than 18?

Figure 3.9 Continued

16) A student that graduated in 2005 scored a 33, while the student that graduated in 2006 scored a 32. How did you show that this did not strengthen Mr. Lehman's belief that the ACT scores are going down? Show your calculations to support your case.

17) When solving the Murder Mystery we used Newton's law of cooling, which is $T = S + (T_0 - S)e^{-kt}$. Explain what each of these letters stands for.

18) Explain how we found the value for e. Use the formula for compound interest, $A = P\left(1 + \dfrac{r}{n}\right)^{nt}$, to complete the table below and use it as part of your explanation.

Suppose you invest $1.00 at 100% interest for 1 year. Complete the following table that outlines your investment.

Number of times compounded per year	Work using compound interest formula	Value of investment
Annually		
Semiannually		
Quarterly		
Monthly		
Weekly		
Daily		
Hourly		
Minutely		
Secondly		

19) Explain what a logarithm is. Use the fact that $10^{0.3010} = 2$ in your explanation.

20) Explain the difference between a logarithm and a natural logarithm.

21) Explain why $\ln e = 1$.

22) What was the time of death? Use the data given for the body to show how we found the time of death.

23) What was the time of death? Use the data given for the can of coke to show how we confirmed the time of death.

24) If the room temperature had been 72° instead of 75°, what would have been the time of death? Use the information given about the body to do your calculations.

25) For the Birthday Problem we used permutations instead of combinations. Explain what permutations and combinations are and how they are different. Give the formula for both.

26) For the Birthday Problem we developed a formula that given the number of people in the room (n) we could calculate the probability that two of the people would have the same birthday. What is that formula and show how we developed it using n = 4.

27) If there are 19 people in the room, what is the probability that two of them will have the same birthday?

28) What would be your answer to problem #27, if we had used 366 days per year instead of 365?

29) At a certain point our calculators crashed as we were computing the probability of two people having the same birthday given a certain number of people in the room. Using n = 45, show how we got around this problem. What is the probability of two people having the same birthday if there are 45 people in a room?

30) When dealing with probability, we have three (3) types of probability. State what these three types of probability are and explain each one.

Figure 3.9 Continued

31) Explain why there is a 2/3 chance of winning on the Three Door problem if you switch doors instead of a 50% chance.
32) When playing the Mega Millions game, what is the probability of winning the jackpot?
33) When playing the Mega Millions game, what is the probability of winning the $5,000.00?
34) When playing the Mega Millions game, what is the expected value for each $1.00 played? Why is this value negative?
35) The Mega Millions game recently changed to 56 white balls and 48 gold balls. What is the new probability of winning the jackpot?
36) With the new lottery game, what is the new expected value?
37) List the rows 0 through 5 of Pascal's Triangle
38) Show how combinations can be used to find row 6 of Pascal's Triangle.
39) Show how Pascal's Triangle can be used to expand $(x + y)^4$.
40) What is the function for the diagonal number 3 of Pascal's Triangle.
41) If you roll a single die 15 times, what is the probability that you get a 5 six times?
42) If you roll a single die 15 times, what is the probability that you will get a 5 more than 2 times?
43) We found functions for the diagonals of Pascal's Triangle. What was our function for the 4th diagonal?
44) Given the following data set find the correlation coefficient using the formula. Show your calculations.

X	1	2	3	4
Y	2	4	6	7

45) What is the formula for calculating the slope for the line of best fit?
46) Using the data from problem #44 and the formula you gave in problem #45, find the slope for the line of best fit.
47) Using your results from problem #46, find the line of best fit for the data given in problem #44.

This has been a good year. We have accomplished a lot. Thank you for all the work you have done. Good luck next year and in the years to come. Mr. Lehman

Notice how many times Michael used the word "we" to refer to work he did along with the students. In partnering with his students to prepare and develop tools for assessment and providing multiple opportunities for his students to be successful in applying mathematical processes, Michael incorporated what Stiggins and Chappuis (2006) call "assessment *for* learning," rather than assessment *of* learning:

Assessment *for* learning happens in the classroom and involves students in every aspect of their own assessment to build their confidence and maximize their achievement. It rests on the understanding that students, not just adults, are data-driven instructional decision makers. . . . In this case, students and their teachers become partners in the classroom assessment process, relying on student-involved assessment, record keeping, and communication to help students understand what success looks like, see where they are now, and learn to close the gap between the two.

(11)

Figure 3.10 Algebra 2: "The sound of music"

Algebra II
"The Sound of Music"

In this project we will be investigating the properties of circular functions as they relate to sound waves. We used a CBL, TI Interactive and a TI 84 calculator, and tuning forks to collect data from sound waves.

Download the Sound Wave data from your teacher's computer.
(http://www.phy.mtu.edu/~suits/notefreqs.html)

1. For the note that you are assigned:

   - Create a scatter plot of the data.

   - Write a sine function and cosine function that model your note's data.

   - Calculate the error for your models.

2. Calculate the frequency of your note.

3. Identify your note using the following formula: freq = $220(2)^{x/12}$, that we developed in class, where freq represents the frequency of your note and x is the number of half steps your note is from an **A**, which has a frequency of 220 Hz (hertz).

4. Using MS Word and the Nspire Computer Link Software print a copy of your scatter plot and a copy of each of your functions graphed on the scatter plot, state the error of your function showing your calculations, and state the letter of the note your data represents including the calculations you used.

NOTE TO READERS FROM MICHAEL:

The data for the Musical notes came from tuning forks we used in class. I had a CBL with a microphone and a TI 84. (If you have access to a TI Nspire CX calculator I do have some of the data on my laptop that I use with the teachers.)
I had a tuning fork with slides on it so we could set the note, collect the data on the calculator and then pass it on to the students. I also had a set of 8 tuning forks that were not labeled. We would collect data from those forks and the student would write a model for the data then use their model to tell me what note the tuning for was.
This was an awesome project. The students loved it. They would explain how octaves worked. I would play dumb and eventually they would just tell me to sit down and they would take over. This worked so well because of the size of our bands and choirs at Holt. I always had students who could explain how octaves worked. They would then research how frequencies changed with in an octave and we would develop the formula for that.

I got this idea when talking to the choir director. He is an awesome teacher so he and I would collaborate so that when I was teaching this unit he would do a unit on music theory in his classes. This was a great collaboration. He taught me a lot.

1

Figure 3.11 Algebra 2 Project: Chapter 4

Name _____

Hour _____

Granger Construction, the company that built the current track at Holt High School, has recently been contracted by Michigan State University. MSU wants Granger to plan and construct a new track that is similar to Holt's that meets the criteria of the NCAA. The track will consist of two straight sections and two semicircle curves. Although Granger's blueprints contain the dimensions of the track, they are still in need of assistance on some crucial aspects of the track design. Previous Algebra 2 classes have helped Granger in many ways, such as deciding where to place starting positions or how much track material to order. Again, Granger needs our advice.

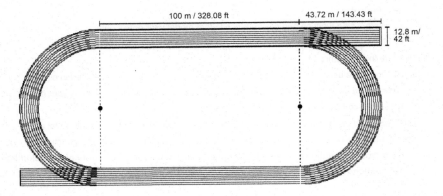

a. Why do the starting marks need to be staggered?
b. The track being built at MSU is a 400m track with 8 lanes. Each lane is 4.5 ft wide, and there is also a 3-ft border on the inner and outer edges. You need to decide where the starting position should be for the 100m, 200m, 400m, and 800m events. The finish line for all races will be at the end of the straightaway on the audience's side. Give precise directions that a sports official could easily follow. When placing the starting positions, keep the audience's view in mind.
c. The following diagram shows which materials will be placed underneath the track to prevent it from cracking during the winter and for drainage. Compute how much of each material will be required for the construction. U.S. tons are the industry's standard units for such quantities. You should report the necessary amount of each material in these units. You will need the densities shown in the table to make calculations. Finally, the inside of the track is intended to be used as a football field and should therefore be a grassy area. Compute how much sod (in square yards) you would have to order to cover the inside area of the track.

Cross-section of Track   ———— 7/8" Track Running Surface

4" Bituminous Top Course 1100T with ruberized Coating
9" Bituminous Base Course 1100L
12" Aggregate Subbase 22A

Material	Density^{-1} (cubic yards/ton)
Rubberized Track Surface	1.979
Bituminous base 1100T	0.534
Bituminous Base 1100L	0.521
Aggregate Sub-base	0.623

d. Write a paper discussing why the track needs staggered starting blocks and the amount of materials needed to construct the track. In your paper, describe the mathematics you used to decide where to put the starting blocks and calculating the amount of materials to be used. Finally, explain how you know your solution is correct and why you chose the methods you used. Include in your paper any mathematics you have done and any drawings that will help in your explanation.

Write this paper as if you are laying out the details for the Asphalt Company to follow as they build the track. Assume this company has not built a track previously; you will need to be very precise in your explanation. **Include a detailed diagram with your instructions.** Also, tell where you would want to put the stands for the audience to be able to get the best view of the races, including the start and finish of the races. Be sure to explain any terms you use.

Please **_type_** and **_double-space_** your paper. If you do not have access to a computer, please see me before the paper is due and I will try to arrange for you to use a school computer. This paper is due on Monday, September 10. We will give full-earned credit to papers handed in prior to 3:00 P.M. on the due date. If you are going to be absent on that day, be sure to hand it in prior to the due date. If you are unexpectedly absent on the due date, send it in with a friend, have your parents drop it off in my mailbox, or fax it to me. The school fax number is ###-####.

Figure 3.12 Algebra 2: Chapter 2 Project—Correlation and modeling of data

Name _____

Hour _____

In the movie *Pretty Woman,* there is a scene where Julia Roberts's character states, "Do you know your foot is the same as your arm from your elbow to your wrist?" This idea of body proportions comes from the work done by Leonardo da Vinci. Not only was da Vinci an outstanding artist of his time, but he was also a brilliant mathematician in his own right. Since movies are not always mathematically accurate, we should do some research to find out if Julia Roberts's character is correct when describing da Vinci's proportions. Below are some of his observations that we are particularly interested in confirming and reporting on.

1. The foot is the same as the arm from the elbow to the wrist
2. The length of a man's outspread arms is equal to his height.
3. The greatest width of the shoulders contains in itself the fourth part of the man.
4. The foot is the sixth part of the man.
5. Kneeling reduces ones height by one-fourth.

In your report include the following:

♦ A description of the methods you used to conduct your research.
♦ All of the data that you collected.
♦ A scatter plot and line of best fit for the data used in each of the observations.
♦ The error of each of the lines of best fit. Was your model a good fit? Confirm or contradict da Vinci's claims?
♦ A discussion about the correlation coefficient for each of the observations. Was the correlation positive or negative? How is this connected to the line of best fit?

Figure 3.12 Continued

- A discussion of the coefficient of determination for each of the observations.
- Are there any outliers in any of the data sets collected? If there were outliers, how did they affect the line of best fit and correlation coefficient? What method did we use in determining the outliers?
- An explanation of any terms that you use.
- A discussion of all the methods of finding the functions we discussed in class.

Your report should be **TYPED and DOUBLE-SPACED**. If you do not have access to a computer, please see us before the letter is due and we will try to arrange for you to use a school computer. This paper is due on **Monday, February 17.** We give full earned credit to papers handed in before 3:00 p.m. on the due date. If you are going to be absent on the due date, send it in with a friend, have your parents drop it off in our mailbox, or fax it to us. The school fax number is ###-####.

Figure 3.13 Algebra 2: Chapter 6 Project—The mathematics murder mystery

Name _____

Hour _____

NEWS BULLETIN: Hello, this is Nancy B. Chung. I am here with some late-breaking news from the World Mathematics Conference being held in downtown Holt, Michigan at the beautiful new education facility this community built for its students. We are now going to switch you live to Matt Mauer, who is at the scene. Matt, first of all, I didn't know they had Mathematics Conferences. That sounds like the coolest thing ever. Do they actually just get together and talk about mathematics?

Matt: Nancy, yes they do. It is the neatest thing I have ever seen! If I had known that I could just talk about mathematics all day, I would never have become a meager reporter. Oh well, I made my choices and have to live with them now! Nancy, I am on the scene because there has been a very sad incident here at the seminar that may detract from its true joy. It has been reported that one of the attendees has been found murdered.

Nancy: Matt, are you sure? How could someone ever consider murdering a professional mathematician? That is the lowest you can go. What is society coming to these days?

Matt: Well, Nancy, this is what I know so far. The police are reporting that a body was found in the snack room at 11:18 a.m. The victim was in the process of purchasing a refreshing Coca Cola when the deed was committed. The police report that at the time the victim was found, the body temperature was 34.4 Celsius degrees. One hour later it was down to 32.2 Celsius degrees.
          They also report that there was an unopened Coke on the floor beside the victim. How cruel is that. Not only did the evil person murder the victim who was probably experiencing one of the happiest times of their life just doing mathematics, but the victim was also preparing to enjoy the cool refreshing taste of a Coca–Cola. Is there no compassion left in this world?

Nancy: Matt!! Matt!! Back to the facts please. We are on international TV. So tell me, are police offering any speculations as to how this could have happened?

Matt: I am sorry. I got carried away with the totally unbelievable emotion of this incident. I've managed to track down the manufacturer of the Coke machine, and she told me the Coke machine usually keeps the soda at 42 degrees Fahrenheit. The police have reported that it was already warmed up to 8.89 Celsius degrees when they found the victim. An hour later the soda was up to 11.7 Celsius degrees. The police are also reporting that the convention center is kept at a very comfortable 75 degrees Fahrenheit.

Nancy: Uh . . . no, Matt. I meant the *crime*, not the *Coke*. Do the police know how such a heinous crime could have been committed?

Matt: Yes, well the police have announced that they have narrowed the search down to four suspects, all of whom are prominent mathematicians attending the conference. Naturally, since the victim here was a dedicated mathematician, the public is in an uproar and is demanding swift justice. The District Attorney is expected to announce later today in a press

Figure 3.13 Continued

conference that she will seek the maximum penalty allowed and would seek the death penalty in this case, if it were an option. Since the death penalty is not an option in Michigan, this person will be sent to prison for life and, worst thing of all, will not be allowed to think, write, or even talk about mathematics for the rest of their life.

Nancy: Wow, that punishment is worse than death itself. Well, it sounds like the police are really under pressure to find out who did this. What do they know so far?

Matt: Here are the stories given by the suspects.

Alibis

Euclid: We all travel in a parallel universe, so I guess this victim has moved to the next level. Well, from 8:00 to 9:30 I was presenting our theory on Infinitesimals with my colleague Liebniz. After that I went and had Coke with my friends Leonard Euler and Isaac Newton until 10:00. I then stepped out for a breath of fresh air until around 10:30 when I met Liebniz and Euler to attend Newton's presentation on something to do with apples. This guy actually thinks that an apple falling from a tree is news.

Liebniz: I started my day presenting with my good buddy Euclid until 9:30. We presented a fantastic paper on our theory of Infinitesimals. After the presentation I went back up to my room and worked on a problem I've been puzzling over. I met Euler around 10:05 to help him carry some of his equipment out to his Volvo. Euler and I then joined Euclid at Newton's outrageous presentation about gravity. This presentation was finally over at 12:00.

Euler: I overslept and missed the presentation by Liebniz and Euclid. Once I arrived at the convention I met Newton and Euclid for Coke. I then met Liebniz at 10:05, when he helped me carry out my equipment from my presentation to my car. We had to hurry so we could attend Newton's presentation on gravity.

Newton: After my early morning constitutional, I had to hurry to attend the presentation by Euclid and Liebniz. After this presentation I was lucky enough to be able, even if it was only for 30 minutes, to join Euclid and Euler for Coke. I had to cut our conversation short because at 10:10 I had to make a telephone call back to England to ask the queen for extra funding to continue my work. I finished just in time to get to my presentation on gravity.

Matt: Well, Nancy, there you have it. This is an amazing mystery. I sure hope someone can bring this fiend to justice.

Nancy: I agree, Matt. What a terrible tragedy to have happen at such a wonderful get-together. Is it true the police have called on some students who actually attend that educational institution to solve this mystery?

Matt: Yes it is. I was amazed when I heard the police were completely stymied by this crime, but a group of students in a world-renowned FST (Precalculus) class stepped forward and said they could figure it out. What surprised me was that in this little community of Holt and Dimondale there are students who are so well respected that they are known all over the world. They must have one amazing teacher.

a) Newton's Law of Cooling states that the difference in the temperature of a warm body (or drink) and its surroundings changes exponentially. Determine two equations to represent this situation (one for the body and one for the can of Coke). Explain in more detail Newton's Law of Cooling. Also, explain exponential functions and how they apply to this situation. Include in your explanation what each part of the equations represents.

b) Graph your equations in Part A. According to your equation and/or graph, what is the lowest temperature the body can reach? What is the lowest temperature the Coke can reach? Why? At what times do these occur?

c) Determine who "dunnnit." Use math to justify your conclusion. (HINT: The normal internal temperature of the human body is 98.6° F.) Your explanation should consist of an explanation of the mathematics that is used to solve for the time of death including use of logarithms.

d) What generalizations can you make about the effects the surrounding temperature has on the rate in which something cools? How would a change in location's temperature affect your work? How would your result change instead of drinking a Coke the victim was getting a hot coffee? Support your claims.

Figure 3.13 Continued

e) Write a paper summarizing your results. Be sure to explain any terms you use. Also please **_type and double-space_** your paper. If you do not have access to a computer, please see me before the paper is due and I will try to arrange for you to use a school computer. This paper is due on Monday, March 8. We will give full credit earned to papers handed in by 3:00 p.m. on the due date. If you are going to be absent on that day, be sure to hand it in prior to the due date. If you are unexpectedly absent on the due date, send it in with a friend, have your parents drop it off in my mailbox, or fax it to me. The school fax number is ###-####.

We would like to thank Ms. Beth Pulver for the original idea for this project.

Figure 3.14 Algebra Project: Bicycle project

Name _____

Hour _____

Your intern, Ms. Chadwick, has a dear friend who was Sparty (the MSU Mascot) at MSU. While she was on a bike ride across the MSU campus one day, she ran into Sparty. Quite literally, she ran into Sparty. Please don't blame Ms. Chadwick. It is not totally her fault. She was leaving the MSU-versus-U of M game, and she was very distraught when she ran into Sparty. Not only had MSU lost to U of M again, but it had also lost to Notre Dame and Illinois, with Ohio State on the horizon. So you see the only thing Ms. Chadwick had to look forward to was Northwestern, and she was worried that it may not be too good for the Spartans also. So as she rode along she saw a group of MSU fans chasing Sparty, who was running at a dead sprint and was not paying attention to where he was going. You see these fans caught Sparty begging some U of M fans to take him home with them and give them some of their nice blue clothes to wear. When these fans heard this conversation, they took off after him. So he ran out right in front of Ms. Chadwick. Both Sparty and Ms. Chadwick are okay, physically, but Ms. Chadwick's bicycle was completely ruined, and she was even more of a wreck emotionally. The bicycle was her favorite, and she didn't know where she could get a good replacement. That's when Ms. Lehman assured her that you, a bike design specialist, could help her out. She did not have the exact plans for the bike but from her wrecked bike came up with a few specifications of the bike and she found a graph showing the ratio of the gear to the rear tire.

Ms. Chadwick gave you the results from the test below.

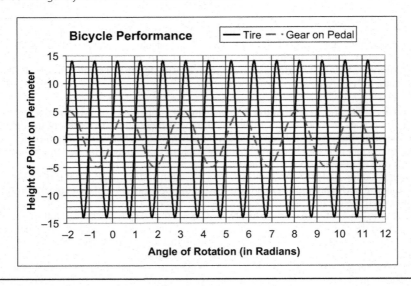

Figure 3.14 Continued

Ms. Chadwick also remembered that the frame of the bike was basically just a triangle, with the horizontal crossbar forming the base of the triangle and the angle formed near the pedals equal to 62°. She knew the horizontal cross bar on the bike was 33" off the ground. She also remembered that the front and rear tires of the bike just missed hitting this triangular frame by one inch (1"). Last, Ms. Chadwick knew that the chain that went from the top of the gear on the pedal to the top of the gear on the wheel was parallel with the ground.

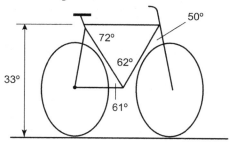

She drew you this sketch showing the frame with no gears or chains.

It is your job to design this bike for Ms. Chadwick. She needs the dimension of every major side on the bike and the measure of all of the angles formed between these sides. She also wants the design to include the size of the gears--both the gear hooked to the pedals and the gear that is hooked to the rear tire. Only one rear gear and one pedal gear were damaged in the accident. The rest of the gears survived and are usable on the new bike. She sincerely hopes that the information she has given you is enough to design a replica of her lost ride.

1) Based on the graphs what is the radius of the gears attached to the pedals? What is the radius of the tires? Explain how you know.
2) Based on the graphs what is the turning ratio of the pedals to the tires? By this ratio what is the radius of the rear gear?
3) Calculate all the missing lengths and angles of the bike frame and size of the gears. Do not worry about the measurements for the handlebar or the seat. Insert your results on the extra sketch for Ms. Chadwick attached to this project. Show and explain your work. Include an explanation and proof of the Law of Sines and the Law of Cosines.
4) Write a paper summarizing your results. Be sure to explain any terms you use. Also please **_type and double-space_** your paper. If you do not have access to a computer, please see me before the paper is due and I will try to arrange for you to use a school computer. This paper is due on Monday, November 7. We will give full credit earned to papers handed in before 3:00 P.M. on the due date. If you are going to be absent on that day, be sure to hand it in prior to the due date. If you are unexpectedly absent on the due date, send it in with a friend, have your parents drop it off in my mailbox, or fax it to me. The school fax number is ###-####.

In doing his best to integrate research results into practice, Michael exemplified teachers who work hard to improve their teaching, often in the face of uncertainty and frustration. The keys to Michael's success included his perseverance and patience—changing a little at a time—and his willingness to enlist the help of colleagues.

Unit Overview

Group Performance Assessment

Aim: How can we promote student learning through performance assessments?

Objective: Students will demonstrate their understanding of a topic through performance assessments.

Course: All courses but examples are for Algebra, Algebra 2, and Precalculus.

Source: Original.

Grade Levels: All.

Number of 90-Minute Periods: One to two.

NCTM/CCSSM Standards: Varies with the course.

NCTM Processes/CCSSM Mathematical Practices: Mathematics as Problem Solving, Communication, Reasoning, Connection/SMP1–SMP6.

Mathematical Concepts: Varies with the course.

Materials and Tools

- ◆ Packet of six questions per group of three to four students plus one extra problem for the group to process
- ◆ Instructions for students
- ◆ Three judges per group of students
- ◆ Instructions, grading rubric, score sheet for judges

Management and Assessment Procedures

- ◆ Develop sets of problems for the groups.
- ◆ Allow class time for students to prepare.
- ◆ Develop instructions, rubric, and student grade sheet for judges.
- ◆ Solicit the help of parents, colleagues, business associates, and faculty from area universities and colleges to serve as judges.
- ◆ Assign three judges per group.
- ◆ Put students in groups of three or four. Students in each class are judged at the same time. Eight groups of students present each period.

- ◆ Share instructions and rubric given to the judges with students.
- ◆ Collect, read, and return judges' responses to students.

Resources

1. Black, P., & D. Wiliam. (1998). Assessment and Classroom Learning. *Assessment in Education* 5(1), 7–74.
2. Wiliam, D. (2014). The Right Questions, the Right Way. *Educational Leadership* 71(6), 16–19. www.ascd.org/publications/educational-leadership/mar14/vol71/num06/The-Right-Questions,-The-Right-Way.aspx. Retrieved April 2014.
3. Chapter12, this volume. From the Web: Google the names if the links have changed.
4. Mathematics Assessment Project: http://map.mathshell.org/materials/index.php Prototypes for summative assessments are at http://map.mathshell.org/materials/tests.php.
5. NCTM's *Navigation Series* for grades 9–13: www.nctm.org.
6. TIMSS (Trends in International Mathematics and Science Study) questions: www.edinformatics.com/timss/timss_intro.htm.
7. Charles A. Dana Center: www.utdanacenter.org/ http:www.ccsstoolbox.com/.
8. Mathematics Assessment Resource Service (MARS). High school math tasks are at www.scoe.org/docs/mars/course-1.pdf http://www.scoe.org/docs/mars/course-2.pdf.
9. Illustrative Mathematics Program: http://illustrativemathematics.org.**Figure 3.14** Continued

4

Mark Lonergan: The Mathematics of the Theater

The mission of the Boston Arts Academy is to be a laboratory and a beacon of academic and artistic innovation for any student interested in coming to our school. When we first opened, we thought that this meant teaching through the arts. The original vision, as I understand it, was to incorporate the arts into all of the academic subjects and to try to make every class period an interdisciplinary learning experience. This was, as you may imagine, a very challenging task. For science classes, this meant that sometimes they would study chemistry and tie it back to learning about pottery glazes. For humanities classes, it meant learning about different cultures through their music and dance as well as researching about them. But for math class, this always felt like a bit of a tug-of-war. There are many, many times where math connects to the arts. There are also times when we really think of math as an art unto itself. But the truth is that most of the places where there is true overlap between math and arts are places where either the math is very simple or very complex. For years, we have asked our Geometry students to imagine an event that will take place on stage in our theater and then use equations of circles to map out the lighting plan for this event. This stage is a place where there is rich interdisciplinary overlap between math and theater. Our hanging spotlights are a real-world version of conic sections and the metal grid that hangs on the ceiling above the theater is a real-world example of Cartesian axes. The students really enjoyed developing their own use for the space.

Mark Lonergan, Boston, Massachusetts

Boston Arts Academy (BAA) was founded in 1998 as a public high school for the visual and performing arts in Boston. It is part of the Boston Public School system and a pilot school, which means teachers have special autonomies around governing the school and are able to deviate from the district calendar, curriculum, and course schedule. As an example, ninth-graders take Geometry before Algebra, and the classes are 85 minutes long. When I asked Mark about how his school differs from others having art as a focus, he said:

> The population of BAA is somewhat unique. Most arts schools across the country want to teach arts to students who are well prepared academically. That means that to gain admission, students have to have a minimum GPA in their academic classes, which is not a requirement for BAA. This increases the challenge for us to give our students a world-class arts education that prepares them for a college or conservatory when they graduate and to also give them a college-prep academic education that prepares them to continue on to a selective college or university.

A project that Mark has taught for several years with ninth-graders is the Lighting Design project where students are asked to create an event that will be performed on BAA's stage, which is called a "black box." The black box, so called because all of its interior walls are painted black, is a small but flexible performance space that can be adapted depending on the type of performance. It has been used many times as a typical theater but can also be reconfigured by arranging the staging, risers, and seating into arrangements that can accommodate fashion shows with a catwalk, theater, dance, or music shows, and even exhibitions for science fairs.

Background on the Project

The task that the students are given is to think about developing an event for the black box. Their job on this project has three different parts. The first is to develop an imaginative event; the second is to include the lighting, which means determining where lights are hanging, how wide their radii are and their related equations; the third is to communicate the results through a short summary and a poster presentation.

The project is part of a circles unit in ninth-grade geometry class. Before the circles unit, students have studied basic planar geometry, including definitions of points, lines, rays, planes, shapes, coordinate graphing, and the distance formula as part of the triangles and the Pythagorean Theorem. Early in the circles unit, students learn about the definition and development of π and the area and circumference formulas.

Preparing for the Launch

Mark starts the lighting project with the traditional approach of introducing a warm-up consisting of equations of circles to reinforce the definition of a circle as all the points that are the same distance from a center point (see Figure 4.1). As students

Figure 4.1 Circle equation notes

_____   Name:

> ### THE "real" CIRCLE EQUATION
>
> If you have a circle on the coordinate plane whose radius is *r* and whose center is the point (*h*, *k*), its equation is:

The Proof: Given a circle on the coordinate plane whose radius is *r* and whose center is the point (*h*, *k*). Let (*x*, *y*) be the coordinates of a point on the circle.

$$r^2 = (\qquad)^2 + (\qquad)^2$$

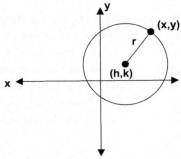

Directions: Write the equation for the circle described below and sketch the circle on the coordinate grid.

Ex 1
What is the equation of a circle whose center is at (4,1) and whose radius is 3 units?

Equation:

Ex 2
What is the equation of a circle whose center is at (−2, 4) and whose radius is 5 units?

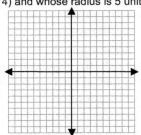

Equation:

Figure 4.1 (Continued)

Directions: Fill in each of the rows below with descriptions, graphs, and equations.

Description	Graph	Equation
Center point: (1, 0) Radius: 2		
Center point: _____ Radius: _____		
Center point: _____ Radius: _____		$(x+3)^2+(y-1)^2=9$
Center point: (0, 0) Radius: 1		
Center point: _____ Radius: _____		$(x+1)^2+(y-2)^2=25$

Figure 4.1 (Continued)

1. Circle P has a radius of 4 and is drawn to the right.

    a. What is the **equation** of circle P?

    b. For each of the following points, determine whether
       they are **inside**, **on** or **outside** of circle P.

Point	Inside, On, or Outside the circle
(4, 0)	
(0, 4)	
(−4, 4)	
(3, 1)	
(4, 3)	

2. The point (1.5, *b*) is on Circle P. Find the value of *b*.

3. The point (*c*, −2.5) is on Circle P. Find the value of *c*.

Figure 4.1 (Continued)

PUSH YOURSELF

4. Nine circular tiles are arranged as below as part of a pattern in a floor design. Each tile has a diameter of 1 inch. If the group of 9 tiles is enclosed by a diamond-shaped border that lies tangent to the exterior tiles, what is the total length, in inches, of the border?

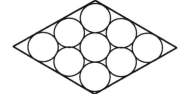

(A) 4
(B) 6
(C) 8
(D) 9
(E) 12

5. Points D and B lie on the circle below with center A. If square $ABCD$ has an area of 16, what is the length of arc BD?

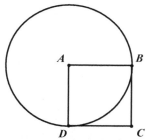

(A) 2π
(B) 4
(C) 8
(D) 4π
(E) 8π

6. A circle's diameter is divided in the ratio of 3 to 4, and semicircles are drawn on each segment, as shown. What is the ratio of the upper area to the lower area?

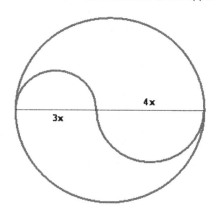

review the distance formula, they consider finding the distance from a point (h,k) to a constant number (r). What follows next is a straightforward review prompted by the following questions:

1. Given the center and radius of a circle, how can you write its equation?
2. Given the equation of a circle, how can you determine its center and radius?
3. What if I give you just a picture of a circle? How can you find its center, radius and equation?
4. Is the point (3,2) on this given circle?

Most students see the patterns and are able to decode the equation of a circle fairly quickly. But Mark says:

The most challenging question for students at the outset is determining if a point is on circle. It is tricky for students to understand how to substitute a given coordinate point into the equation of the circle and how to use their algebra skills to decide whether or not this is a true statement. We find that it helps to first ask the question with a graphed circle because students can often answer this question with an eyeball estimate. To help them see the need for algebra, we give them some points that are too close to call and so it becomes necessary to learn how to substitute into the equation of the circle and to check more closely. For homework, students are asked to graph equations of circles whose end result is a series of circles, as in Figure 4.2.

The Launch

Mark launches the project by saying, "For the next couple of days, you will work on the job of developing an event for our black box." Students' interest piques and their minds are full of questions:

Shanette: Can we design anything we want?
Mark: Yes.
Lamonte: Like a play?
Kevin: How about a dance or musical recital?
Meredith: How about staging a circus?
Mark: Your choice.

Mark smiles as he comments, "Many students like to think about a connection to their arts major, so they suggest the above but staging a circus would be a tight fit—honestly—but who am I to stifle creativity on this hypothetical project?" He does indirectly help students think through the process by observing, "We will need to consider what is doable for us in this project since we do not have a Hollywood stage! What are some things we may have to simplify or alter?" On the second day, to provide

Figure 4.2 Circle project preparation

Name:

Math 1 HW   Date:

1. Rectangular black box theater is being used for a fashion show. The lighting director has written the equations of the circles that will be created by the spotlights. Sketch the circles on the grid below. The first one has been done for you.

Equation	Center & Radius
1. $(x-3)^2+(y-3)^2=1$	Center: (3, 3) Radius 1
2. $(x-7)^2+(y-3)^2=4$	
3. $(x-12)^2+(y-4)^2=9$	
4. $(x-12)^2+(y-15)^2=9$	
5. $(x-12)^2+(y-10)^2=16$	
6. $(x-17)^2+(y-3)^2=4$	
7. $(x-21)^2+(y-3)^2=1$	

Figure 4.2 (Continued)

2. Another production is going on in a rectangular black box theater. Given the equations of circles, sketch the circles on the grid below:

Equation	Center & Radius
1. $(x-8)^2 + (y-17)^2 = 4$	
2. $(x-12)^2 + (y-19)^2 = 9$	
3. $(x-16)^2 + (y-7)^2 = 4$	
4. $(x-12)^2 + (y-11)^2 = 16$	
5. $(x-12)^2 + (y-14)^2 = 81$	

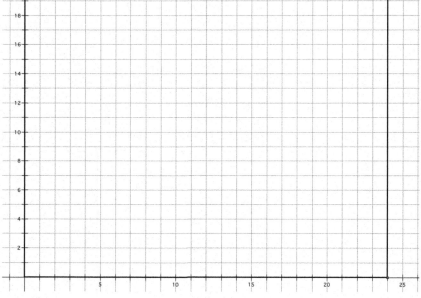

students with an overview of the project's requirement, he distributes Figure 4.3, which shows the project's assessment criteria.

Mark then takes a trip with students to the black box, where he has various resources to help with the project that include a short video narrated by Gary Gonzalez, a BAA graduate. Gary's video is a tour of the lighting booth that shows how lights are chosen, adjusted, and hung from a metal grid that is suspended from the theater ceiling. He shows how the lighting circle can be made bigger or smaller just by pulling some tabs or by using a wider light source. He also shows the number and letter labels that are hidden near the top of the walls in the theater. "The numbers are on this side, the letters are on the other side. The numbers and letters help you locate where you're going to put your lights. Instead of using x,y coordinates, we use a letter and a

Figure 4.3 Lighting design project

Math 1 Project

Name:
Date:

For this activity, we will try to come up with a lighting design for the Black Box Theater, which is a rectangular theater. We will be using coordinate geometry to help us find the equation of the circles made by lights hanging overhead.

Diagram Artwork   (20 points)

❏ Practice Lighting Diagram (3)
❏ Rough Draft of Lighting Design (2)
❏ Includes at least 5 circles (1)
❏ Includes at least 3 different sizes (1)
❏ Circles accurate sizes/shapes (5)

❏ Space for both exhibition & audience (1)
❏ Audience less than 90 + Calculations (2)
❏ Neatness/Craftsmanship (2)
❏ Artistry/Invention/Color (2)
❏ Labeled circle spotlights (1)

Math Requirements   (20 points)

Light 1 Info	❏ Radius (1)	❏ Center point (1)	❏ Area (1)	❏ Equation (1)
Light 2 Info	❏ Radius (1)	❏ Center point (1)	❏ Area (1)	❏ Equation (1)
Light 3 Info	❏ Radius (1)	❏ Center point (1)	❏ Area (1)	❏ Equation (1)
Light 4 Info	❏ Radius (1)	❏ Center point (1)	❏ Area (1)	❏ Equation (1)
Light 5 Info	❏ Radius (1)	❏ Center point (1)	❏ Area (1)	❏ Equation (1)

Analysis and Evaluation Requirement   (30 points)

Paragraph 1: Problem Statement (4)
❏ What were you asked to do for this assignment?
❏ What choices did you make?

Paragraph 2: Event Information (10)
❏ What is your scene/event?
❏ How did you decide where to put the stage/audience/lights?
❏ How did you decide what colors and sizes to use?
❏ How does your lighting design enhance the event?
❏ What will the audience remember about your design?

Paragraph 3: Process (8)
❏ How/why did you use trigonometry?
❏ How did you find your equations of circles?
❏ What parts were challenging? What parts were easy?
❏ Did results match expectations? Why or why not?

Paragraph 4: Evaluation (8)
❏ Proud of your final artwork? Why or why not?
❏ Proud of your math work? Why or why not?
❏ Proud of your work process? Why or why not?
❏ Should we do this project next year? Why or why not?

Presentation   (10 points)

❏ Main title & subheadings (1)
❏ Name (1)
❏ Include lighting diagram (2)

❏ Include all information from Paragraph 2 (5)
❏ Image/artifact connected to your event (1)

PROJECT TOTAL	/80 points

number to show where it is on the grid," he says while standing on a ladder and pointing to the labels. Mark says, "Usually, the ninth-graders can't quite believe their eyes because they've only been in the black box once or twice since coming to BAA. They don't realize how flexible the space really is or how all of the changes are designed and built by students working with teachers."

Mark also asks the lighting design teacher, Dan Jentzen, to come to class or shows a video that Dan made so that the class learns about lighting techniques and some examples of good and bad lighting from different movies and TV shows. Many students say that they haven't really noticed lighting before, but when Dan shows a couple of clips from some well-lit music videos, students marvel at how much of an impact the lighting can make. Dan shows a clip from the movie *Rent* (available on YouTube at www.youtube.com/watch?v=UvyHuse6buY), which starts with a completely black screen and then shows eight small circles on an empty stage. As the music builds, the lights rise up toward the ceiling and reveal the eight main characters in the story, standing in a row and singing the opening song of the movie.

It's both simple and incredibly dramatic, and, as Dan points out, the only thing that is moving in the scene are the lights. "At the end of this scene, students begin to see the value and the power of lighting design," Mark adds. He then initiates a discussion to highlight the important points:

Mark:	Who can describe the effect of the lighting in the *Rent* clip?
Kyle:	It started on the floor and then moved up, I think.
Jacobie:	I think they were adjusting the tabs on the light or something, to make the circles get bigger, until you could see the actors standing there.
Mark:	But what was moving? Did the actors move at all?
Cynthia:	No. They didn't move but I think the lights did.
Mark:	And what shapes did you see as the lights moved?
Jacobie:	I saw circles.
Maya:	I saw cone shapes coming from the light to the floor.

Mark: Good. Let's agree that, for this project, we only focus on overhead lighting that creates circle graphs. In the theater world, there is usually a mix of overhead lighting and angled lighting—sometimes called "three-point lighting." But let us think about lighting for one key scene of a play instead of thinking about how to stage an entire production. It is also true that most lighting designers are reliant on technology to model their lighting plans instead of doing the calculations by hand, and few lighting designers are interested in writing down the equation of the circles—but that could change if they knew how cool equations of circles really are. Before we move further, we need to review and extend some mathematics we have used before. Mark uses this discussion to guide students into the mathematics required to explore lighting and spends a big chunk of the second day with a review of trigonometry. He distributes and has students read the important aspects of lighting as shown in Figure 4.4, which is Part I of the project. He tells students, "It is very important that you be able to determine the area of the spotlights on stage for your project. Before completing the problems in Part 1, let's work on one where the spotlight is hanging 15 feet above ground and the angle measure of 18 degrees is between the two rays from the vertex of the fixture" (see Figure 4.5).

To help students see the embedded right triangle in Figure 4.5, Mark tells students to label the light source "theta" so that the adjacent side of the triangle is the height of 15 feet, the opposite side of the triangle is the radius of the circle, and the

Figure 4.4 Part 1: Lighting info

1. The lighting that we can use is the **LEKO spotlight**.

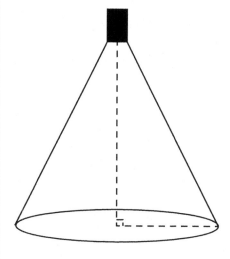

➢ When pointed straight down, each of these lights will make a circle on the stage.

➢ You have five different light degree widths possible for this assignment:

- 10 degrees
- 18 degrees
- 26 degrees
- 36 degrees
- 50 degrees

➢ Each light hangs from 15 feet overhead.

2. You can use color gels to change the light color.

3. In a real show, the angle of the lights can change as well as the location of the lights. Sometimes, lighting can come from the sides or the bottom of the stage. **For this project, we are only changing the location. The angle will be fixed and all lights are pointing straight down.**

Calculations
We want to calculate how big the spotlights will show up on the stage in order to decide what size lights we want/need.

For all the lights, calculate the radius and area of the spotlight. Remember that each light hangs from a height of 15 feet from the floor:

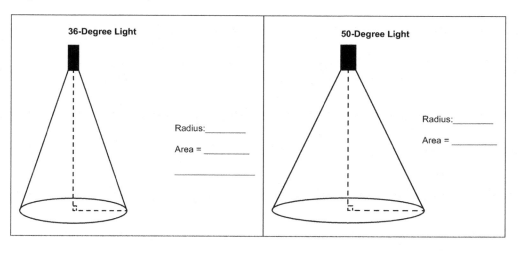

Figure 4.5 Guided example: 18-degree light

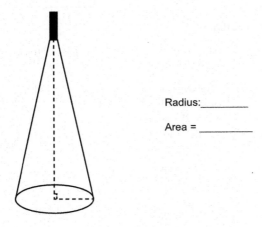

Radius:_____

Area = _____

hypotenuse is the edge of the cone (which is not really useful). Students work in small groups to complete the problem as Mark listens to their processes:

Joshua: I think we should find the tangent of 18 degrees.

Mayte: I agree.

Sara: Let's see, tan18 = 0.3249, and the opposite side . . . is the radius of the circle.

Mayte: We know the adjacent side is 15 because the lights are 15 feet overhead.

Mark notices that many students do use the 18 degrees as a starting point, and he usually lets them finish the process before reminding them that the 18 degrees is not the size of the angle in their triangle:

Mark: Can we look at the board for a minute and focus on the light circle or light cone? What does the 1-degree opening really mean?

Adonis: That's how wide the light is . . . going across the circle.

Mark: And where on my figure can I label the 18-degree angle?

Annie: It's there, at the very top of the cone.

Mark: Sure, but that means that my triangle can't also have an 18-degree angle at the top.

Annie: Yeah . . . I see. . . . It's cut in half because the triangle only takes up half of the cone.

Mark: What do you think about Annie's thinking?

Shanette: Annie is right. Let's all use 9 degrees to help us find the radius of this light circle.

Once students understand the math for Figure 4.5, he has them practice problems for other degrees of light similar to those in Figure 4.4. Students are relieved (some are disappointed) that the other examples are very similar, with only the angle size changing. Having found the radius for each spotlight, students begin to plan their own use of the space and start with thinking about what they'll present. Mark helps by having them complete a description of the black box and how it compares to and contrasts with the coordinate plane (see Figure 4.6, which shows Parts 2 and 3 of the project). Mark provides several options, including scenes from *Romeo and Juliet* or a design of their choice. He distributes Part 4 (Figure 4.7) of the project, which delineates the requirements for the project, suggestions for events, and the specific mathematics that need to be considered such as spaces between chairs and the maximum number of people the theater can seat. Students busily brainstorm ideas for their projects and think about the math they need to include while Mark circulates to guide students when necessary.

Mark:	Jonathan, your numbers look good, and it looks like you're ready to start thinking about what kind of presentation you'd want to make in the black box. Do you have any ideas of what you want to do? In a bit, I will borrow your calculations to share with the class (see Figure 4.8).
Jonathan:	I don't know, but maybe some kind of music concert. I was thinking maybe the jazz band could play?
Mark:	I think that will work. You can think about whether you want to have the performers in the front of the audience or in the middle. Also you might want to have some spotlights for soloists. And if you know what songs, maybe you can include some special lighting—something moody or dramatic, maybe?
Mayte:	What are you thinking of doing, Antony?
Antony:	I think I am going to do a catwalk for a fashion show. How about you?
Mayte:	Maybe something from *Romeo and Juliet*. See what I have already staged?
Mark:	It looks like you are taking up most of the space with the stage and set. Where's the audience going to sit? Remember that we have to fit an audience in this space as well.
Mayte:	They're going be over here by the door . . . and some of them are going to sit on benches on the stage. Some benches are going to be red for Capulet, and some are blue for Romeo.
Mark:	That sounds cool. Can't wait to see your finished diagram. Can you add those colors to the lighting as well?

Mark is careful to notice whether any of his struggling students are lost or overwhelmed, and when he finds that to be so, he provides specific suggestions for them, like a benefit karaoke performance! Mark says, "When I give them this idea, students always suddenly realize that they have a better idea in their head!" Mark gives students Part 6 of the project (Figure 4.9), which is a checklist of the important element of the project to ensure that students do all that is required.

Figure 4.6 Part 2: Black box info; Part 3: Lights and blackboard practice

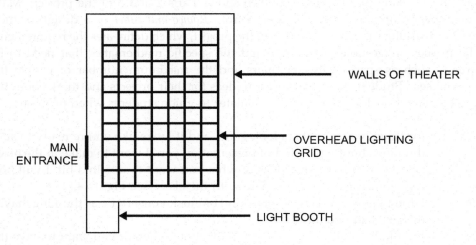

1. BAA's Black Box Theater is **46 ft by 36 ft.**

2. A square grid hangs **15 feet** overhead used to hang the lighting.
   ➢ The grid is made of metal poles and does not move.
   ➢ The grid lines are 2 feet apart.

4. The grid has an x-axis and a y-axis. The location of the light source can be listed using coordinates.
   ➢ *So (4, 6) means over 4 feet to the right and 6 feet up from the origin.*

5. Because the grid is hanging in the air, either the x-coordinate or the y-coordinate must be an even whole number.
   ➢ *So the coordinate (3.5, 6.2) would be an impossible location for a light source because there is no way to attach this light to the grid.*

6. The Black Box can seat 90 people at most.

<u>*Use the floor plan and table on THE NEXT PAGE*</u>

1. Using the Black Box floor plan on the next page, sketch a graph of the spotlight circle if I hang the 10-degree light from the point (8,10). **Label this circle A.**

2. Add a seating area for your audience. If **each person takes up 2ft by 3ft** when seating, how many people can your audience space seat?

3. Add four more spotlight circles to your practice lighting design. Make sure to only use the available spotlights and to **label** each spotlight circle.

4. For each spotlight circle, use the table on the next page to record the degree of light you used, the radius of the spotlight, the area of the spotlight, the center point of your light and the equation.

Figure 4.6 (Continued)

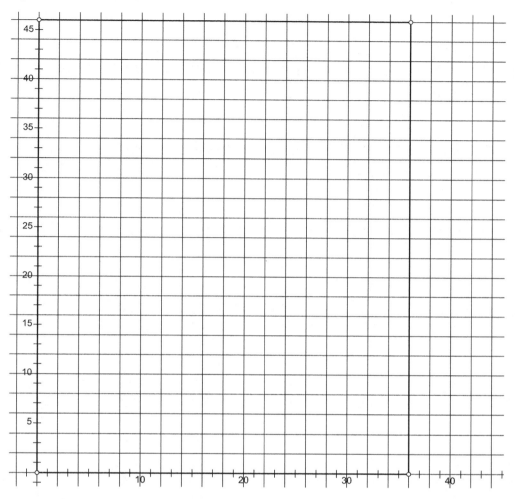

Circle	Degree	Center	Radius	Area	Equation
A	10	(8, 10)			
B					
C					
D					
E					

Figure 4.7 Part 4: Your assignment

You have two options for this project:

1. For your final product, you can create a lighting design for one scene of *Romeo and Juliet*. After watching the Balcony Scene, the Party Scene, and the Death Scene, which scene will you create a lighting design for? You can also pick another scene from *Romeo and Juliet* that you are more interested in.
   ➢ How will you use lighting to enhance the scene? Explain with detail below.

OR

2. If you do not want to create a lighting design for *Romeo and Juliet*, you can create a design for another event—a play, a fashion show, a fundraiser, etc. Write your idea below and explain how you plan to use lighting to enhance your event.

_____

_____

_____

_____

_____

_____

_____

_____

_____

_____

REMEMBER THE FACTS:

❑ This Black Box has a grid that hangs from the ceiling 15 feet above the ground.

❑ The grids are spaced **2 feet apart.**

❑ The lights that are available are 10-, 18-, 26-, 36-, and 50-degree lights.

❑ You may use different filters to change the color of your light circles.

❑ The Black Box can seat up to 90 people.

❑ Each person, when seated, takes up a 2 ft by 3 ft space block.

Figure 4.7 (Continued)

Lighting Design Sketch

SKETCH:
Look back to Part 1 to find the radii of your lights. *List them in the chart below to help you when creating your sketch.*

Light's Degree	Light's Radius
10 degrees	
18 degrees	
26 degrees	
36 degrees	
50 degrees	

LIGHTING DESIGN REQUIREMENTS:

❑ Your design must include **at least 5 circles.**

❑ Your spotlights have to be **at least 3 different sizes.**

❑ You don't have to use every size of light.

❑ You can use the same light sizes more than once.

❑ **Label** all spotlight circles (A, B, C, . . .)

❑ Your diagram must have space for both performance/exhibition and audience.

❑ Your audience space must hold **90 people or less.**

❑ Your final lighting design should be **neatly** done and use appropriate light **colors.**

Audience:
How many people do you want to fit into your design? _____

How much area will you utilize in audience space? Show your calculations below.

Figure 4.7 (Continued)

BLACK BOX THEATER—The grids are spaced **2 feet apart.**
- ✓ Use this as your **ROUGH DRAFT** diagram for your lighting design plan.
- ✓ **FINAL DRAFT** should be done on a separate grid (provided by your teacher) or Geometers Sketchpad.

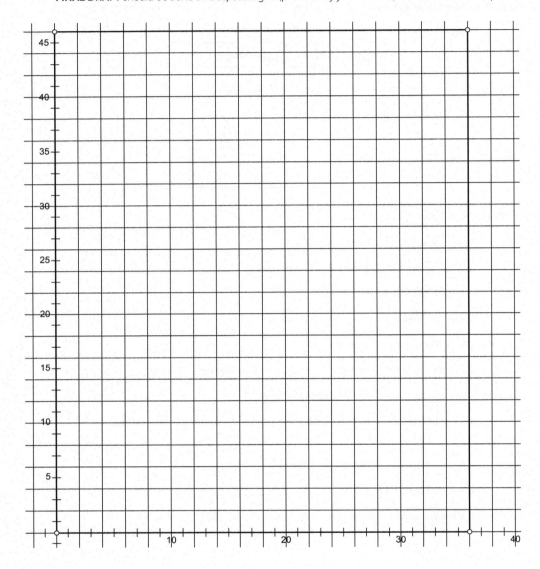

Figure 4.8 Sample student spotlight calculations

CIRCLE SPOTLIGHT AND AUDIENCE					
INFORMATION					
Spotlight Label	Light's Degree Size	Light's Center Point	Light's Radius	Light's Area	Light's Equation
A	10°	(12,34)	13.1 ft.	5.39 ft.²	$(x - 12)^2 + (y - 34)^2 = 1.77$ ft.
B	18°	(24,30)	2.37 ft.	17.71 ft.²	$(x - 24)^2 + (y - 30)^2 = 5.62$ ft.
C	26°	(14,24)	3.46 ft.	37.61 ft.²	$(x - 14)^2 + (y - 24)^2 = 11.97$ ft.
D	36°	(24,14)	4.87 ft.	74.57 ft.²	$(x - 24)^2 + (y - 14)^2 = 23.72$ ft.
E	50°	(14,8)	6.99 ft.	153.5 ft.²	$(x - 14)^2 + (y - 8)^2 = 48.86$ ft.

Figure 4.9 Part 6: Analysis and evaluation

Final write-up should be typed.

PARAGRAPH 1: Problem Statement
☐ What were you asked to do for this assignment (artistically, mathematically, etc.)?
☐ What choices did you make while doing this assignment (the event, set-up, etc.)?

PARAGRAPH 2: Scene/Event Information
☐ What is the scene/event you chose to create a lighting design for?
☐ How did you decide where to put the stage, audience, and lights?
☐ How did you decide what colors and sizes of the lights to use?
☐ How does the lighting design that you created enhance the scene/event?
☐ What will the audience remember about the lighting design you created?

PARAGRAPH 3: Process
☐ Why/how did you need to use trigonometry to find the dimensions of the circle?
☐ How did you find your equations for the circles?
☐ What parts of the process were challenging? What parts were easy?
☐ Did your end result match your original expectations? Why or why not?

PARAGRAPH 4: Evaluation
☐ Were you proud of your final artwork? Why or why not?
☐ Were you proud of your final math work? Why or why not?
☐ Were you proud of the way you worked on this project? Why or why not?
☐ Do you think Math 1 students should do this kind of project again next year? Why or why not?

Depending on time, Mark uses one of the following strategies for having students share their project with the class:

◆ Making a poster/gallery walk. After students complete their lighting plan, they put their final work on a poster and hang it in the room. Students then do a gallery walk. One of Mark's colleagues gives her students three Post-it notes and asks them to critique their peers, writing positive and negative feedback on the Post-it notes and posting them next to the posters. (See Figures 4.10 and 4.11.)

◆ Making a digital representation. Using a program like Geogebra, students can create a simple grid and graph the equations of their circles.

Marks adds, "Using Geogebra is a terrific way to make sure that the graphs and equations are equivalent, and that the final product can be printed and added to a poster. In the next years, some students will be encouraged to make a 3D representation of their lighting plan using Google SketchUp."

Discussion between Colleagues

Tell us a bit more about your school.

Knowing our school and our students may help make sense of some of the curricular choices that we have made along the way. First of all, because of our school philosophy (and our small size), we do not believe in tracking students, and we prefer whenever possible to have a diverse mix of ability levels all in the same classroom at the same time. Because we admit students from all across the city, some have had very strong middle school math experiences (which usually means that they have strong Algebra skills), and others have only minimal exposure to Algebra. For this reason, we decided that ALL of our ninth-grade students would take a semester of Geometry when they enter the school. We like Geometry for ninth-graders because it allows us to push the well-prepared students without excluding the ill-prepared students. Geometry is a new subject for almost all of the students, but it is also a familiar subject, since shapes, area, volume, and other Geometry concepts are introduced in elementary math classes.

The school is a full-inclusion school?

We are full inclusion, which means that there is no separate track for students with IEPs or disabilities. Instead, these students are mainstreamed and work alongside all of the other students in their grade. Many ninth-graders with IEPs have a concurrent class called Learning Center that helps provide organization skills and other supports for students in Geometry class. In a class of 24 students, we can have up to a third of the class who has an IEP or 504 plan.

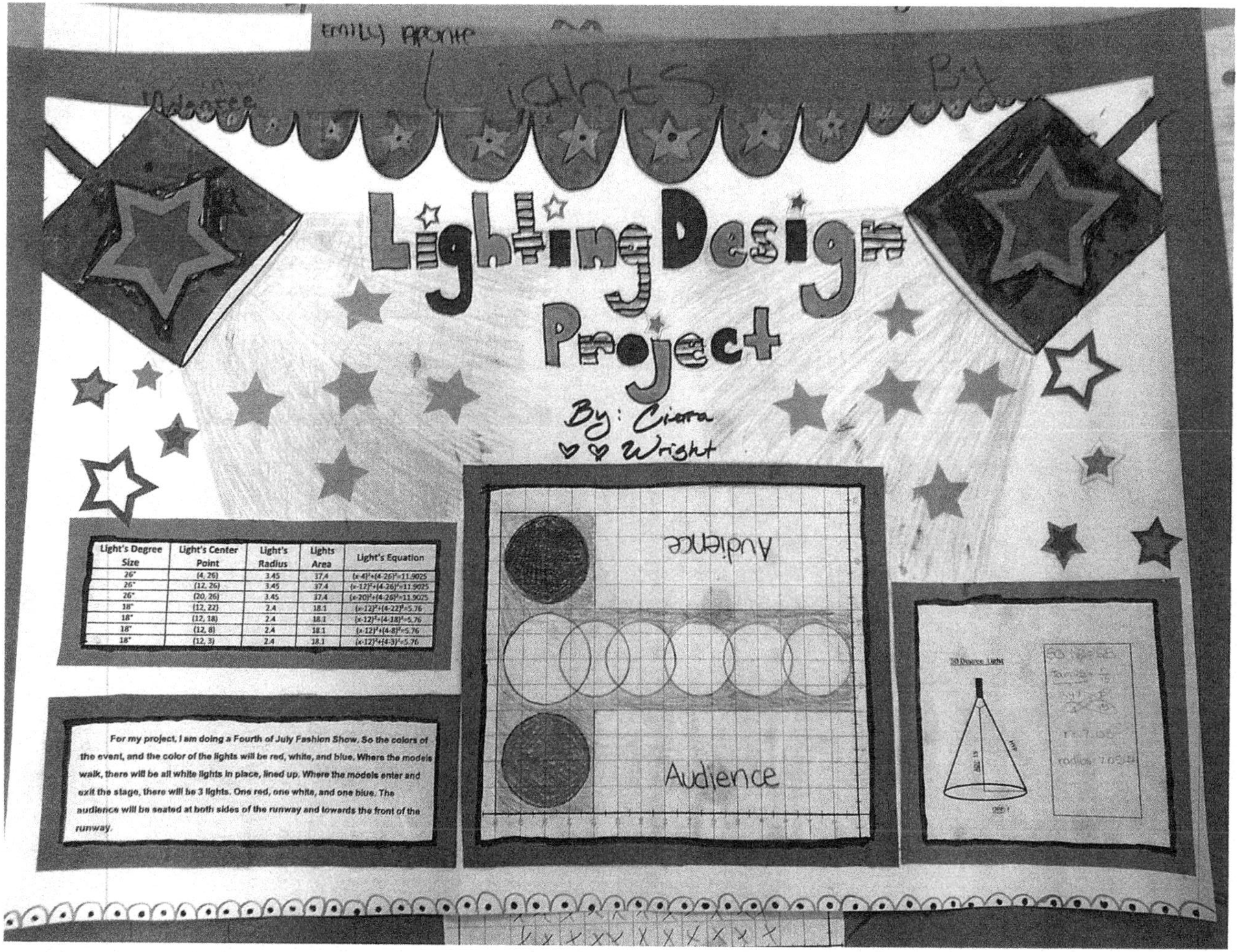

Figure 4.10 Student poster

Figure 4.11 Student design summary

ABOUT MY DESIGN

My scene is based on a catwalk fashion show. I decided where to put my stage, audience and lights by making a rough draft of everything to see if it'll work out how I planned. I decided on which colors and sizes to use by just thinking off the top of my head about what colors I like and would fit best. I found the sizes by using the previous sizes from my rough draft. The lighting design enhances the event by focus. Certain colors mean certain things and there is usually a lot of people at fashion shows who remember the size of everything, so that would be something to remember.

Students seem to have done well with the project and learned from it as well, but what are the most common student errors you and your team observed?

We found that some students:

— struggled to compare the area of the stage and the area of the audience. They made the stage huge and didn't realize they just had a few seats available for audience. Some forget to include space for the audience at all.

— hang lights off the grid. They are shooting for perfect symmetry in their lighting design and end up putting a light where it can't be hung.

— graphed the radius as the diameter and got a massive light for the stage.

— just didn't realize that the grid is counting by 2s, and they assume it's by 1s.

— just don't have a very feasible design. As examples, most of the stage is black, and, either the lights are super concentrated and the rest is black, or the lights are super-spread out and there's a lot of black space between them.

How do you support struggling students?

For this project, because there are multiple entry points, it's easy to get students started. Often students are able to complete most of the assignment before they hit a wall with confusing math concepts. Most often, though, we find that students that struggle with the traditional mode of the class can usually excel in project mode (especially on this project) because the math sneaks in at the last minute. Surprisingly, the less constraints I give to students the more creative they're able to be. So, for the past two years, we've offered two different project options: Students can either design a scene for a specific play or they can create another use for the black box space. When students get stuck, we can either steer them to one of the scenes of the play (for example, the balcony scene from *Romeo and Juliet*) or ask them what else they'd do if they were planning a fund-raising concert/performance or event. The goal is to give students choices and a chance to invest a bit of their own identity in the project but not so much freedom that they become paralyzed by all the choices and spend the whole time deciding what to do. Often, I give a five- to eight-minute window of time to plan and say that if they haven't decided on their event by the end of eight minutes then I will tell them what to plan.

How did the ideas for this project emerge?

Several years ago, I was at a performance and just turned my head to look up. I noticed that there was a metal grid hanging overhead, which reminded me of a coordinate plane. In talking to our lighting and theater teachers later, I realized that the metal grid truly is a coordinate grid. Near the roof of the room there are letters and numbers next to each beam of the metal grid, which is to help lighting designers and directors communicate about where to hang lights.

Point (B,6), for example, is a specific place on the grid where a student can move a hanging spotlight. In talking about the similarities, I realized that this concept really overlaps with our work on the geometry of conic sections. Instead of abstract cones meeting planes, we can look at cones of light coming from a spotlight and meeting the planes of the floor or walls of the black box theater. Once we had the overlap, then it took a few iterations to think about how to turn this into a meaningful learning experience for our students. What we've developed now as the Lighting Design project took a few tries to get right, and every year we still work as a team of Geometry teachers to try to improve it in some small way.

Please comment on the necessary school infrastructure that helps in getting such an elaborate unit completed.

For the past three years, Tess Mandell, Ibeth Jaime, and Chris Flaherty have worked with me to plan curriculum, create assignments, and share assessments. We find that this daily collaboration has become an essential element of our practice, as it gives us a chance to improve on each other's work. I am the veteran teacher in the group and am able to provide some experience and wisdom, but each of the other members of the team brings their own insights and perspective to the endeavor. By meeting daily, we are able to create a culture of collaboration, to troubleshoot, and to constantly refine our lessons and approaches. This team approach also has allowed us to create some innovative approaches to teaching. In addition, our math courses are 85-minute periods, five days a week. We have a semesterized schedule, so our Geometry class runs roughly half the year, from September until late January. Most of the time, we are able to group students in grade cohorts, so that all ninth-graders are taking math at the same time and all ninth-grade math teachers share a common prep period. We group all ninth-grade classes together for a common end-of-semester exhibition called the Math Fair. We also are able to flexibly regroup students at some points during the term.

How does your team structure the projects?

We no longer try to have every lesson address both arts and academic concepts. Instead, we try to create projects that closely connect to our math content that are opportunities for the students to apply their math learning and also to apply some creative thinking. Our best projects also seem to have some arts element attached. An extensive library of our projects can be found on our STEAM department website at tinyurl.com/baasteam.

Talk about the interdisciplinary aspects of the project

Over the years, we've tried to make this more and more of an interdisciplinary project. Last year, we wanted students to get a sharper sense of what the black box looks like and what our theater technicians do to make the lighting happen for a typical show. With the help of one of our twelfth-graders, we created a 10-minute documentary that shows what the space is, how the lighting is controlled, and what sizes of spotlight are available. The purpose of this movie wasn't really about getting better math results. Instead, it was about developing a stronger interdisciplinary learning for the students. The thought was that if they get a better understanding about the lighting world or if they're more enthusiastic about the creative part of the project, then they'll also be more inspired to work on the math part of the project. Not to privilege the "fun" stuff over the math stuff, but to somehow acknowledge that both are happening, and we need to give teaching time to learn about both disciplines if we really want it to feel like an interdisciplinary project.

What is the teacher's role during the project?

When a project is going well, it can be a tough time for a teacher. We want to be helpful and work with students, either one-to-one or a whole class. But there's often a moment (or a whole class period) during our project times when the best thing that a teacher can do is just keep quiet and not say anything. Project work time requires me to shift from teacher to coach—I'm there if you need me but also need to give you enough space to make it through on your own. Sometimes, I make sure that students see me working on my own example of the project and if I'm working with a student teacher, I often ask them to do the project themselves. Doing the work that we give the students gives us a perspective on the challenges and also allows us to create models/exemplars for the students.

What are strategies for assessing the projects?

With all of our projects, we have moved away from using rubrics and instead try to create a checklist or grade sheet at the start of each project that lists each step of the process and each sub-task necessary to complete it. This allows us to check off the complete elements of the project and show students where their work is not yet complete or up to standards. We encourage students to refine their work and find that the simplicity of a checklist helps students to see what they still need to work on for future revisions of the assignment.

How is technology integrated in the project?

We have students who finish early use Geogebra to map their graph onto a computer. In planning the task, we also use iPhones and iMovie to create and edit a documentary explanation of how lighting designers work.

What resources do you use?

I should have mentioned earlier that we don't use textbooks. We opened the school using the Interactive Mathematics Program (IMP) first edition. Much of the skeleton of our math curriculum comes from IMP: teaching content that connects to a summative unit project. We found that our school population was better served with some different projects and we also reshuffled much of the four-year sequence of IMP so that it better aligns with our state test, which takes place at the end of tenth grade. The Lighting Design project, for example, would replace a project in IMP Year 3 unit called "Orchard Hideout." This project dealt with graphing trees as they expand in circumference and studying the angles of visibility. It's a rich problem, but this lighting problem is much more relevant for our student body.

Comment on the process for improving the project.

Over the many iterations of this project, we've tried to make sure that our numbers and constraints are as realistic as possible. We have students hang "LEKO" lights, which are sold based on the degree size of the opening of the light. This allows us to do some great trigonometry review at the start of the unit, because we know the light angle and know the ceiling height and use trig to find the radius of the light circle.

We've also gotten better about using real numbers for the length and width of the room and the height of the ceiling. This year, we used the fire code restriction that there can be no more than 90 people in our black box theater. We also told students to think about how much space seating can take up (typically a theater seat takes up about 5.5 to 6 square feet).

We've also had fun in the last couple of years trying to tie this project to an upcoming BAA production. When we know, for example, that our theater department will be producing *Romeo and Juliet,* we introduce students to a few key scenes from the play and ask them to develop the staging, seating, and lighting that would work best for one of these scenes. This allows our project to feel less hypothetical and much more practical.

Commentary

The Lighting Project begins by having students take a careful look at the equations for circles and searching for patterns to facilitate quick graphs of circles (SMP8). It then poses a problem to students that requires thinking about creating an event, applying and explaining the mathematics and processes used, and creating a presentation to display results which students can critique (SMP1–SMP6). While one would think that such a project would engage students in most of the mathematical practices, it depends on Mark's pedagogical actions to make this happen. Note that Mark is careful to let his students own the problem by working on the project at his desk so as not to help too much. He also encourages students to invent their own event and has them draw their representations while he circulates and asks questions to deepen their understanding when necessary.

Mark and his colleagues demonstrate how fruitful collaboration can help teachers create or modify projects to engage students at a level that allows all students to use mathematics to solve interesting and worthwhile problems. Although the team is fortunate in having access to CCSS-based units such as those by the Interactive Mathematic Program (IMP), the team nonetheless models how important it is for teachers to continually focus on students and their environment to help determine revisions that can make a good resource even better.

Changing the traditional order of the high school curriculum shows that the team's focus on students' success supports the recommendations of Seymour Papert, who is a computer scientist, educator, and mathematician. In his article on project-based learning, Curtis (2011) quotes Papert's supposition on why students are turned off by school:

> "We teach numbers, then algebra, then calculus, then physics. Wrong!" exclaims the Massachusetts Institute of Technology mathematician, a pioneer in artificial intelligence. "Start with engineering, and from that abstract out physics, and from that abstract out ideas of calculus, and eventually separate off pure mathematics. So much better to have the first-grade kid or kindergarten kid doing engineering and leave it to the older ones to do pure mathematics than to do it the other way around."

The Lighting Project provides the background students need so engineer their own event out of which they apply the appropriate mathematics they need to complete it. In addition, help for students at varying levels of understanding, when necessary, is interspersed throughout the project so that students can continue to persist toward the goal.

Unit Overview

The Mathematics of the Theatre

Aim: How can properties of circles help us design an event to present on stage in our black box theatre?

Objectives: Students will apply equations of circles and right triangle trigonometry to plot a lighting plan for an event in the school's theater.

Course: Algebra/Algebra 2.

Source: Original.

Number of 85-Minute Periods: Three to five.

NCTM/CCSS Standards: Functions: F.IF.1–F.IF.5: Interpret Functions; Geometry: SRT.C.8: Solve Problems with Right Triangles; Geometry: MG.A.1, A.3: Modeling; Geometry: GPE.B.4: Express Geometric Properties with Equations.

NCTM Processes/Mathematical Practices: Mathematics as Problem Solving, Reasoning and Proof, Communication, Connections, Representation/SMP1–SMP6, SMP8.

Mathematical Content: Students begin with properties and equations of circles, which they use to plot placement of lights using right triangle trigonometry.

Prerequisites: Students should have already studied right-triangle trigonometry and also have been introduced to areas and equations of circles.

Materials and Tools

◆ Project packet. This includes the assessment rubric, introduction to the project, practice problems, and handout for students' final write-up and final diagram.
◆ Video links
   1. www.youtube.com/watch?v=oZAu_r5Pi70&feature=plc.. This is the YouTube by twelfth-grader Gary Gonzalez, who led the tour for the students. Students visit the lighting booth and learn about the types of lights and how the grid locates the lights. They climb ladders and see parts of the space that they would not normally get to see.
   2. www.youtube.com/watch?v=ZsvWl0AHUpc&feature=youtu.be. The YouTube video is by lighting designer Dan Jentzen, who explains how geometry is connected to designing the lighting for the theater.
   3. www.youtube.com/watch?v=syzKexuEy64. YouTube clips from *Rent* or *Glee*.

4. https://sites.google.com/a/bostonartsacademy.org/baa-steam/math-initiatives/lighting-project-2012. This site has an overall summary of project with all handouts.
5. Additional supports: Scaled cut-out models of the different light circles. These are a useful support for students who need additional help. For most other students, it is easier to use a compass to sketch the lighting circles.

Management Procedures

◆ Have students visit the theater and view videos of how lighting is hung and impacts production. Assign the project design sheets and discuss with students.

Assessment: See Figures 4.3 and 4.9.

Resources

1. NCTM Resources: www.NCTM.org.
2. Literature—Chapter 8, this volume.
3. Music: Chapter 3, this volume.
4. Alexandra Pannoni is an education intern at U.S. News. See her blog, *3 Ideas for Incorporating Music into Core High School Classes,* www.usnews.com/education/blogs/high-school-notes. Retrieved March 13, 2014.

5

Henry Kranendonk: Raisin Geometry—Exploring the Balance Point and Its Applications

What is so remarkable about the idea of "center"? After all, center is simply the midpoint of the diameter of a circle—or the mean of a data set—or a median value of a sorted list—or the location that minimizes the sum of distances—or . . . ? Exactly! The concept of "center" is not as simple as we thought. Its meaning depends on the context of the application. When it is used to summarize and analyze an entire set of data, it can be a powerful tool for investigative student projects.

Henry Kranendonk, Milwaukee, Wisconsin

As part of a research project that focuses on the exploration of data in high school mathematics courses, Henry Kranendonk was invited to develop a module that targeted the concept of *center* for a geometry class. Henry's added challenge was to maintain meaningful connections with preceding modules that involved algebra. Key questions included were: *Center as a geometric concept often designates the "middle" of a data distribution or locations on a number line. However, is it strictly a middle? What if the locations of points are weighted? In what context is a center more appropriately a measure of weight and distance? Finally, how do we interpret a center as a meaningful statistic?* The module that emerged is called *Data Driven Mathematics: Exploring Centers* by Henry Kranendonk and Jeffrey Witner. For updated information about this module, please e-mail Henry (kranendonk@earthlink.net).

Ten lessons of *Exploring Centers* are designed to connect a geometric center to an important summary of a population distribution represented on a coordinate plane. The first two lessons set the stage for defining center as the typical value of a data distribution. The applications in these lessons provide practical examples of using mean, median, or mode to summarize the typical value of a data distribution. In lessons 3 to 8, students investigate the balance point of raisins taped to poster-paper cutouts of specific geometric shapes. The investigations guide students toward understanding that the balance point is the weighted mean of the coordinate locations of the raisins; this point is defined as the centroid. In lessons 9 and 10, raisins are used to represent population distribution. Students explore the significance of the centroid in population studies, applying the properties they studied in the geometric models.

Henry originally taught the activities for this chapter to students at Rufus King High School, Milwaukee, Wisconsin, which was renamed Rufus King International School—High School Campus in 2010–2011. To start the activities, he gave groups of four students a small box of raisins and different polygons cut from poster board. He instructed them to select raisins of similar size, tape one raisin at the vertex of each shape, and then balance each shape on the eraser end of a new pencil. Intrigued, they accepted the challenge.

The next step was to mark the approximate location of a balance point, B, on each shape. He initiated a discussion of the properties of balance point, B. His students concluded that B was determined by the distance of each raisin from a center location. Next, they placed the polygons on a coordinate grid and recorded the coordinates of each vertex and the approximate coordinates of B (see Figure 5.1). How does the centroid C compare to the balance point B? Students discovered that the two locations are very close.

The next step was to vary the weights at the different vertices of a convex pentagon. On a grid, students taped additional raisins to several vertices of a convex pentagon, whose coordinates are:

P_1 (–7,6), P_2 (1.5,y_2), P_3 (7.5,y_3), P_4 (3.5,y_4), P_5 (–5.5,y_5).

Students followed these instructions:

Create a pile of four raisins (one on top of each other), and tape this stack as close as possible to vertex P_1. Tape a stack of three raisins at P_2. Tape one raisin at P_3, one raisin at P_4, and one raisin at P_5.

"How do these additional raisins change the location of the balance point of the model?". He directed the students to predict the new balance point on the grid. Henry listened carefully to students' predictions to determine whether they integrated concepts from previous lessons. He commented that students are generally able to predict the shift of the balance point toward the heavier points. The students then balanced the unevenly weighted pentagon on a pencil. Interestingly, the new balance point clearly *appeared* to be off center. However, the students recognized that this new point still meets the definition of a center.

The next task was directed at calculating the centroid from the values on the coordinate grid. To organize their information, Henry had students complete Figure 5.2, which shows how the location of a point is weighted by the number of raisins taped to the point.

After calculating the weighted means of the x and y coordinates, the students compared the locations of the centroid and the observed balance point. Again, the

Figure 5.1 Triangle fit to a grid

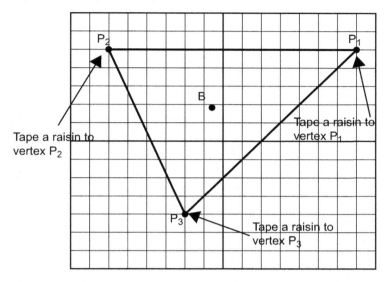

For the triangle shown in Figure 1, the centroid C is:

$$\bar{x} = \frac{(7 + -6 + -2)}{3} = \frac{-1}{3} = -.33$$

$$\bar{y} = \frac{(5 + 5 + -4)}{3} = \frac{6}{3} = 2$$

For raisins of approximate weight, the balance point is determined by the location of the raisins. In this case, the **centroid** is defined by the **means** of the x and y values of the vertices:

$$\bar{x} = \frac{(x_1 + x_2 + x_3)}{3}$$

$$\bar{y} = \frac{(y_1 + y_2 + y_3)}{3}$$

y-value
5
5
−4
2

very close. Henry monitored the ensuing discussion. "I allow time for students to verbalize and write clearly that the x and y coordinate values of the centroid are formed by the sum of the weighted values for each coordinate divided by the total number of raisins taped to the polygon." Once they could do so, he guided them to express the process symbolically as shown:

$$\bar{x} = \frac{\sum_{i=1}^{5} WiXi}{\sum_{i=1}^{5} W1} \quad \text{and} \quad \bar{y} = \frac{\sum_{i=1}^{5} WiXi}{\sum_{i=1}^{5} W1}$$

In the final lesson of the module, the significance of the centroid is explored within the context of population centers. Henry posed this problem:

Figure 5.2 Calculating the weighted means

Points P_i (x_i, y_i)	Number of Raisins W_i	X coordinate values x_i	Y coordinate values y_i	Weighted x values $W_i x_i$	Weighted y values $W_i y_i$
P_1 (−7,6)	4	−7	6	−28	24
P_2 (1.5, y_2)	3	1.5	y_2	4.5	$3y_2$
P_3 (7.5, y_3)	1	7.5			
P_4 (3.5, y_4)	1	3.5			
P_5 (−5.5, y_5)	1	−5.5			

Let's suppose that you have been appointed by the governor of Wisconsin to head a committee to determine the location of an important job agency, which will serve the communities of Milwaukee, Waukesha, Port Washington, Belgium, Beloit, and Racine. Figure 5.3 shows a map of this area of Wisconsin, along with population statistics. The recommendations of your committee are expected to service the people of this area for at least the next 20 years. You have an interest in running for governor yourself at some future date, and you want to identify a location that is "fair" to these communities (and their voters).

Figure 5.3 Area map with population statistics

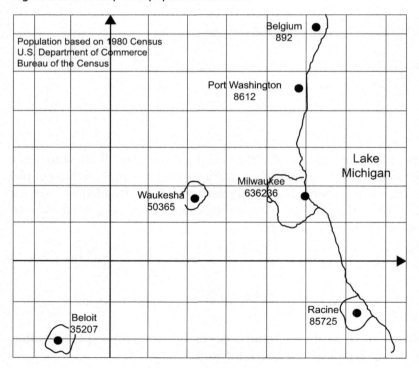

Henry asked, "How can our model with the raisins help us approach this problem?" One students laughed, "Who wants to stack up over 600,000 raisins to represent Milwaukee?" Others were quick to suggest that replacing the number of raisins with the number of people and calculating the weighted means will describe a "center" that balances the locations and populations of the towns and cities. Students indicated that the model from their work with the geometric shapes could also be applied to this problem. As one student indicated, "Raisins are people too!" They made the connection between the model and the real world and the modeling cycle outlined in the CCSS high school conceptual category "Modeling."

Referring to their raisin model, the students construct a table to represent the data (see Figure 5.4). Now they are prepared to use tools other than paper-and-pencil calculations as they solve the problem.

Real-world problems such as the one posed here require different mathematical tools. Data that are organized in a chart lend themselves neatly to the use of a typical spreadsheet application. Henry used this lesson to introduce students to spreadsheets and their graphing capabilities. In this instance, his students applied a spreadsheet application to set up the data, perform the calculations, and produce the graphs. One of the advantages of spreadsheet programs is their speed at processing data. To exploit this potential, Henry has students explore several "what if" questions. He required them to write their responses, not only to review the activities and connect the concepts of the lesson but also to serve as an assessment tool.

1. What happens if Belgium is not considered in the determination of the population center?
   Using a spreadsheet, determine the location of the population center without Belgium.
2. What happens if Milwaukee is not considered in the determination of the population center?
   Using a spreadsheet, determine the location of the population center without Milwaukee.

Figure 5.4 Table representing data

Community	Population P_i	x coordinate value (x_i)	y coordinate value (y_i)	$P_i x_i$	$P_i y_i$
Belgium	892	10.5	12.3	9,366	10,972
Port Washington	8,612	9.8	9	84,398	77,508
Waukesha	50,365	4.5	3.3	226,643	166,205
Milwaukee	636,236	10.0	3.3	6,362,360	2,099,579
Beloit	35,207	−2.7	−4.0	−95,059	−140,828
Racine	85,725	12.5	−2.8	1,071,563	−240,030

3. Develop a drawing that shows each of the cities/towns, the population center of the six cities/towns, the population center *without* Belgium, and the population center *without* Milwaukee.

4. What if during the next 10 years the population of Milwaukee decreases by 20 percent, the population of Racine increases by 30 percent, and the populations of each of the other cities increase by 5 percent?

5. Briefly describe how the population center is similar to the center that you calculated in the weighted means lesson involving the raisins on the card stock paper cutout.

6. Recall that your original task was to identify a "fair" location for a job agency. Political "fairness" is a very difficult (maybe impossible) goal to achieve. Describe in what way the population center might be a fair location. Describe in what way it might not be a fair location.

As they developed their answers, students become engaged. The location of the new population center did not visibly change if Belgium was removed from the calculation. In contrast, there was a major shift when Milwaukee was removed. Most students thought this method of determining the agency's location was "unfair" to Belgium. But, one said, "The people in Belgium choose to live there, away from the positive and negative aspects of a city such as Milwaukee. They shouldn't expect the job agency to come to them."

Another student agreed. "There are probably more jobs and more people looking for jobs in the more populated areas. It makes sense that this agency should be closer to the more populated communities."

Because the population center determined from the population data was southwest of Milwaukee, one student commented:

I think it is actually unfair to Milwaukee to locate this agency at the population "center." It should be located in the city, or at least close to transportation. Maybe a more weighted determination is needed—one that counts only the unemployed or doubles the value for a person who is unemployed. It would be interesting to compare this new center to the previous one.

Clearly these students were applying the mathematics they learned in earlier lessons as they explored possible solutions to a real-life situation.

Discussion between Colleagues

How did you manage the class during the project?

The beginning lessons combine individual work with small group work and class discussion. All students were expected to complete problems that were specifically designed to complement the group work. As the population issues were introduced, the students were involved in more discussion and were expected to write summaries to their ideas.

How do you assess the students as they participate in the discussions?

As the geometric concepts were introduced in the early lessons of the unit, I observed how students talked about balance and center. As the later applications focus more on the population examples, the ability to articulate the meaning and significance of a population center was important. Although assessing through discussion was not the main objective of the lessons, my informal assessment helped me keep track of the students' progress. Many of the questions that were addressed in discussion appear again in the exercises. My informal assessment was based primarily on students' written responses.

Please comment on where your project best fits into the curriculum.

The word "center" naturally arises in many geometry topics and problems. Those lessons in a geometry class can be coordinated with the center problems. For example, most geometry students will study the special properties of the unique point that results from the intersection of a triangle's medians. This point has a property of center that is addressed in the lessons. Supplementing the study of triangles with this material complements any curriculum with a data-driven theme.

Many high school mathematics courses are integrating the subjects of mathematics. Data-driven topics are critical to all areas of mathematics; these lessons enrich the study of measurements, coordinate geometry, and plane geometry. They fit best into a mathematics course after students have mastered a few prerequisite skills. However, these skills are actually supported by the lessons. For example, angle and side properties of triangles are discussed in several investigations that lead to the special properties of a centroid. These investigations could be used to introduce the study of these properties as well as to expand the possible applications of these topics.

The school has a large minority population. Describe their participation.

The school has an African American student population of approximately 60 percent and a white population of approximately 20 percent. Mixed groups, Native Americans, Asians, and other groups comprise the remaining 15 percent. The students in most of my classes represented these percentages.

In general, I find student participation and evaluation of the project to be quite positive among all student groups. In particular, discussions related to history and geography generated more ideas from the minority students. I noticed a more active participation in the class discussions on the part of my African American students. The results of the project as determined by my assessments were not significantly different among the groups.

What is your primary vision as a teacher?

My primary vision is to promote a curriculum that provides students with a model of research and communication. My goal is to help establish a process by which the tools of technology are used in our schools to lead high school students to master the ability to question, articulate, listen, and reason.

For all the new ways to create a beautiful paper, it is still the content, the reasoning expressed by the students, that matters. Similarly, for all the new ways to solve an equation, what matters is still the information or insight that the equation communicates. Education must not lose track of the core of its purpose: to prepare citizens to deal with the complexities of a world that constantly demands higher-level integrated thinking. Although the "how to's" remain important, they must also be balanced with "why?" and "for what purpose?" The latter questions are not only more exciting, more interesting, and more entertaining for students, but they are rapidly becoming basic skills for the twenty-first century. In my experience as a math teacher, the most meaningful connections with my students were developed when I was able to provide a meaningful context for the topics they studied. This is not always easy, but the effort to develop these connections is increasingly important.

Commentary

The Common Core State Standards for Mathematics state that "statistics provides tools for describing variability in data and for making informed decisions that take it into account" (National Governors Association & Council of Chief State School Officers, 2010, 79). Its recommendation that students study the measures of center is supported in Henry's unit as students work together on tough issues that require knowledge of the statistical tools to help develop an understanding of this concept. This application represents a connection to the Modeling conceptual category of the CCSS that links geometry and data to the modeling cycle.

Henry's project models good teaching that engages students with the mathematical practices. He begins with raisins on poster board and ends with discussions to determine the location of a job agency near an urban center. It is structured to make best use of instructional time and encourages participation from a diverse student group through the use of challenging experiences (SMP1). He could have started the project with a real-world application but preferred to begin with appealing manipulatives to help students connect what they already know to the challenges of the real-world application (SMP4). The manipulatives were continually used as visual reminders of what the students were investigating and further connected to the modeling conceptual category.

An observer who causally observes Henry's class might see students who are eager participants in a discussion that has little to do with mathematics. A longer stay or deeper insight would soon reveal that worthwhile mathematics underlies their ideas, debates, and solutions (SMP3, SMP6). They use mathematical models to validate and generalize their own thinking and answers (SMP2, SMP4, SMP5), and they engage in a curriculum that fosters sound "habits of mind," as described by Cuoco, Goldenberg, and Mark (1996):

A curriculum organized around habits of mind tries to close the gap between what the users and makers of mathematics do and what they say. Such a curriculum lets students in on the process of creating, inventing, conjecturing, and experimenting; it lets them experience what goes on behind the study door before new results are polished and presented. It is a curriculum that encourages false starts, calculations, experiments, and special cases.

Henry's application of the collaborative process is not what is typically found in schools that are composed largely of minority and working-class students. In the article "The Pedagogy of Poverty versus Good Teaching," Haberman (1991) remarked that almost every form of pedagogy is observable in urban classrooms. However, he noted that a collection of teacher acts formed the primary means of instruction in urban schools and that "not performing these acts for most of each day would be considered prima facie evidence of not teaching" (291). He defined these acts as a "pedagogy of poverty" that includes the routine in which teachers give information, ask questions, give directions, make assignments, monitor seat work, review assignments, give tests, settle disputes, punish noncompliance, grade papers, and give grades. He rightly noted that, taken individually, each act appears to be an appropriate teaching behavior for daily classroom life. "However, taken together and performed to the systematic exclusion of other acts, they have become the pedagogical coin of the realm in urban schools. They constitute the pedagogy of poverty—not merely what teachers do and what youngsters expect but, for different reasons, what parents, the community, and the general public assume teaching to be" (291).

The implications of Haberman's article for the education of working-class students continue to be discussed by educators as an equity issue that raises concerns about whether standards-based practices widens the achievement gap (see research discussion on teacher race and belief section by Clark, DePiper, Frank, Nishio, et al. [2014], 273; see also Rogers 2013). However, research by Boaler (2002) showed that working-class students were able to engage in problem solving and be successful in their math classes when taught by teachers whose teaching reflected the NCTM standards.

Unit Overview

Raisin Geometry—Exploring the Balance Point and Its Applications

Aim: How can the concept of "center" help us make strategic decisions about population centers?

Objective: Starting with a geometric, manipulative-based representation of the center of a polygon, students explore properties of means, weighted means, and the centroid of polygons, and their relationships to the interpretation of real-life applications.

Course: Geometry.

Source: Adapted from Kranendonk and Witmer, *Exploring Centers* (Dale Seymour Publications, 1998).

Grade Levels: Ninth and tenth.

Number of 50-Minute Periods: About 10; it depends on how lessons are approached, how much time is allocated to discussions, and how some of the problems are addressed.

CCSSM Standards: Statistics: S.ID.2: Use statistics appropriate to the shape of the data distribution to compare center of two or more different data sets; S.ID.3: Interpret differences in shape, center, and spread in the context of the data sets. Modeling: G.MG.3: Apply geometric methods to solve design problems.

NCTM Process Standards/Mathematical Practices: Mathematics as Problem Solving, Communication, Reasoning, and Connection/SMP1–SMP6.

Mathematical Concepts: Students use coordinates of points to determine the weighted means and centroids of polygons. They apply the mathematical formula for weighted means to solve problems that require the computation of population centers.

Prerequisites: Knowledge of operations with signed numbers, identification and classification of geometric shapes, plotting and interpreting points in a coordinate system; familiarity with medians of a triangle, distance formula.

Materials and Tools

- ◆ One small box of raisins for each group of two to three students
- ◆ Ten geometric shapes cut from a heavyweight paper. Any interesting geometric shape works. Examples:
  - – Equilateral triangle, sides = 3 inches
  - – Obtuse triangle

- – Acute triangle
- – Right triangle
- – Parallelogram
- – Trapezoid
- – "Boomerang" quadrilateral (concave quadrilateral)
- – Pentagon
- – Hexagon
- – Nondescript quadrilateral
- ◆ Graph paper that will fit each shape
- ◆ An overhead projector
- ◆ A graphing calculator with TI-84 functions
- ◆ Classroom set of scissors, tape, and new pencils to balance the shapes
- ◆ A box or location where each group can store models
- ◆ A sandwich bag (or zip bag) in which to store models while working on other activities
- ◆ Optional: computers with a spreadsheet software (e.g., ClarisWorks)

Management Procedures

- ◆ Before the activities that involve the triangles, quadrilaterals, and polygon, prepare copies of the shapes on poster paper.
- ◆ Several of the models developed by the students become excellent examples to display on a bulletin board. Although most models will be similar, the bulletin board is a good summary of the entire project.
- ◆ Provide bags and/or waste receptacles to place the scraps of cut paper, raisins, and such. This is a messy project at times!

Assessment

Have students answer the "what if" questions. Collect and grade their work.

Resources

1. For other lessons on Henry's content topic, visit LearnZillion (http://learnzillion.com/lessons/2899-find-population-percentages-using-technology) and Statistic Education website (www.amstat.org/education/stew).
2. NCTM: www.nctm.org.
3. NCTM's Core Math Tools: www.nctm.org/standards/content.aspx?id=32706.

6

Virginia Highstone: Equations That Model Growth and Decay

The NCTM/CCSSM Standards call for greater emphasis on the use of technology to develop conceptual understanding. The problems presented in this project are inaccessible without the use of technology, but are easily approached with its use. The project fosters viewing a problem from numerical, algebraic, and graphical perspectives as well as writing about one's understanding.

Virginia G. Highstone, Glen Ellyn, Illinois

Virginia Highstone attended the University of Chicago School Mathematics Project's (UCSMP) summer and fall conferences for a number of years, and then, in 1993, she began writing for the project. When she began teaching from the UCSMP text *Algebra* (Scott Foresman, 1996), she made a conscious decision to be mindful of moving all of her students to the higher thinking levels supported by the program. She taught this lesson to students at York High School, in Elmhurst, Illinois.

Having just taught a chapter on linear change, slope, and lines, Virginia designed a project to focus students' attention on studying functions from four viewpoints: numerical, graphical, algebraic, and written. She wanted students not only to analyze and synthesize results but also to create new problems that required similar mathematical processes. Her students had studied topics that required extensive work in writing and graphing linear change situations and using spreadsheets, graphing calculators, and hand-sketched graphs. Before they graphed lines and learned about slope, they were required to write expressions for problems such as:

Each minute a computer prints out six sheets of paper. Suppose the printer starts with 1,100 sheets of paper. Write an expression of the amount of paper P left in the paper well after m minutes.

Figure 6.1 Eight problem situations on growth and decay

1. Two nearby villages listed their population in 1995 as follows: Athabaska (Situation **A**) has a population of 15,500, and Bayou Bay (Situation **B**) has a population of 150,000. Both towns want to increase their population. Athabaska has decided to offer each family that moves in a free parabolic dish that gets 400 TV channels. Bayou Bay has decided to offer each family that moves in a hammer and a bag of 10,000 nails. It is expected that Athabaska's population will increase at a rate of 20 percent each year, while Bayou Bay will gain an average of 11,400 people each year.
2. Hearts-A-Fire (Situation **A**) and Diva Brava (Situation **B**) are two popular local rock bands. Hearts-A-Fire had a fan club following of about 1,250, but they have a new hit album and their membership is growing by 35 percent each month. Diva Brava's recent fan club count is at 59,500; however, due to bad press about a missed gig and two lost guitars, it is losing an average of 1,467 fans each month.
3. Alphonse (Situation **A**) likes to invest in the stock market. Starting with an initial investment of $8,500, Alphonse has lost 25 percent of his investment each month. His young brother Bertrand (Situation **B**) has a piggy bank with $124. Since he is only eight, Bertrand earns money by visiting his grandparents and looking cute. Bertrand earns an average of $6 a month from his doting grandparents.
4. Triple AAA Corporation (Situation **A**) is conducting a search for the best citizen in the country. It has received 415,000 applications to date, and each day the 200-person Review Committee eliminates 40 percent of the applicants. BBBB INC. (Situation **B**), located in a small community, is conducting its own search for the best citizen in its community. It has received 450 applications, and the one-person Review Committee eliminates 17 applicants each day.
5. Two candidates running for office hire pollsters to conduct a survey to see who is in the lead. Alfred Albemarle (Situation **A**) just spoke out against mothers and apple pie; the poll taken this week showed that he had 225,555 votes, a 5 percent loss of voters compared with the poll conducted last week. On the other hand, Bertha Brandonton (Situation **B**) had 72,315 votes, a 2 percent increase over the poll taken last week because she promised voters a chicken in every pot. The pollsters say that these trends will continue until the election, which is 20 weeks away.
6. Archibald (Situation **A**) and Bellerophon (Situation **B**) inherited money from a rich uncle. Neither believed in banks, so they placed their inheritances in paper bags they kept under their mattresses. Archibald, who received $9,000, is spending his money at the rate of 1.5 percent a month. Bellerophon, who received $15,000 (he was the uncle's favorite), is spending his money at the rate of 4.5 percent per month.
7. Bacterium Alpha (Situation **A**) and Bacterium Beta (Situation **B**) share the same petri dish that is filled with peanut butter broth. Bacterium Beta loves peanut butter and its starting colony of six bacteria grows at a rate of 15 percent per hour. Bacterium Alpha, on the other hand, likes only peanut butter and grape jelly broth and its starting colony of 50 bacteria grows at a rate of 2 percent per hour.
8. Alex (Situation **A**) buys a new Alfa-Romeo for $25,000. Its value depreciates 7.5 percent every year that it is driven. The same year, Bernadine (Situation **B**) buys an old beater of a car for $1,000. Soon after she buys it, she realizes that it is a classic car and will increase in value by 15 percent every year.

With two other colleagues, Virginia created a project to extend the text's chapter on exponents and powers. "We all began brainstorming ideas in the office one day; Mike Guccione and Sue Brown helped me flesh out the idea of a project that would use technology to compare growth situations." They wrote a set of problems to explore the nature of exponential and linear growth functions (see Figure 6.1; answers are found in Figure 6.3). These eight problems were written to encourage students to practice thinking about a variety of configurations of growth and decay versus linear climb and fall; the problems also ensured that there was not a single set of correct equations during a semester for a project, even when more than 200 students took the same course.

To begin her project, Virginia distributed a sheet describing the eight situations, randomly assigning one to each student in her freshman algebra class. Those students who were working on the same problems were then told to form groups of three to four to write and correct each other's equations. "Although I sometimes let students choose their own groups, I also wanted them to experience sharing information with a number of different students. The randomness forced a new configuration of work groups and required students to move out of their comfort zone."

At first the debates revolved around whether the problem required an exponential or linear change model. At this stage Virginia often noticed students correcting each other and even checking with other groups. Once they agreed on the type of equation, they focused on writing the correct equation. "What is the starting value? What is the rate of change—or what is the growth factor?"

Students did not easily process answers to these questions without help from the group. One major issue was in the writing of the *number* for the growth/decay factor and whether to *add* or *subtract* the percent change. Virginia writes, "Students wrote $y = N(1 + r)^x$ or $y = N(1 - r)^x$ and would often remind themselves, and others, to include the number one as a starting point of constant change. Also, they still needed to remind themselves about the difference between growth and decay. Many did not remember to subtract the decay factor from 1."

As she moved around the room, Virginia noticed that students had trouble with example five—they read the problem situation and immediately became confused. To help them along, she asked questions:

◆ "What are the essential facts of one situation?"
◆ "What does Alfred have now?"
◆ "In an equation, where would that number appear?"
◆ "What is changing?"
◆ "Is the change a gain or a loss?"

She also noticed the dynamics within the groups. For example, some students began by writing $y = 225555(5)^x$. Another remembered that 5 percent is really .05, so the group changed the equation to $y = 225555(1 + .05)^x$. Incorrectly believing that they had the answer, students moved on to situation B. Here they easily wrote, $y = 72315(1.02)^x$ on their own—and they paused because they saw that the equations were similar even though one was meant to represent decay. At that point, students returned to situation A to change the equation to $y = 225555(1 - .05)^x$.

For the next lesson, Virginia reserved the computer lab. She distributed an instruction sheet that provided details on the various aspects of the situations to explore (see Figure 6.2). Students create spreadsheets and graphs to compare the situations numerically and graphically and to find the point of intersection to the nearest tenth. Once they finished this step, Virginia required that they check, verify, evaluate the graph of their situations at a point of inequality, write a complete sentence that expresses the time of equality, and write a paragraph that expresses when each situation is greater. Figure 6.3 shows the solutions to the problems.

Figure 6.2 Directions for the Growth and Decay project

Algebra 1

Each of you has been given one of eight problem situations that compare exponential growth, exponential decay, constant growth, and constant decline. This project requires you to examine the relationship between the situations and determine when the y-values are the same. All the problems will have a solution for some x-value between 0 and 20. Please follow the instructions below for each situation.

Part I. Using Technology to Find an Intersection

1. a. Write an equation in x and y for the situation described as **A**.
   b. Write an equation in x and y for the situation described as **B**.
2. Create a spreadsheet using 0 to 20 for x to evaluate your situations numerically.
3. Create a graph using 1 to 20 for x-axis values to graph your situations. Trace to find the point of intersection.
4. Print out both your spreadsheet and your graph.

Part II. Drawing Conclusions

1. Where do the graphs intersect?
   a. Mark the spreadsheet cells that show the time interval when the graphs cross. Use a highlighter.
   b. Circle the point of intersection of your graphs with a colored pen or pencil.
   c. Write a sentence, using your problem situation, that explains when situation A is equal to situation B.
2. Find the y value for each situation when $x = 9$.
   a. On the Spreadsheet: Mark the cells that show these values with a highlighter.
   b. On the Graph: Draw the line $x = 9$ and mark the points of intersection on the two graphs.
   c. Use your equations to find y when $x = 9$. Show your work below.
3. Give the x value (to the nearest tenth) where your equations intersect.
   a. Use your point of intersection and write a brief paragraph that tells someone in words when situation A is less than situation B and when it is greater than situation B.
      For example: During the first 100 hours, the Dingbats have more salt than the Bebops. After 100 hours the Bebops have more salt than the Dingbats.
   b. Mark your graph along the x-axis in two colors, one that shows when situation A is less than situation B and one that shows the opposite.
   c. Write an inequality using only x that gives the values when situation A is less than situation B.
   d. Write an inequality using only x that gives the values when situation A is greater than situation **B**.

Part III. Create Your Own Problem

1. Create a sensible problem situation from the real world that compares two kinds of growth/decay. One type of change must be exponential.
2. Write the two equations that express your problem. Label them with words from the problem. For example: the Dingbats and their salt and the Bebops and *their* salt.
3. Use either a graphing program or a spreadsheet to find the point of intersection of your problem. Attach a printed copy of your solution, with the point of intersection marked for full credit.
4. Draw a cartoon that represents your situation. Make it clever and colorful!

Figure 6.3 Solutions to the Growth and Decay project

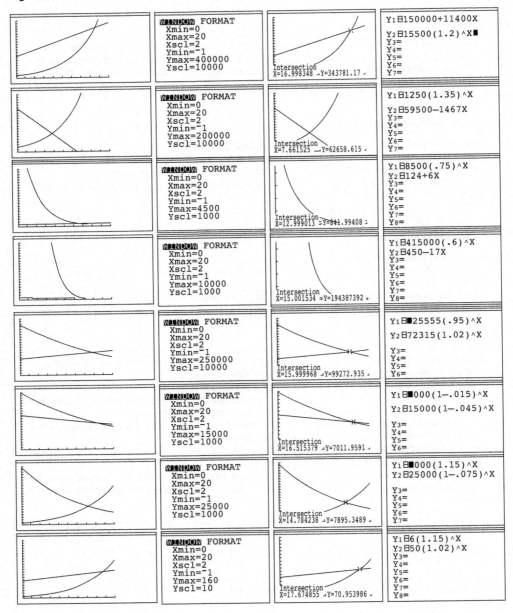

As they worked, Virginia noticed that students were quite adept at using spreadsheets tables and the graphing program because they had used them in previous classes. Problems arose only when students incorrectly typed the formula. The graphs followed easily as well, and within a single period students had two printouts to represent their situations numerically and graphically. They used different colored pencils to mark the spreadsheet, the graphs, and the x coordinates of times when the two situations are not equal.

The final challenge was to write two inequalities in x to describe the relationships when the situations are unequal. This was when they really needed Virginia's help. She writes:

> Originally we had them simply write an inequality; but we found that they had great difficulty doing this. We modified it to require that they express the inequality first in words, and then color and mark their graph. This helped them visualize the situation. Although most students clearly understood the solution (verbal response) and could read the solution on their graphs (coloring response), the leap to a more abstract algebraic representation seemed to elude our freshmen. It may simply be that they were not ready cognitively to see this relationship. We continued to ask the question, because it gave students practice in abstract thinking; and we accepted the fact that some students may not arrive at the correct response. In the last part of the project, each group decided on who will present the various sections of the problem. The class then reviewed and discussed all of the problems.

To gauge the level of students' understanding, Virginia assigned independent work that required each student to write a new and creative problem in growth, decay, and/or constant change. They were to solve the problem on a spreadsheet and with a graphing utility. An unusual addition to this assignment was that students had to produce a cartoon of their original situation. Samples of students' cartoons included hoarding piles of money or spendthrifts gleefully throwing it away. Virginia comments: "Some boys wrote about hoarding meat and had cartoons of butchers in their shops. One young man drew a cartoon of a garden with piles of vegetables and dirt that were growing and decaying. I think it is important to find ways for my students to express themselves creatively."

Discussion between Colleagues

Did you always teach like this? Have you tried amusing projects in other courses?

I reentered the teaching profession after a long hiatus to raise my three daughters. Returning as a mature woman who had spent years as a self-employed math tutor, I wanted to move away from a test-driven assessment model. Early on, I began thinking of creative ways to have students demonstrate their understanding. In my other classes, students wrote illustrated technical papers, did posters and drawings using their calculators, made models, gave oral reports—any form of mathematical exposition or expression I could find. Certainly my department coordinator, Dr. Susan Brown, was positive about such a change. In every course I taught, there was a nontraditional component made up of projects and other problems. I purposely kept the percentage of a student's grade from testing per se at below 50 percent.

Comment on how this project fostered a conceptual understanding of relationships among the various rates of change.

In general, I sensed a real gain in understanding from this project. Seeing the numerical and graphical solutions to the problem side by side clarified the meaning of setting functions equal to each other and prepared students for systems of equations later in the year. The concrete approach to answering the questions "Which is greater?" and "When?" was also helpful. The project was structured to move from the specific to the general, using kinesthetic (tracing and marking), visual (coloring), and oral (group work) means to express the solution. By the time the students had to write the inequalities, they had approached the answer from a variety of viewpoints and had used a variety of inputs.

Comment on the process for creating the problem situations.

Mike Guccione wrote three, and I wrote the rest. We shared comments about which would be included and then made little changes here and there. Getting two graphs that crossed within the domain of $0 \leq x \leq 20$ was not always easy—and we did a lot of adjusting of numbers to make them come out in a reasonable way. We simply tried to make the topics a bit funny but still real world in the sense that they could possibly happen.

Did students find the problems amusing or approachable?

The students did think some were funny—or at least interesting. They particularly liked the one about the classic car and the one about the rock bands. They also seem to find them approachable—not because of the problem situations themselves but because our text uses real-world word problems within each lesson rather than in a special section. Writing equations from a real-world situation was and still is routine for students in UCSMP.

What difficulties did students encounter?

Requiring students not only to analyze and synthesize results but also to create new problems that required similar mathematical processes presented a challenge. The proposed new problem must be checked to see the potential domain before the students moved on to graphing and using a spreadsheet. The key is to find the domain in which the situations will trade places—"When will Al have more than Bob?" or vice versa. Students wrote an interesting situation and then they couldn't find the appropriate window in which to draw their graphs. The idea of discrete versus continuous phenomena also played a role here because they had to choose quantities that could show continuous growth.

How did students react to this project?

They reacted in a variety of ways. The students found interpreting the graph more difficult than one might imagine. Although it seems obvious to us where $f(x) > g(x)$, in general, it is not clear to beginning algebra students or even more advanced students. We continued this kind of thinking in Advanced Algebra with a line crossing a cubic function, asking "Where is f(x) <5; where is f(x) >5?" The answer requires three open intervals. It is surprisingly nonintuitive for students. Even more difficult was the process of writing correct inequalities in x to represent the domain where $f(x) > g(x)$ or $f(x) < g(x)$. Because the projects asked them to do a variety of activities, some would love one part and hate others. For example, the mention of a cartoon brings either squeals of delight or cries of "I can't draw!" Students did enjoy creating their own problem situation and seeing the result solved for them by computer.

In the directions to students you write, "This project requires you to examine the relationship between the situations and determine where the y values are the same." Why is it necessary to give such explicit instructions about a key understanding of the mathematics?

By this time in the second semester, students have become quite familiar with looking at computer- and calculator-generated lists of range values to see where they are equal. They have mastered this skill for homework and test problems. However, we did not assume that this mastery would translate to a more complex and richer problem environment. Yes, students quite easily found the intersection point of the two curves from the spreadsheet—that is exactly why we choose to do that piece of technology first. But, even there, writing a correct expression for the spreadsheet program could be tricky. These students had not yet studied systems of equation, so they had not seen two curves intersect on a plane—and they certainly had not seen an exponential curve intersect with a line. There the software presented challenges as well.

Even more important to understanding why we choose to "give away the game" at the beginning are some fundamental truths about our students and their cognition:

- ◆ We were dealing with ninth-graders, not twelfth-graders. Algebra was new to them.
- ◆ We were dealing with average students, not honors students.
- ◆ This seemingly simple lesson contains some very tough ideas—independent versus dependent variables, domain versus range. Even eleventh-graders in advanced algebra with trigonometry still struggle with these ideas—and twelfth-graders in college algebra finally seem to master them.
- ◆ The problem situation was a rich one. It began with a word problem from which equations must be written; it required the use of two types of technology with different symbols and menus. They had to write about their findings in complete sentences and then go on to use the coordinate plane to understand what it meant when one curve lies below or above the other. This last idea is not an easy one for average or honors students.
- ◆ In all, we found that telling students what they must look for in no way diminished the problems that the project presented, because they were doing so many varied tasks and tying them all together into one broad report.

How has the cartoon requirement enhanced the project? What insights about students have you gained from the cartoons?

More and more, I desire to see the side of my students that was not ordinarily apparent in math class. It helped me to value them as fully rounded persons rather than to simply rate them as algebra students. Drawing a cartoon engaged some students who are seldom interested in participating. For others, it was a worrisome chore—they were far too judgmental of their abilities as artists. The insights I gained are less mathematical than personal. Giving an artistic student a chance to excel is important, I think, both for self-esteem and peer acceptance. For example, a few years ago, one sophomore did a poster project in my class that was exceptionally artistic. I encouraged him to take art—he had never taken a formal course. By senior year he was not taking math, but he was taking AP Art and applying to serious art schools. That's the kind of interaction that helps a teacher guide the "total" student.

Please comment on your algebra curriculum.

The University of Chicago School Mathematics Project texts introduce the topic in first year algebra, in conjunction with the study of rules of exponents. In Algebra 2, the topic is revisited again in more depth using a function approach; logarithms are introduced at this time.

Some teachers may want to use this project for Algebra 2. I believe it would fit quite well. Many texts do not begin the study of exponential growth until that level.

How often did you engage students in projects?

I tried to do two projects per quarter in each class. Sometimes there were more, sometimes less, depending on the length of the project. For example, in College Algebra, two technical papers per quarter are expected. In an Enriched Precalculus course, longer technical papers using *Mathematica* to explore types of functions were assigned to partners. Shorter theoretical papers, which I called theory discussions, were also assigned. Students found the latter very difficult. A typical theory discussion posed the question "Which is the dependent variable on the unit circle? Which the independent?" and then asked the student to relate the point moving about the unit circle to the sine and cosine waves. The best students noted the change in acceleration on both figures.

Elaborate on your assessment of the project.

We did not use a formal grading rubric for this project but agreed as a teaching group about points to assign for each part of the project: correct tables, graphs, inequalities, etc. The assessment of the student-created problem was harder. We graded it on correctness in language, equations, solutions from technology, and creativity and originality. The cartoon was assessed in the same way. Did it fit the problem situation? Was it clever? Was it original? Was it neat and done with craftsmanship (i.e., care, time spent)? Because we had a number of these projects that require a creative touch, we had gotten used to more subjective assessment. We also saved work from year to year to show students both good and poor examples.

Any other comments?

I would like to stress the importance of teamwork in the way we ran our courses. At times during the conception process, I was informally running ideas by two other teachers, and together we refined the project. We all talked about it as our students were doing it too, and I took notes about where there were problems and where it went well. At every step I received input from others. This kind of collegial atmosphere where one teacher is responsible for a course but all do the same projects made change easier, I believe.

Commentary

Virginia's project is rich in opportunities for helping students enhance and extend their understanding of the relationship between varying rates of growth while actively engaging in the six stages for a complete cycle of modeling as listed by CCSS:

1. Identifying variables in the situation and selecting those that represent essential features;
2. Formulating a model by creating and selecting geometric, graphical, tabular, algebraic, or statistical representations that describe relationships between the variables;
3. Analyzing and performing operations on these relationships to draw conclusions;
4. Interpreting the results of the mathematics in terms of the original situation;
5. Validating the conclusions by comparing them with the situation, and then either improving the model or, if it is acceptable;
6. Reporting on the conclusions and the reasoning behind them. (CCSSM)

The graphing directions provide opportunities for students to practice these steps for modeling, and the requirement that students analyze and synthesize their results helps them internalize the key ingredients that underlie the mathematical structures of the problems (SMP1, SMP2, SMP6, SMP7). The role of Virginia and the actions of her students throughout the project are also recommended by NCTM as examples of appropriate use of the graphing calculator (SMP4):

Using technology to display multiple representations of the same problem can aid in making connections. . . . When technology allows multiple representations to be linked dynamically, it can provide new opportunities for students to take mathematically meaningful actions and immediately see mathematically meaningful consequences—fertile ground for sense-making and reasoning activities.

(NCTM, 2010, 14)

Virginia's use of whimsical problems may at first seem out of step with current emphasis on real-life problems. Many of her situations are not the typical "real-life" problems found in textbooks. However, according to Hiebert et al. (1996):

> The value of a problem depends on two things: whether students problematize the situation and whether it offers the chance of leaving behind important residues. . . . We argue only that the mathematical content be considered seriously when selecting tasks and that the definition of usefulness be expanded to a variety of problem situations. The important questions are:
>
> 1. Has the student made the problem his or her own, and
> 2. What kind of residue is likely to remain?

These are the criteria that address, respectively, whether problems are appropriate and whether they are important (20–21).

The problem situations that are posed to students in this project meet these criteria. Because they are assigned after students have worked on the real-life applications of growth/decay functions found in her text, Virginia's students had already engaged in a variety of different real-life problem situations. Second, precisely because they are whimsical, the problems appeared friendly and thus more approachable to students and thus are key features that encourage students to take ownership of their work.

How can a teacher best determine if a student has understood a lesson? Major criteria include the student's ability to explain, use, and apply the concept taught. A specific litmus test for deep conceptual understanding is whether students can transfer their understanding of the concept to novel situations. However, creating a novel situation is daunting, if not difficult, for most students—they may not have a good understanding of the underlying structures of real-life situations that connects to a specific concept, even though they may apply the concept well to a problem that is given to them. Virginia's requirement that students create a novel situation eventually focused students' attention to the critical elements of the problems so that the process of writing their own stories reinforced their understanding of the essential concepts.

Although Virginia has retired from teaching, she leads professional development workshops for teachers on precalculus and on how to attain National Board certification. Her project is still used at York High School.

Unit Overview

Equations That Model Growth and Decay

Aim: How can we model situations representing growth and decay?

Objective: Students use technology to explore different representations of growth/decay functions to explore differences between exponential and constant rate of growth.

Course: Algebra 1/Advanced Algebra.

Source: Original.

Number of 50-Minute Periods: One to two.

NCTM/CCSSM Standards: Algebra: Patterns and Functions: F.IF.8,.9; F.BF.1; Modeling: HSF_LE.A.1–.3.

NCTM Process/Mathematical Practices: Mathematics as Communication, Problem Solving, and Reasoning/SMP1, SMP2, SMP4–SMP7.

Mathematical Concepts: Students interpret numerical and graphical output in terms of a given word problem. They pose and solve problems in exponential growth/decay and/or constant change, using graphical and numerical methods.

Prerequisites: Familiar with definitions and application of slope formula, constant rate of change, exponent, exponential growth decay factor; able to solve one-variable inequalities; able to write equations that express linear change and exponential growth/decay; able to use spreadsheet and graphing technology; able to read graphical and numerical representations of a problem situation; substitute in linear expressions and exponential expressions.

Materials and Tools

- ◆ Access to computer lab with spreadsheet and graphing software or TI-Interactive's graphing and table making capabilities
- ◆ Rulers, colored pencils, markers, highlighters

Management Procedures

- ◆ Day 1: about 15 minutes at end of a period—students randomly choose one of eight different problem situations and work with others to write and correct equations that represent the given word problem

- Day 2: full period, of lab day—students use technology to complete part I of instruction sheet (Figure 6.2)
- Day 3: about 50 minutes, which may be spread throughout several periods—students complete parts II and III of the instructions

Assessment

Assign points for each part of the project: correct tables, graphs, inequalities, language, equations from the problem situation, correct solutions from technology, creativity and originality. The cartoon is assessed on the degree to which it fits the problem situation and is clever or original.

Resources

1. Chapters 5 and 9, this volume.
2. NCTM's Illumination site: National Debt and Wars. http://illuminations.nctm.org/Lesson.aspx?id=2272.

   NCTM's Core Math Tools: http://www.nctm.org/standards/content.aspx?id=32706. Retrieved April 7, 2014.

3. Science Education Center at Carleton College (2014). *Teaching Exponential Growth and Decay*, http://serc.carleton.edu/quantskills/methods/quantlit/expGandD.html. Retrieved April 6, 2014.

7

Craig Jensen: A Dice Game for Engaging Teachers in Discourse

One of the challenges for me as a mathematician interested in professional development of teachers is finding or creating an engaging lesson that is in the high school curriculum and yet will challenge high school math teachers so that they engage in the mathematical practices at an authentic level. By authentic, I mean that teachers truly do not have an algorithm to apply to the problem and thus have to think deeply and share ideas with colleagues. As part of a Louisiana Systemic Initiative Program (LaSIP) mathematics grant for professional development of high school teachers that Yvelyne, Ivan, and I codirected, I shared a lesson on discovering the Sicherman dice which are two six-sided cubes, with the first labeled 1, 2, 2, 3, 3, 4, and the second labeled 1, 3, 4, 5, 6, 8. They are the only dice with positive integer labels having the same probability distribution for its sum as a pair of normal dice labeled 1 to 6. This lesson provided the type of challenge necessary for engaging the teachers in authentic discourse.

Craig Jensen, Ph.D., New Orleans

Background

The goal of our project was to enrich 30 high school teachers' content and pedagogical knowledge through engaging activities the teachers could later adapt for their students. Our pre-observations of many of their teaching showed the traditional style; that is, very teacher centered, with little significant student discourse. In addition to a session on promoting discourse in the classroom, we wanted teachers to experience the benefits of discourse to the development of shared understandings and to use "mathematical discourse to make conjectures, talk, question, and agree or disagree about problems in order to discover important mathematical concepts" (Stein, 2007, 285). But this required that we engage them at appropriate levels of challenge.

Because it is particularly challenging to find activities that allow multiple entry points for teachers who may teach only algebra or only calculus, our strategy was to use the Launch-Explore-Summarize lesson process (Lappan et al., 2002) to model best pedagogical practices for our teachers by immersing the content within an engaging launch, followed by explorations and then a summary (LES). Craig's lesson on discovering properties of the Sicherman dice provided the type of challenges necessary for engaging the teachers in authentic discourse that they could later adapt and implement with their students.

We began with a warm-up to review the concepts necessary for the launch.

Warm-up

1. There are three ways to roll the number 4 on two dice, corresponding to the pairs (1,3), (2,2), and (3,1). That is, the first die is 1 and the second die is 3; the first die can be 2 and the second die 2; or the first die can be 3 and the second die 1. Complete the entries for the table in Figure 7.1 and leave the third column blank for now.
2. Factor completely: $x^4 - 1$.
3. Determine $f(x)$ given that it is a polynomial with integer coefficients and that $(f(x))(x+1) = x^4 - 1$.

The groups had no problem constructing the table of probabilities and we had a teacher show her results as shown in Figure 7.1.

For example 2, most factored $x^4 - 1$ as $x^4 - 1 = (x^2 - 1)(x^2 + 1) = (x - 1)(x + 1)(x^2 + 1)$. Teachers assumed that "fully factor" meant over the real numbers, and thus no one continued to factor $(x^2 + 1)$ as $(x + i)(x - i)$, which is consistent with most assumptions made in high school mathematics. The third problem of determining $f(x)$ in $(f(x(((x + 1) = x^4 - 1$ was the most difficult, and some could not solve it. We circulated to listen to the discussions.

Group 1

Henry: Okay. So we have to solve for $f(x)$ in $(f(x))(x + 1) = x^4 - 1$. From example 2, we already know that $(x^4 - 1) = (x - 1)(x + 1)(x^2 + 1)$.

Kettly: Yeah, so, if x is not -1, divide by x+1 to get $f(x)$ having to be $(x-1)(x^2 + 1)$ or, $f(x) = x^3 - x^2 + x - 1$.

Group 2

Sam: What is $(f(x))$? Is that different from $f(x)$?

Dean: I think the extra parentheses are there to show multiplication.

Sam: Makes sense, thanks. What do we do from here?

Group 3

Chris: Let's start by factoring $x^4 - 1$ to $(x - 1)(x + 1)(x^2 + 1)$.

Figure 7.1 Answers for probabilities of roll sum on normal dice

Sum	Roll Sum on Normal Dice		Number of Ways	Probability
2	(1,1)		1	1/36
3	(1,2),(2,1)		2	2/36 = 1/18
4	(1,3),(2,2),(3,1)		3	3/36 = 1/12
5	(1,4),(2,3),(3,2),(4,1)		4	4/36 = 1/9
6	(1,5),(2,4),(3,3),(4,2),(5,1)		5	5/36
7	(1,6),(2,5),(3,4),(4,3),(5,2),(6,1)		6	6/36 = 1/6
8	(2,6),(3,5),(4,4),(5,3),(6,2)		5	5/36
9	(3,6),(4,5),(5,4),(6,3)		4	4/36 = 1/9
10	(4,6),(5,5),(6,4)		3	3/36 = 1/12
11	(5,6),(6,5)		2	2/36 = 1/18
12	(6,6)		1	1/36

Marisa: So, $f(x) = (x^4 - 1)/(x + 1)$, we get, $(x - 1)(x + 1)(x^2 + 1)/(x + 1)$ which is . . . $x - 1)(x^2 + 1)$ . . . or . . $f(x) = x^3 - x^2 + x - 1$.

Joseph: Okay, but we can't have $x = -1$, right?

Charles: Nope, since that yields a zero denominator.

Group 4

David: We know that $x^4 - 1$ factors into the irreducibles $(x - 1)(x + 1)(x^2 + 1)$. Let me think . . . since $x^4 - 1 = (f(x))(x + 1)$ we have that the factor $(x + 1)$ isn't in $f(x)$, so . . .

Dinah: I see where you are going . . . so $f(x)$ has the other factors and that means . . . $f(x) = (x - 1)(x^2 + 1) = x^3 - x^2 + x - 1$.

The groups share and, interestingly, about half of the teachers who solved it stated that $f(x) = x^3 - x^2 + x - 1$ provided $x \neq -1$. This was said even by very talented teachers and shows good awareness of the perils of division by zero but weak knowledge of polynomial factorization. To help clarify the situation, Craig leads the following discussion on this incorrect response.

Craig: It looks like many of you wrote $f(x) = (x^4 - 1)/(x + 1) = (x - 1)(x + 1)(x^2 + 1)/(x + 1) = (x - 1)(x^2 + 1) = x^3 - x^2 + x - 1$
What is the domain of $f(x)$?

Joseph: Since we divided by $(x + 1)$ and we can't divide by 0, then $f(x) = x^3 - x^2 + x - 1$ has domain all x such that $x \neq -1$.

Craig: Who agrees with Joseph? (many hands rise)

Dinah: But . . . if $f(x) = x^3 - x^2 + x - 1$, it should have all real numbers as its domain. That's just a polynomial—we are not dividing by 0 or anything there, right?

Sam:	But we divided by $x + 1$ to get there, so that means x can't be –1.
Craig:	Let's go back and look at the original statement we were supposed to solve. What was it?
Eva:	$(f(x))(x + 1) = x^4 - 1$.
Craig:	What values can x take in that equation?
Genevieve:	It can take on any value.
Craig:	Does anyone disagree? (pause). If that is so, what is the domain of $f(x)$?
Liberty:	It has to be all numbers?
Craig:	If that is so, what led most of us to believe that to be false?
Doug:	We divided by $(x + 1)$ where x couldn't be negative 1.
Craig:	Okay, and how does that affect the domain of the function $f(x)$?
Steven:	The original domain, all real numbers, should still be the same.
Dinah:	In my group, we connected this to prime factorizations. For example, (she goes to the board to write) if n is an integer, say, $3n = 60$ then we can factor 60 into the primes, $60 = (3)(4)(5)$ And so if $3n = 60$ then by the Fundamental Theorem of Arithmetic, $3n$ factors uniquely into a product of primes as $3n = (3)(4)(5)$. So . . . if there is a 3 already on the left *and* on the right-hand side, then n must contain the remaining factors, so that n has to be (4)(5) or 20.
Craig:	Thanks, but how does that connect to our problem?
Sara:	I see, I see. In $(f(x))(x + 1) = (x - 1)(x + 1)(x^2 + 1)$, we know that the $(x+1)$ is already on the left- and right-hand side, so $f(x)$ must contain the other factors and that means $f(x) = (x - 1)(x^2 + 1) = x^3 - x^2 + x - 1$.
Craig:	Does that make sense? (pause) Any questions?
Mark:	Interesting. I would not have thought to solve it like that.

Launch

Craig starts the launch with this question: "Figure 7.1 has the various probabilities of the sums that can occur for rolling a pair of normal dice. Is there another way to number these two dice to get the same probabilities occurring for the sum of the two dice?"

Megan:	What do you mean?
Craig:	Take the normal two six-sided dice. Now, cover the sides with masking tape and then use a pen to write a different number of dots on the faces. Here is the question: Can we get the same probabilities for the sums as in Figure 7.1?
Megan:	Using any numbers?
Craig:	For this question, let's assume the number of dots on each face is a positive integer. Discuss this in your groups. There are wooden cubes and masking tape on the tables so that you can label them with the new numbers and experimentally see if they seem to have the same probability distribution for their sum as a normal pair of dice. First, can someone clarify what I mean by "same probabilities occurring"?

Andre:	If you look at Figure 7.1, the probability of getting a sum of, say, 4 is, 1/12. If we use different numbers on the dice, would that still be true for a sum of 4?
Craig:	Provide another example of what Andre just said in your groups, and then try to solve the problem.

Group 1

Jerry:	Let's subtract 1 from every number on one die and then add one to every number on the other die. So we will use labels like 0, 1, 2, 3, 4, 5 and 2, 3 ,4, 5, 6, 7.
	(After a while, Jerry raises his hand to say that his group found labels that do produce the same distribution. Craig asks him to write his labels on the board for all to see.)
Kay:	Careful, because this would not answer the question because 0 is not a positive integer.
Jerry:	Oh no! You are right!
Jean:	Our group also made the same mistake.
Craig:	It is great that you came up with an example of two different dice that give the same probability as the sum of a pair of normal dice. Unfortunately, Kay pointed out the problem that one of your dice has 0 as a label, and that is not a positive integer. Was anyone able to get labels that do work? No hands yet, please, as we allow for think time. (pause)
Liberty:	We tried several different labels but couldn't come up with anything.
Andre:	We don't think it possible to come up with an appropriate alternate labeling scheme.
Craig:	Okay. Well, in today's lesson, we will explore how factoring and multiplication of polynomials may support or refute your statement, Andre.

Explore—Part A: Patterns in Products of Polynomials

We next have the teachers work in groups on the following problems.

1. Multiply $(x^1 + x^2 + x^3 + x^4 + x^5 + x^6)(x^1 + x^2 + x^3 + x^4 + x^5 + x^6)$.
2. What properties did you use to multiply the expression? What patterns do you notice? Why do these patterns occur?
3. How does this relate to the probability of rolling a given number on two pairs of normal dice?
4. In your group, choose a reporter to show your work on the document reader.

As we circulate, we notice that teachers are seeing interesting patterns. Craig invites the groups to share.

Dan:	We got $(x^1 + x^2 + x^3 + x^4 + x^5 + x^6)(x^1 + x^2 + x^3 + x^4 + x^5 + x^6) = x^2 + 2x^3 + 3x^4 + 4x^5 + 5x^6 + 6x^7 + 5x^8 + 4x^9 + 3x^{10} + 2x^{11} + x^{12}$

We do see that the exponents of the product are consecutive integers beginning with 2, but were we supposed to find an easier way to multiply these polynomials?

Sam: No. I think it's just brute-force application of distributive and commutative property.

Dean: I used the Binomial Theorem to figure out the coefficients.

Craig: Can you explain that to the class?

(Dean briefly goes to the board and explains his method.)

Craig: Thanks! Now what connection does this have to rolling a pair of dice?

Eva: The coefficients are connected to the table. For example, the coefficient of x^4, which is 3, is also the number of ways to roll a sum of 3. In general, it seems like the coefficient of x^i gives the number of ways to roll a sum of i.

Henry: Wow!

Craig: Interesting results. Can someone explain this connection to me a little bit more?

Eva: Well, there are three ways to roll a 4: (1,3), (2,2), and (3,1). And the coefficient of x^4 is 3 because there are three ways to get a x^4 . . . look at this (she writes on the board) $(x^1 + x^2 + x^3 + x^4 + x^5 + x^6)^2 = (x^1 + x^2 + x^3 + x^4 + x^5 + x^6)(x^1 + x^2 + x^3 + x^4 + x^5 + x^6)$

Now the three ways to get x^4 comes from multiplying
x^1 from the first factor by x^3 from the second factor, and
x^2 from the first factor by x^2 from the second factor, and
x^3 from the first factor by x^1 from the second factor.

Liberty: And . . . the probability of rolling a sum of 3 is the number of ways to get 3, which is 2 divided by 36. The probability of rolling a sum of i is that number of ways divided by 36.

Craig: Fantastic! Please write some sentences with examples to paraphrase what Eva and Liberty said and share with your partner. (pause)

Now let's investigate some patterns when factoring polynomials. Work in your groups to answer the second exploration.

Explore—Part B: Patterns in Factors of Polynomials

1. Fully factor the expression: $(x^1 + x^2 + x^3 + x^4 + x^5 + x^6)$.
2. What tools and/or facts did you use to factor it?
3. Now fully factor this expression:

$(x^1 + x^2 + x^3 + x^4 + x^5 + x^6)^2 = (x^1 + x^2 + x^3 + x^4 + x^5 + x^6)$
$(x^1 + x^2 + x^3 + x^4 + x^5 + x^6)$

As we circulated, we noticed that different teachers used different methods to do factor example 1. Craig asked volunteers to share.

Amber: I first factored out an x, like this: $x(1 + x + x^2 + x^3 + x^4 + x^5)$. Then I factored out $(1 + x + x^2)$ to get $x(1 + x + x^2 + x^3 + x^4 + x^5) = x(1 + x + x^2)1 + (1 + x + x^2)x^3) = x(1 + x + x^2)(1 + x^3)$.

My next step was to factor the $(1 + x^3)$. I don't know if you guys use this with your students to help remember the signs for factoring $(1 + x^3)$. I use SOAP: "Same, Opposite, Always Positive." This gives $(1 + x^3) = (1 + x)$ $(1 - x + x^2)$. Pulling it all together, I get $x + x^2 + x^3 + x^4 + x^5 + x^6 = x(x + 1)(x^2 + x + 1)(x^2 - x + 1)$.

Craig: Any questions? Does any one have a different approach?

Jennifer: My method is different in that I factored $(1 + x)$ to get $x + x^2 + x^3 + x^4 + x^5 + x^6 = x(1 + x) + x^3(1 + x) + x^5(1 + x) = (x + x^3 + x^5)(1 + x) = x(1 + x^2 + x^4)(1 + x)$.

I then rewrote $1 + x^2 + x^4$ as $1 + 2x^2 + x^4 - x^2$ to factor it as the difference of two squares, $1 + x^2 + x^4 = 1 + 2x^2 + x^4 - x^2 = (1 + x^2)^2 - x^2 = (1 + x^2 + x)(1 + x^2 - x)$.

I then get $x + x^2 + x^3 + x^4 + x^5 + x^6 = x(x + 1)(x^2 + x + 1)(x^2 - x + 1)$.

Sam: That is really good work! I got as far as the x^4 expression, and then I got stuck here: $x + x^2 + x^3 + x^4 + x^5 + x^6 = x(x + 1)(x^4 + x^2 + 1)$.

Dean: Yes. I thought we were done at that point.

Craig: I noticed some teachers also reached this stage and thought it was fully factored. Who remembers how to tell when we have factored an expression completely? (silence)

Craig: This shows the value of understanding the unique factorization theorem for polynomials over the reals.

(Craig writes on the board, "Every polynomial of degree greater than or equal to one over the real numbers can factor uniquely (up to the order of the factors) into irreducibles as $c(x - a_1) \ldots (x - a_r)(x^2 + b_1 x + c_1) \ldots (x^2 + b_s x + c_s)$ where the integers $r, s \geq 0$, $c \neq 0$, all of $c, a_1, \ldots, a_r, b_1, \ldots, b_s, \ldots, c_1, \ldots, c_s$ are real numbers, and $b_i^2 < 4c_i$ for all i." That is, you can factor it as a product of linear factors and quadratic factors. From the quadratic formula, we know that the quadratic factors above have nonzero imaginary parts because $b_i^2 < 4c_i$ for all i.

Dean: Had I remembered that, I would have realized that I had more work to do, even if I didn't know how to factor $x^4 + x^2 + 1$ further.

Craig: That does help. Next, how about factoring $(x^1 + x^2 + x^3 + x^4 + x^5 + x^6)^2$?

Genevieve: Now that's not a problem since we already know how to factor $x^1 + x^2 + x^3 + x^4 + x^5 + x^6$. Its square would be $(x + x^2 + x^3 + x^4 + x^5 + x^6)^2 = x^2(x + 1)^2(x^2 + x + 1)^2(x^2 - x + 1)^2$.

Explore—Part C: Back to Dice

Craig: Any questions? (pause) Well, the work we have done so far has prepared us to again consider the launch problem, which was to determine if there are any other ways of rolling two six-sided dice with positive integers on their faces and still get the same probability distribution as a normal pair of dice. Who can restate the connection between these factors and sums of dice?

Mark: Okay, let me show this on the board. Here we have this expression $(x^1 + x^2 + x^3 + x^4 + x^5 + x^6)(x^1 + x^2 + x^3 + x^4 + x^5 + x^6) = x^2 + 2x^3 + 3x^4 + 4x^5 + 5x^6 + 6x^7 + 5x^8 + 4x^9 + 3x^{10} + 2x^{11} + x^{12}$

where the numbers 1 to 6 are on the surfaces of a regular pair of dice. Eva said that the coefficient of a term tells the number of ways to roll the exponent of the term. So, for $6x^7$, there are six ways to roll a sum of 7. (Craig next asked the class to work in small groups to reconsider the launch.)

(Readers: Please note that the teacher responses presented are reconstructed from memory and are not exact quotes. For this next section, however, we videotaped one of the groups to capture their discussion.)

Craig: Now back to the dice-rolling problem. We want to discover if there are any other ways of rolling two six-sided dice with positive integers on their faces and still getting the same probability distribution as a normal pair of dice. What is the connection between this problem and that of determining the number of ways we can factor the following expression where the exponents are all positive integers: $(x^1 + x^2 + x^3 + x^4 + x^5 + x^6)^2 = (x^a + x^b + x^c + x^d + x^e + x^f)(x^p + x^q + x^r + x^s + x^t + x^u)$.

We observed that teachers had little trouble with this after the preparation in the previous section.

Katherine: We already know that each of a pair of normal dice represents $(x^1 + x^2 + x^3 + x^4 + x^5 + x^6)$ so that rolling two normal dice is $(x^1 + x^2 + x^3 + x^4 + x^5 + x^6)^2$. So a die corresponds to a factor of $(x^1 + x^2 + x^3 + x^4 + x^5 + x^6)^2$ and if you had different dice they would correspond to a different way of factoring it.

Craig: Now consider the function $f(x) = (x^a + x^b + x^c + x^d + x^e + x^f)$ corresponding to one of the two dice above. What could it be? Some questions to consider:

1. Does our factorization of $(x^1 + x^2 + x^3 + x^4 + x^5 + x^6)^2$ restrict what $f(x)$ could be?
2. What other facts can you use to restrict what $f(x)$ can be?
3. Is there a pair of weird dice that is different from normal dice?

If you think you have come up with such a pair, try to create them with those numbers placed on masking tape over the normal dice. Now roll the new dice several times and use a table to record the outcomes. Are the probabilities close to what they should be?

(We observed that this small group exploration is where all of the material comes together and teachers are asked to create a solution to the main problem.)

David: Its factors will be coming from the factors of the whole thing so it will be like $f(x) = (x^a + x^b + x^c + x^d + x^e + x^f) = x^g(x + 1)^h (x^2 + x + 1)^i(x^2-x + 1)^j$.

Craig: What if you substitute the number 1 into both sides?

David: (Does calculations silently. Then discusses with his group.) When you plug 1 into the left-hand side you get 6, but when you plug it into the right-hand side you get 2^h3^i. So h = I = 1.

Amber:	We still have to find g and j, and then we will be done. Then we will know what f is.
Craig:	What happens if we substitute 0 into both sides? So far you got h = I = 1 and $f(x) = (x^a + x^b + x^c + x^d + x^e + x^f) = x^g(x + 1)(x^2 + x + 1)(x^2-x + 1)^j$.
David:	If we plug 0 in we get $0 + 0 + 0 + 0 + 0 + 0 = 0$ for the left-hand side and $0(1)(1)(1) = 0$ for the right-hand side.
Craig:	Remember all of variables *a-f* are the digits written on the side of the new die. Because the rules say these have to be positive, all of them are positive. And as you already observed, 0 to a positive number is 0. So the left-hand side is 0. But for the right-hand side, each of g, j can be from 0 to 2. What happens if g is 0?
David:	Well, zero to the zero is undefined.
Craig:	Remember that we are trying to see which of the factors x, (x + 1), (x² + x + 1), and (x²-x + 1) from $(x^1 + x^2 + x^3 + x^4 + x^5 + x^6)^2$ actually appear in f. So if g = 0, then that really means that the factor x does not appear in f and that f would be $f(x) = (x^a + x^b + x^c + x^d + x^e + x^f) = (x + 1)(x^2 + x + 1)(x^2-x + 1)^j$.
	This can't happen, though, because then, when we plug 0 into the left-hand side, we get $0 + 0 + 0 + 0 + 0 + 0 = 0$ but when we plug it into the right-hand side we get $(1)(1)(1) = 1$.
	(At this point Craig circulated to another table to let this group make sense of the problem and when we returned later we heard the following.)
David:	f(0) did not make any sense to me either.
Katherine:	Well, I figured out why he does the f(0) because when this is factored, if you put in the 0 here it makes the product 0, and if g is allowed to be 0, then you would have a 1 right here and your product would be 1 instead of 0.
David:	Well, zero to the zero is undefined. Anything else to the zero is one.
Katherine:	Yeah, and so that's why I'm saying is that . . . um . . . well . . . that would be the other option, because that's why we do the f(0) because it forces g not to be 0.
Amber:	To be 1?
Katherine:	Well, it just can't be 0. So we didn't even have to go back to the original one to find out that g was not 0 if we looked at f(0). Because the product had to be 0.
Amber:	Oh, so that would be the reason we got this to be x into x + 1 into x² + x + 1, and that's gone so we get our dice from this multiplication.
	(Later, Craig asks Katherine to summarize her group results for the class, and Amber continues from there.)
Amber:	We know that g = 0 is false which means g > 0. Since this is true for both dice, we have g = 1. So each die must have the form $f(x) = x(x + 1)(x^2 + x + 1)(x^2-x + 1)^j$ and the only difference is what value j has.
David:	If j = 1 for both factors, we get a normal pair of dice.

Amber: Otherwise, j can be 0, and we get a die $f(x) = x(x + 1)(x^2 + x + 1) = x^1 + x^2 + x^2 + x^3 + x^3 + x^4$.
which means it has labels 1,2,2,3,3,4 on its sides. And if j is 0 for one of the dice, it has to be 2 for the other. So the other die is $f(x) = x(x + 1)(x^2 + x + 1)(x^2-x + 1)^2 = x^1 + x^3 + x^4 + x^5 + x^6 + x^8$
with labels 1,3,4,5,6,8.

Craig: (to whole class) Are there any questions? Figure 7.2 is a handout that explains more formally why $0^0 = 1$ in this application. Colonel George Sicherman invented these dice. Please, make them up and roll them a few times to see if you can experimentally verify that they have the same probability distribution as a pair of normal dice. Enter the results in column 2 of Figure 7.1 (see Figure 7.3 for a summary of the table).

(The class fills out the table.)

Figure 7.2 Interpreting empty products and empty sums.

If S is a finite set like $S = \{a_1, a_2, a_3, \ldots, a_n\}$, we know that the sum of elements in D should be interpreted as

$$\sum_{x \in S} x = a_1 + a_2 + \cdots + a_n$$

However, if S is some other set (say, the empty set or an infinite set), we have to do more work to define what the sum of elements in S should be. One formula we would like to be true (for finite sums at least–infinite ones are more problematical) is that if $S = A \cup B$ then

$$\sum_{x \in S} x = \left(\sum_{x \in A} x\right) + \left(\sum_{x \in B} x\right)$$

One can now see that if we let A be the empty set then

$$B = \varnothing \cup B = A \cup B = S$$

so that $\sum_{x \in B} x = \sum_{x \in S} x = \left(\sum_{x \in \varnothing} x\right) + \left(\sum_{x \in B} x\right)$

Hence we see that to make this formula be true we have to define

$$\sum_{x \in \varnothing} x = 0$$

A similar situation arises with products. If S is a finite set like $S = \{a_1, a_2, a_3, \ldots, a_n\}$ then we should interpret the product of elements in S via

$$\prod_{x \in S} x = a_1 \cdot a_2 \cdot \cdots \cdot a_n$$

As before, if $S = A \cup B$ then we want

$$\prod_{x \in S} x = \left(\prod_{x \in A} x\right) \cdot \left(\prod_{x \in B} x\right)$$

and so we see that if we let A be the empty set, this means

$$\prod_{x \in B} x = \prod_{x \in S} x = \left(\prod_{x \in \varnothing} x\right) \cdot \left(\prod_{x \in B} x\right)$$

so that we have to define $\prod_{x \in \varnothing} x = 1$

Figure 7.3 Probabilities for roll sum on normal and Sicherman dice labeled

Sum	Column 1 Roll sum on normal dice	Column 2 Roll sum on Sicherman dice with labels: (1, 2, 2, 3, 3, 4) and (1, 3, 4, 5, 6, 8)	Column 3 Number of ways	Column 4 Probability
2	(1,1)	(1,1)	1	1/36
3	(1,2),(2,1)	(2,1),(2,1)	2	2/36 = 1/18
4	(1,3),(2,2),(3,1)	(1,3),(3,1),(3,1)	3	3/36 = 1/12
5	(1,4),(2,3),(3,2),(4,1)	(1,4),(2,3),(2,3),(4,1)	4	4/36 = 1/9
6	(1,5),(2,4),(3,3),(4,2),(5,1)	(1,5),(2,4),(2,4),(3,3),(3,3)	5	5/36
7	(1,6),(2,5),(3,4),(4,3),(5,2),(6,1)	(1,6),(2,5),(2,5),(3,4),(3,4),(4,3)	6	6/36 = 1/6
8	(2,6),(3,5),(4,4),(5,3),(6,2)	(2,6),(2,6),(3,5),(3,5),(4,4)	5	5/36
9	(3,6),(4,5),(5,4),(6,3)	(1,8),(3,6),(3,6),(4,5)	4	4/36 = 1/9
10	(4,6),(5,5),(6,4)	(2,8),(2,8),(4,6)	3	3/36 = 1/12
11	(5,6),(6,5)	(3,8),(3,8)	2	2/36 = 1/18
12	(6,6)	(4,8)	1	1/36

Summarize—Content

1. What is the distributive property, and how was it applied today?
2. What is probability, and how was it applied today?
3. What does it mean to factor expressions, and how was it applied today?
4. What tools can you use to factor expressions, and how was it applied today?

There was a lot of discussion here. Many teachers discussed their factoring methods and the particular methods they had used to factor expressions throughout the lesson.

Amber wanted to know what would happen if it were possible for one of the two dice to be a four-sided tetrahedron. Could you still get the standard distribution for a pair of normal six-sided dice this way? This sparked some discussion among the class (for example, the other die would be an octahedron) about how one would show this was possible or not possible, with varying opinions among them. They then discussed what is meant by a probability distribution.

Summarize—Pedagogy

1. Reflect on and share about the elements of this lesson that you can take back to your students.
2. What were factors that motivated you to engage in discussing the content with your peers? Which would you try or adapt to use with your students? (see figure 7.4 for a teacher's reflection.)

Figure 7.4 Amber's reflection

The connection between the factoring and the probability is amazing. Most people do factoring is over here [gestures with one hand], and probability is over there [gestures with the other hand], and Craig just did this [puts hands together]. The interconnectedness we see in math between seemingly different activities is amazing. I love it. I do. . . . When we first started this I'm going "I don't like probability because I never had a course in formal probability but it's okay . . . two dice . . . I can handle this, and so I think even my kids in my Algebra 2 class should be able to handle the probability aspect of it with a little encouragement similar to what Craig provided us.

Discussion between Colleagues

Where did you get the ideas for this lesson?
I was motivated to write the lesson from a problem from an earlier edition of Gallian's abstract algebra book, which is listed in the reference section.

What made you decide to teach this particular lesson?
I thought it would be fun for teachers to engage in factoring polynomials to find the solution to a concrete problem. Students spend so much time learning to factor polynomials, and yet very few factoring problems have a meaningful context.

Were there any surprises when teaching the lesson?
Yes. When teachers reached the factored form for $f(x)$ as
$$f(x) = (x^a + x^b + x^c + x^d + x^e + x^f) = x^g(x + 1)^h(x^2 + x + 1)^i(x^2 - x + 1)^j,$$
I was surprised that few thought to use a simpler problem to get a feel for how to proceed. The hint to look at f(1) and f(0) helped, although looking at f(0) was confusing for most because while substituting 0 into a polynomial was a direct exercise, determining what the result meant was not. In this particular context, the 0^0 should be interpreted as 1, because it is indicating that x is not actually a factor of f(x). Again, this is so because in the context of products, a term to 0th power should be interpreted as 1. This is common knowledge among mathematicians but apparently not among high school mathematics teachers (see Figure 7.2, from Knuth 1992).

What would you do differently?
I would rephrase some of the statements in the handouts to minimize confusion on the above issue. My goal would be to make it more natural and "obvious." So the new handout would include the following:
What happens when we calculate f(0)? Note that there are two cases.
Case 1: g > 0. Then $f(x) = (x^a + x^b + x^c + x^d + x^e + x^f) = x^g(x + 1)^h(x^2 + x + 1)^i(x^2 - x + 1)^j$.
Substitute x = 0 to see what happens in this case.
Case 2: g = 0. So the factor x^g does not occur and $f(x) = (x^a + x^b + x^c + x^d + x^e + x^f) = x^g(x + 1)^h(x^2 + x + 1)^i(x^2 - x + 1)^j$.

Substitute x 0 to see what happens in this case.

Based on what you observed, which of case 1 and/or case 2 actually occurs? What can you conclude from this?

Note that the appendix is intended for those wanting a thorough treatment of this discussion.

But wouldn't this revised handout eliminate or reduce the opportunity for teachers to engage in productive struggle and worthwhile discourse?

That is always the danger when you simplify a problem or provide too much direction. I think many learners may shut down when they get too frustrated, however, and that this extra guidance would thus be helpful for them. The problem would still be rich enough for the teachers to engage in worthwhile discourse.

How do you assess teachers?

We had both pre- and postassessments, homework, and of course we observed them as they participated in the lesson.

As a Ph.D. mathematician, compare and contrast teaching teachers versus teaching mathematics majors.

From my experience, some secondary school teachers sometimes assume that if they don't know something, it must not be useful, because—after all—they are already good math teachers (which they are). So they sometimes shut down and lose interest. Math majors, on the other hand, tend to have an implicit attitude that the material is appropriate and useful–even if they are not motivated to learn any particular content. Thus, it takes much more time to prepare a lesson for the teachers than my math majors since I have to think and do research to find motivating links to the content the teachers want or need to teach.

Commentary

Students spend much of their middle and high school years doing various factoring problems, and, while the usual application of factoring to finding zeros of polynomials is tremendously useful, the Sicherman dice provide an application that is more concrete and yet a genuine application of the factoring process itself that challenged the teachers. This contrasts with many factoring exercises where the real goal is to factor the polynomial into linear factors and find all real zeros of the polynomial. An added bonus is that the dice connect higher algebra to probability through the process of reasoning and sense making as recommended by NCTM's *Reasoning and Sense Making* document (2009). Upon finding how they should be labeled, teachers then use the dice as manipulatives experimentally to verify their results and to foster better understanding.

Craig's lesson engaged teachers in content from the CCSSM function standards. Teachers used multiple representations of functions arising from the context of the weird dice as well as using that context and manipulatives to make sense of contradictions arising from misconceptions of definitions (SMP1–SMP7). He chose a high-level task appropriate for the high school teachers and encouraged participation through the use of questioning and small-group work (SMP1, SMP2). His strategies are consistent with NCTM's (2000) *Principle and Standards* recommendation for having students share strategies:

◆ Elicit students' mathematical ideas
◆ Represent students' diverse strategies
◆ Make connections between mathematical ideas
◆ Compare similarities and differences across strategies
◆ Develop students' repertoire of strategies and flexible thinking

These strategies encouraged the teachers to engage in meaningful discourse that helped them to solve a challenging problem because they asked and answered each other's questions, shared the mathematical authoring, and challenged one another's mathematical ideas (MP6). According to DeJarnette, Dao, and González (2014), those actions are ingredients necessary to helping middle grades student function productively in small groups, but, as Craig's lesson demonstrated, they are also appropriates for adult learners.

In many instances throughout this lesson, teachers tried to make sense of an arbitrary rule they learned within the context of a new problem and tried to connect their existing knowledge of factoring to make sense of the Sicherman dice (SMP1–SMP3, SMP5–SMP7). Their problem-solving process focused on "seeking and using connections across different mathematical domains, different contexts, and different representations." (NCTM, 2009, 10). In so doing, teachers were able to create and justify an algebraic model for determining numbers for a dice with a given property (SMP4). We believe engaging teachers in such experiences together with the time to reflect on how to translate them to their own classrooms, are necessary to helping teachers similarly engage their students in the mathematical practices. According to NCTM's *An Administrator's Guide to High School Mathematics: Making Reasoning and Sense Making a Focus in Mathematic* (n.d.):

Many teachers may not have personally experienced mathematics as a reasoning and sense making endeavor. Consequently, they may have some difficulty in providing their students with the kinds of classroom experiences that are necessary for promoting critical thinking. Teachers should be encouraged to attend workshops and take mathematics courses that help them grow in their ability to reason about and make sense of mathematics. These experiences should help them increase their "content knowledge for teaching," enabling them to connect the mathematics that they are learning with the high school mathematics curriculum and assisting them in examining the ways in which they teach.

(6)

Unit Overview

A Dice Game for Engaging Teachers In Discourse

Aim: Are there dice with positive integer labels having the same probability distribution for its sum as the normal dice labeled 1 to 6?

Objectives: To have teachers work with polynomial functions and apply factoring of polynomials to discover properties of the Sicherman dice.

Course: Algebra 2/Statistics and Probability

Source: Original. These dice were invented by Colonel George Sicherman and first reported by Martin Gardner (Gardner, 1978) in a *Scientific American* article. Other information can be found in Broline (1979) and Fowler and Swift (1999).

Number of 90-Minute Periods: Two

NCTM/CCSSM Standards: Patterns and Functions: F.IF.2, .3, .5, .7, .8, .9; Complex Numbers: NCN.1, .2, .8, .9; Algebra: A.SSE.2, .3: Interpret Structure; Algebra: A.APR.4, .5, .6: Polynomial Identities; Statistics and Probability: S.IC.4, .5: Make Inferences and Justify Conclusions.

NCTM Process/Mathematical Practices: Mathematics as Problem Solving, Reasoning and Proof, Communication, Connections, Representation/SMP1–SMP7.

Mathematical Content: Students work with polynomial functions and Fundamental Theorem of Algebra to interpret the meaning of factored polynomials.

Prerequisites: Experience factoring polynomials and applying fundamental theorem of algebra.

Materials and Tools

- ◆ Lined paper
- ◆ Computer with Internet access
- ◆ Calculators

Management Procedures

- ◆ Have students complete the warm-up problems.
- ◆ Have student work on the Launch.
- ◆ Ask probing questions as student work on finding the numbers for the Sicherman dice.

Assessment

Observe and make note of the methods students use to factor as well as the numbers they try for the Sicherman dice.

Resources

Broline, D. (1979). Renumbering the Faces of Dice. *Mathematics* Magazine, 52 (5), 312–15.

Fowler, B., and R. Swift (1999). Relabeling Dice. *College Mathematics Journal* 30(3), 204–8.

Gardner, Martin. (1978). Mathematical Games. *Scientific American* 238, 19–32.

Knuth, D. (1992). Two Notes on Notation. *American Mathematical Monthly* 99(5), 403–22.

Lappan, G., J. Fey, W. Fitzgerald, S. Friel, and Elizabeth Phillips. (2002). *Connected Mathematics*. Glenview, IL: Prentice Hall.

National Council of Teachers of Mathematics. (2009). *Focus in High School Mathematics: Reasoning and Sense Making*. Reston, VA: NCTM.

Stein, C. C. (2007). Let's Talk. Promoting Mathematical Discourse in the Classroom. *Mathematics Teacher* 101(4), 285–89.

8

Ben Preddy: Integrating Mathematics with Literacy

"I am not good in math. Why are we doing this? When am I ever going to use it? Where does this stuff come from?" My math students can do the drill and practice problems pretty well, but they can't seem to apply them to real-world situations.

—Voices Overheard

Looking upward, I surveyed the ceiling of my prison. It was some thirty or forty feet overhead... . The vibration of the pendulum was at right angles to my length. I saw that the crescent was designed to cross the region of the heart. It would fray the serge of my robe—it would return and repeat its operations—again—and again. . . . Notwithstanding its terrifically wide sweep (some thirty feet or more), and the hissing vigor of its descent, sufficient to sunder these very walls of iron, still the fraying of my robe would be all that, for several minutes, it would accomplish.

—Edgar Allan Poe: *The Pit and the Pendulum*

I challenge my students to stop the lesson whenever they cannot imagine a usefulness, an application, for what we are doing or about to do. In this investigation, Poe's narrative sets the scene. How much time does Poe's condemned hero have to escape the blade swinging from the ceiling of his prison cell?

—Ben Preddy,
Media, Pennsylvania

When the science and mathematics departments at Haverford High School developed the course called "Basic Skills in Math and Science," they identified three objectives:

1. Students will develop basic skills in lab procedures, to include hypothesizing laws of science, designing lab experiments to test those theories, collecting lab data, analyzing the results, and comparing the lab results with their original theories.
2. Students will become familiar with basic problem-solving strategies and with situations to which they can be applied.
3. The course will be offered on a pass-fail basis to reduce anxiety based on grades and to attract the students who need it most.

Highlighting mathematics as the language of science, this integrated approach unites the disciplines and demonstrates their connection so that students gain confidence in their ability to do basic math and science and therefore are motivated to continue their study of both subjects in the future.

If students are to become active participants in math and science, physical space and time are critical factors. Ben's classroom has lab tables as well as a seating area for lectures. When Haverford High School adopted a block schedule with 90-minute periods, Ben and his colleagues jumped at the opportunity to create inquiry-based activities. Rather than presenting a single 90-minute lesson, they partition the time into three flexible sections: Class generally begins with a problem-solving exercise based on the "strategy of the week"; students learn how, when, and where to apply various strategies; they explore and use trial and error, measure and graph results, use a diagram or model, or pursue deductive reasoning. Whenever possible, strategies are selected to complement that week's lab activity. In this lesson, for example, the strategy is "guess and check." Ben starts the class with this problem:

Alex has five more dimes than quarters. The total amount of money she has is $3.30. How many quarters does she have?

Ben asks his students to work together, organizing their guesses systematically. He may guide them, if necessary: "Pick a quantity for one of the coin types; how many of the other must there be? What's the total value? Pick another combination. What is that value? Is it more or less? Are you getting closer to $3.30 or farther from it?" Once they have solved this problem, he assigns two more like it. He keeps the students working, individually or together, until every student arrives at correct answers.

The heart of each lesson is an experiment or lab activity. Topics include density, gravitational forces, Ohm's law of electric currents, and the properties of solutions. This lesson applies the law of the pendulum.

Down—certainly, relentlessly down! It vibrated within three inches of my bosom! . . . Down—still unceasingly—still inevitably down! I gasped and struggled at each vibration. . . . I saw that some ten or twelve vibrations would bring the steel in actual contact with my robe—and with this observation there suddenly came over my spirit all the keen, collected calmness of despair. For the first time during many hours—or perhaps days—I thought.

Edgar Allan Poe, The Pit and the Pendulum

In a brief transition, Ben discusses the process of scientific discovery and experimentation. He points out that scientists wonder and theorize—*guess*—about phenomena and then test—*check*—their hypotheses through experimentation. Now he asks his students to *guess* how much time Poe's hero has to escape. Their experiments will *check* the reasonableness of their guesses.

The class has read *The Pit and the Pendulum* as a homework assignment. Now, one student reads the relevant section aloud for review. Ben notes that the time required for the pendulum to complete a full swing (back and forth) is called its *period*. Students then begin to brainstorm factors that might affect the pendulum's period. The list includes the pendulum's length, its weight, and its arc of swing. Ben asks students to write down why they think these factors are important. Then they discuss how they can check their hypotheses. What laboratory experiments might they use?

The next day, students enter class expecting to conduct experiments. Ben asks them to summarize the important factors from yesterday's list. Once they have shared their ideas, he divides the class into groups of three or four (gender balanced and of mixed grade levels). Each group is given a specific factor to analyze and a set of materials (string, weight, yardstick, stopwatch, clipboard). Ben distributes Figure 8.1, discusses any questions about the lab, and assigns roles to students:

◆ Recorder-navigator—records data and makes sure experimenters follow procedures accurately;
◆ Experimenter #1—sets up equipment, performs lab according to the instructions read by the navigator, and makes appropriate observations;
◆ Experimenter #2—monitors work of experimenter #1, and verifies all data readings.

Students then follow the instructions in Figure 8.1 to determine the effects, if any, of the weight of the pendulum. Ben circulates constantly to assist with problems and to help identify errors. Each group finds an area of the classroom where the pendulum can swing easily. Students carefully attend to their assigned roles as the experiment proceeds. They are surprised that the weight of the pendulum has little effect on the time required for the pendulum to complete a full swing.

Next, the groups vary the angle at which the pendulum starts its swing. Ben distributes a lab sheet similar to Figure 8.1, where Instructions 1, 2, and 4 are the same. He modifies Instruction 3 for a 75-degree angle and Instruction 5 and its related table for 60°, 45°, and 30°. The greater the angle, the longer the path of its arc—but, again, the students are surprised to observe no effects on the period of the pendulum.

Figure 8.1 *The Pit and the Pendulum* lab sheet 1

The Pit and the Pendulum - by Edgar Allan Poe

Name: _____   Group #_____

Question: Does it matter how <u>heavy</u> the pendulum is?

1. Cut a piece of string approximately 36" long. (You will want the length of the pendulum to be close to exactly 24".)

2. Attach one weight to the end of the string, and hang the pendulum so that it is 2 feet from the center of the weight to the top of the string.

3. Use the protractor to start the swing at an approximately 45° angle. Be consistent for each trial!

4. Time 10 complete swings with the stopwatch. (Have a helper time the swings with you.) Do this five times, and record your data in the table.

5. Repeat this experiment for two weights, and then 4 four weights, and record your data in the table.

TRIAL	1 weight	2 weights	3 weights
# 1			
# 2			
# 3			
# 4			
# 5			
total			
average			

45°

start

X

A full swing
returns to the spot
it started from!

Does it matter how heavy the pendulum is? _____

Why do you think you are right?

Ben reviews the list of factors, and students conclude that the pendulum's length is the only important factor that might affect its period. Students then plan the focus and design of the next day's lab.

Down—steadily down it crept. I took a frenzied pleasure in contrasting its downward with its lateral velocity. To the right—to the left—far and wide with the shriek of a damned spirit! To my heart, with the stealthy pace of the tiger! . . .

Yet one minute, and I felt that the struggle would be over. Plainly I perceived the loosening of the bandage. I knew that in more than one place it must be already severed. With a more than human resolution I lay still.

Edgar Allan Poe, *The Pit and the Pendulum*

As they enter class the next day, Ben's students are eager to collect data on varying lengths of pendulums. As an introduction, he has students complete Figure 8.2; to do so they must measure the time it takes pendulums of varying length to swing 10 times. Students are asked to write their conclusion about the effect of varying the length of the pendulum. During the ensuing class discussion, students agree that changing the length of the pendulum changes the time required for a given number of swings.

Now Ben challenges them to predict how long it would take for the pendulum to swing if it were lengthened to 10, 15, 20, 25, and, finally, 30 feet. Their predictions for a pendulum 30 feet long range from 40 to 60 seconds. Students also predict the effects of doubling the length of the string. Most assume a direct relationship between the length of the pendulum and the length of time of its swing.

Ben now restates the big questions: "How long would it take the 30-foot pendulum to swing the 10 times Poe's hero expects? How can we conduct an experiment to help us predict?"

The students are confident about the procedures they must do, but finding a location to swing a string pendulum 10 or 20 feet long is not easy. Fortunately, Ben's classroom is on the fourth floor, with a window that overlooks the schoolyard. Armed with stopwatches and clipboards, his students gather below the window. While Ben swings pendulums of 10, 15, 20, and 25 feet, they time 10 swings, record the results, and refine their estimates for the 30-foot pendulum. Finally, Ben swings a 30-foot pendulum. The students jump with excitement, because the result, 61.9 seconds, is very close to their estimates.

However, they are not sure why doubling the length of the pendulum doesn't double the time it takes to swing 10 times. Back in the classroom, Ben instructs them to enter their data for the 10- to 25-foot pendulums on a graphing calculator, test various functions for a best fit, sketch a graph of the data in Figure 8.2, and again predict the period of the 30-foot pendulum.

As another way to approach Poe's story, Ben shows a video of *The Pit and the Pendulum*. As they time the action, the students find that the hero takes more than five minutes to escape death. At first, they are confused. How could it have taken more than five minutes in the movie but only one minute in their lab? Finally a student

Figure 8.2 *The Pit and the Pendulum* làb sheet 2

The Pit and the Pendulum - by Edgar Allan Poe

Name: _____   Group #_____

Question: Does it matter how long the pendulum is?

1. Cut a piece of string approximately 36" long. (You will want the length of the pendulum to be close to exactly 24".)

2. Attach one weight to the end of the string, and hang the pendulum so that it is 2 feet from the center of the weight to the top of the string.

3. Use the protractor to start the swing at a 45° angle.

4. Time 10 complete swings with the stopwatch. (Have a helper time the swings with you.) Do this 5 times, and record your data in the table.

5. Repeat this experiment for 3′, 4′, and 6′ and record your data in the table.

45°

start

X

A full swing
returns to the spot
it started from!

TRIAL	3ft	4ft	5ft
# 1			
# 2			
# 3			
# 4			
# 5			
total			
average			

Does it matter how <u>long</u> the pendulum is? _____

Why do you think you are right?

_____

_____

_____

Using the data you have collected for 2′, 3′, 4′, and 6′, try to predict the period of a pendulum 30 feet long. How much time would our hero have for 12 swings? Graph the number of swings versus time and sketch the line of best fit?

exclaims, "They violated science in the movie. It couldn't have taken more than 40 to 65 seconds!" That is the level of confidence Ben strives to develop in his students.

> Nor had I erred in my calculations—nor had I endured in vain. I at length felt that I was **free**.
>
> Edgar Allan Poe, *The Pit and the Pendulum*

Once all the results are in, Ben makes sure students know that they have discovered the same scientific principles that Galileo discovered in 1584, when he was only 20 years old—and Galileo is considered to be a genius. He tells them that if they had continued to experiment, they too could have arrived at the formula for the period of a pendulum, $T = 2\pi \sqrt{\frac{L}{g}}$ where T is the period, L is the length of the pendulum, and g is the force of gravity. "You're geniuses, too!"

To conclude this section, Ben asks students to use the formula to recalculate their estimates and compare the outcome with their lab results. He also asks them to explain, from the formula, why the period does not vary directly with the length of the pendulum. Finally, if time permits, students play the game of the week.

Discussion between Colleagues

Is the course achieving its objective?
> This course does give students greater confidence in their ability to do basic math and science. Science teachers have reported that some of my students go on to take science courses that they had not previously planned to take.

It would be great if the class could have actually generated the formula for the period of a pendulum. Is that possible?
> That's not realistic for this group of students. If they can predict the direct relationship between length and period, I'm satisfied—they are using the available data to think algebraically.

How do you assess group and individual student performance on the lab or game portion?
> This is a pass/fail course. Students who complete all the work and attempt all the problems receive a passing grade. It is very rare for a student to fail.

What do you do if some students finish the lab early?
> Frequently, some groups do finish ahead of the others. Suppose a group of students is analyzing the effect of mass on the period of a pendulum, and after completing their lab they return with the conclusion that the period of the pendulum is independent of mass. When I ask them about their results, if they state their conclusion tentatively, I might ask them to repeat the lab and double-check their observations

and calculations. ("How can that be? We all agreed that the weight of a pendulum affects its period—could you have made a mistake?") When they return with confidence in their voices, I congratulate them. If they still have time, they can play the game of the week.

What do you do for students who miss a lab?
Those who are absent must obtain data from a member of their group and be able to answer questions that I have selected to assess their understanding of the process and results. If I see areas of confusion or misunderstanding, they must return to their group for further guidance and try again until they succeed.

Have you been able to get teachers in the other disciplines to work with your course?
Yes. The science teachers have been very helpful and supportive. They guide me in the selection of labs and invite me to share their equipment.

Commentary

The investment of time and energy that Ben and his colleagues put into developing this course specifically designed for students who are typically unmotivated to do mathematics was well worth it. Students are engaged in testing and modifying their own theories and are enthusiastic about the project (SMP1–SMP6). They develop lab skills as they reinforce and extend their mathematics and science skills. And, as Ben hoped, they gain a different view of mathematics—one that dispels the idea that math is a rote process of applying someone else's algorithms to produce correct and unique answers. Instead, mathematics becomes a tool for judging the reasonableness of their own responses to reasonable challenges and to challenge the mathematics presented in a movie!

What is also notable about Ben's course is its pass-fail grading system: It clearly places the responsibility for success on the students because success is based solely on student participation and completion of the lab work. Everyone can succeed because the "test" questions hold no surprises (only the answers!), and collaboration with the teacher and fellow students is encouraged to answer the questions. The course thus creates a welcome mat for the unmotivated students that reads "participate and succeed!" As students continue to experience and learn mathematics in this way, the hostility or dislike that they have toward math is challenged and reduced.

Research has shown that many students believe that solutions to mathematical problems should be obtained in five minutes or less and that creativity in mathematics is reserved for geniuses. Indeed, Schoenfeld and Arcavi's (1988) yearlong observation of geometry students showed that:

Students who have finished a full twelve years of mathematics have worked thousands upon thousands of "problems"—virtually none of which were expected to take the students more than a few minutes to complete. The presumption underlying the assignments was as follows: If you understand the material, you can work the exercises. If you can't work the exercises within a reasonable amount of time, then you don't understand the material. That's a sign you should seek help.

(159–60)

The productive struggling the NCTM/CCSSM calls for is a direct result of such research. Ben's course promotes students' ability to appreciate the varying lengths of time and thinking that are required to do mathematics. Simultaneously, students gain respect for themselves as members of a mathematics community who have the ability to successfully engage in the process of mathematical discovery. They thus are over-coming the notion of "I am not good in math."

In a post by Kimball and Smith in *The Atlantic* (2014), the authors challenge the "I'm not good at math" mindset too often heard when mathematics is discussed outside the mathematics community. They write,

For high-school math, inborn talent is much less important than hard work, preparation, and self-confidence. How do we know this? First of all, both of us have taught math for many years—as professors, teaching assistants, and private tutors. Again and again, we have seen the following pattern repeat itself:

1. Different kids with different levels of preparation come into a math class. Some of these kids have parents who have drilled them on math from a young age, while others never had that kind of parental input.
2. On the first few tests, the well-prepared kids get perfect scores, while the unprepared kids get only what they could figure out by winging it—maybe 80 or 85%, a solid B.
3. The unprepared kids, not realizing that the top scorers were well pre-pared, assume that genetic ability was what determined the perfor-mance differences. Deciding that they "just aren't math people," they don't try hard in future classes, and fall further behind.
4. The well-prepared kids, not realizing that the B students were simply unprepared, assume that they are "math people," and work hard in the future, cementing their advantage.
5. Thus, people's belief that math ability can't change becomes a self-fulfilling prophecy.

Ben's students learn that they can engage in and be successful in solving rigorous mathematical problems. They are good at math—indeed, Ben thinks and tells them that they are geniuses!

Unit Overview

Integrating Mathematics with Literacy

Aim: How can we determine how long it took the hero in *The Pit and the Pendulum* to escape?

Objective: Students will apply the process of trial and error in a lab setting to test hypotheses they have generated and to state conclusions.

Course: Algebra.

Grade Levels: Open (mostly ninth- and tenth-graders).

Source: Adapted from a unit by the Interactive Mathematics Program.

Number of 90-Minute Periods: Three.

NCTM/CCSM Standards: Algebra: A.CED.3: Graph equations—A.CED.2, .3; Modeling: G.MG.1: Use geometric properties to describe objects; G.MG.3: Apply geometric methods to solve design problems.

NCTM Processes/Mathematical Practices: Mathematics as Problem Solving, Communication, Reasoning, Connection/SMP1–SMP6.

Mathematical Concepts: Students conduct experiments to determine the effects of mass, arc of swing, and pendulum length on the period of a pendulum. Using their results, they predict the length of time for pendulums of greater than 10 feet, sketch the line of best fit, and complete labs to test their predictions. They apply the formula $T = 2\pi \sqrt{\dfrac{L}{g}}$ to verify their estimates and compare them with lab results.

Prerequisites: Use of rulers and protractors for measurement; knowledge of how to interpret and compute values for formulas involving square roots determining lines of best fit.

Materials and Tools

- Copies of story *The Pit and the Pendulum* and videotape of *The Pit and the Pendulum* (Caution: Some versions of this story may contain scenes with nudity—skip that portion of the film.)
- One stopwatch, protractor, and yardstick for each group
- Strings for pendulums of various lengths
- Weights (preferably of known value and in multiple units)
- Graphing Calculators

Management Procedures

- ◆ Assign students to read the story two to three days before the lab.
- ◆ On lab day, have students do a problem that requires trial and error and connect their experience to the scientific process.
- ◆ Divide students into groups and have them predict factors that affect the period of a pendulum.
- ◆ Have each group conduct the lab and test their guesses against the results.
- ◆ Have a whole-class discussion of results and summarize major findings.
- ◆ Show students the segment of the video where the prisoner is in the pit and have them note the time it takes the prisoner to escape.
- ◆ Compare groups' results.
- ◆ Present the formula for pendulum swings and have class use that model to recalculate their estimate and compare with lab results.

Assessment

Note students' participation and work throughout the lab.
Collect and grade the lab sheets.

Resources

1. NCTM Resources: www.NCTM.org.
2. Music: Chapter 3, this volume.
3. Theater: Chapter 4, this volume.
4. Alexandra Pannoni is an education intern at U.S. News. See her blog, *3 Ideas for Incorporating Music into Core High School Classes,* www.usnews.com/education/blogs/high-school-notes. Retrieved Mach 13, 2014.

9

Murray Siegel: Discovering the Central Limit Theorem

For years I have sought an activity that would lead students to discover, or at least believe, the central limit theorem. I tried using digits from random telephone numbers and the ages of randomly selected pennies; I also observed Duane Hinders's lima bean sampling. None of these provided a satisfactory result. Finally, at a workshop I attended, Landy Godbold demonstrated a graphing calculator program that sparked ideas for an effective activity. The activity is technology based and definitely student centered.

Murray Siegel, Ph.D., Maricopa, Arizona

Murray Siegel has taught statistics at the high school level for more than 20 years. His beliefs that students learn more through discovery than through lecture and that mathematics is best learned through discourse motivated him to continue to seek ways to actively engage his students. One such activity is described in this profile and was taught to students at the J. L. Mann Academy of Mathematics, Science, and Technology in Greenville, South Carolina.

The central limit theorem is the most important theorem in inferential statistics (i.e., hypothesis testing, confidence intervals, $p < .05$) and all it implies. Given sets of data for which the mean of each set has been calculated, the theorem states that *as the sample size increases, the sampling distribution of the sample means:*

♦   Approaches a normal distribution;
♦   Has a mean equal to the population mean;
♦   Has a standard deviation equal to the population standard deviation divided by the square root of the sample size.

Although Murray's students learned and accepted this theorem, often they did not really understand its underlying concepts, and therefore they were not solidly prepared for the study of inferential statistics. He tried various ways of eliciting the theorem from students, but each method required manual sampling, which restricted the sample sizes to small numbers. As a result, the activity did not fully model the theorem, and at the end Murray still had to tell students what the central limit theorem stated.

Then, at a workshop, he watched Landy Godbold use a calculator program to simulate the theorem. Recognizing the graphing calculator's tireless capacity to generate any amount of random data and then to produce graphs on demand, Murray devised an activity by which students could work with data to discover the central limit theorem without a program.

In a nutshell: Each student is assigned a specific sample size and simulates drawing 25 samples of that size from a population of random digits, 0 through 9. From the 25 means of these simulated samples, the student then determines the mean and the standard deviation for that sample size. Sample sizes range from 5 to 150; students may be assigned more than one of the smaller sample sizes, or they may work together to complete simulations with a larger sample size. The students then combine their data and use a graphing calculator to graph the results. To Murray's satisfaction, students' exploration and analysis of the graphs elicited statements of the three key components of the central limit theorem!

His AP statistics class had already learned about exploratory data analysis, probability, simulation, and sampling when he announced that the subject for that day's lesson was sampling distributions. To clarify and review ideas about sampling distributions, he told students,

Imagine being blindfolded and having to draw a sample of a certain number of marbles from a large barrel full of colored marbles. You remove the blindfold, and after counting and noting the number of each color, you return the marbles, stir the contents and start the process again. Suppose we had the time and motivation to continue this process for a while. What type of data analysis might describe the content of the barrel?

As another example, Murray asked them to consider the same question applied to the height measurements of randomly selected samples of students. When a student suggested computing the mean height for each sample, Murray noted that this would be part of the day's lesson. Next they reviewed the key skills of programming the calculator to perform simulations. Using a simulation of a sample size of 5 and the calculator's overhead view screen, Murray demonstrated how the TI-graphing calculator generated five random numbers from 0 to 9. He defined List L1 as **L1 = "seq(randInt (0,9), x , 1 , 5 ,1)"** and struck the **ENTER** key; five random numbers were generated all at once. Using the **1-Var Stats** choice in the **STAT CALC** menu, he reviewed how the x-bar function of the calculator computed the mean of these numbers, and he had students jot down the means. Returning to List **L1**, Murray struck any key and asked students to comment about the numbers that had been generated. They all recognized

Figure 9.1 Sampling distribution investigation

1. You will be given a unique sample size, n, to substitute in the formula of the next instruction.
2. L1 = **"seq(randInt (0,9), x, 1, n, 1)"**
3. Obtain 1-Var Stats on L1.
4. Record the sample mean for the sample.
5. Press **2nd Enter Enter** to compute the mean of the next sample.
6. Repeat step 4.
7. Continue the process until you have 25 sample means.
8. Press **Clr List L1.** (This clears the formula from L1. If this step is not taken, each data entry into L2 will re-execute the instruction in L1.)
9. Place the 25 sample means in L2.
10. Obtain 1-Var Stats on L2 and record x-bar and s.

that the digits in **L1** were different from the digits in the first sample. Murray explained that the quotation marks in the definition of **L1** told the calculator to execute a new simulation every time a calculator key was struck. Again students noted the mean of the five-digit sample, and Murray entered the two sample means in **L2.**

As he did so, students observed that the entry procedure was delayed. "Why?" one student asked. Murray explained that until they clear the definition of **L1** (using the **Clr List** choice in the **EDIT** menu), each data entry causes a re-execution of the instruction in **L1.** Finally, the mean and the standard deviation of the sample means were obtained using the **1-Var Stats** choice.

Having explained the way the calculator generated and processed random samples, Murray distributed the instruction sheet for the students' work (see Figure 9.1.)

Murray assigned sample sizes ranging from 10 to 150 because these numbers are small but large enough to show a difference in the distributions. Groups or individual students would conduct 25 sample means for each data set assigned. To balance the workload, he assigned individual students the sample sizes of 10, 20, 30, 40, and 50; to a group of two students, sample sizes of 70 and 100; and to a group of three students, sample sizes of 120 and 150. In groups of two, one student performed 12 simulations and the other did 13. In groups of three, two students conducted eight simulations and the third did nine.

After the class completed the simulations, each student or group reported the sample size for the distribution, the mean of their 25 sample means, and the standard deviation of their 25 sample means. Using the calculator's overhead view-screen, Murray entered the sample size information in **L1**, the mean of each sampling distribution in **L2**, and the standard deviation of each distribution in **L3**. He showed students a scatter plot on which the x-axis represents **L1** (sample size) and the y-axis represents **L2** (sample means). The scale on the x-axis extended from 0 to 160, and the values on the y-axis ranged from 3.2 to 5.3. Students' first graph looked like Figure 9.2 without the horizontal line.

Students questioned what they saw in the graphs. "Why were there two points that are off by themselves?" "The graph began like a straight line but then changed." "Why did the graph level off near the end?" The answer to the first question reminded students that experimental errors may be reflected in the data. The deviation from the pattern was related to the relatively small size of the samples and the relatively small number of samples in each distribution. If the students had done 10,000 simulations for each sample size, the patterns would have been more consistent. The last two questions elicited responses that hinted that the means of large samples approach a fixed number.

The class agreed that the plot suggested that as the sample size becomes larger, the mean of the sampling distribution moves closer to a particular number—one of the key aspects of the central limit theorem. In the smaller samples, there were greater differences between the means and the "goal" number, and students discussed why that made sense. Murray asked the class to estimate the goal number for the class's data. One student suggested that it might be the population mean. The class agreed that large samples should have a mean close to 4.5, which is the mean of the entire population of digits from zero to nine. To check the guess, Murray asked students to compare the scatter plot of Figure 9.2 with the line $y = 4.5$ (see Figure 9.3). Once students agreed that this suggestion seemed to be true, he told the class to note this important finding: *As the sample size increases, the mean of the sampling distribution approaches the population mean.* One student wrote this on the board.

The focus of the next key activity was on the standard deviations of the sample sizes. Keeping the x-axis as the sample size, Murray modified the y-axis to represent

Figure 9.2 Distribution of sample means and the line $y = 4.5$

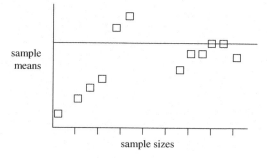

Figure 9.3 Scatter plot of standard deviations

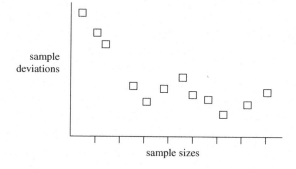

Figure 9.4 Scatter plot of standard deviations and the line $y = \dfrac{2.87}{\sqrt{x}}$

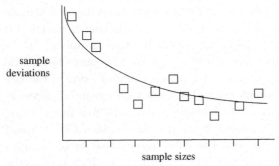

sample deviations

sample sizes

L3, the standard deviations. He told the class to consider the scatter plot for the standard deviations of their collected data, as shown in Figure 9.4. As students looked at this curve, which decreased in value as the sample size increased, he asked questions to guide their explorations. "What is the standard deviation if the sample size equals 1? Is this the graph of a decreasing or increasing function?"

Students provided these explanations:

◆ If the sample size were 1, then we would be looking at the distribution of the individual random digits in the entire population. We can compute that standard deviation (2.87) by getting the **1-Var Stats** for a sample that has one of each of the 10 digits. Thus we know that when x is 1, our y should be 2.87.

◆ The standard deviation is decreasing as we increase the sample size; in Figure 9.3, as you move from left to right on the x-axis, the sample size is going from 5 to 150 and the y values are generally decreasing.

The sequence of questions and answers helped students remember that decreasing functions are typically obtained by subtracting or dividing by the variable (in this case, the sample size). However, they noted that subtraction can be eliminated, because the decrease is not constant. Thus the sample size must be in the denominator of the function.

Making use of a calculator's quick responses to "what if" questions, students embarked on a series of conjectures to find an equation that best fits the graph of their data: "Try $y = 2.87/x$," one student suggested. However, a quick glance at its graph showed that it did not fit the data points of Figure 9.3. Another suggested 2.87 divided by the square of the sample size, but she commented, after viewing the resulting graph, "That is even worse." A third proposed putting the square root of the sample size in the denominator. Figure 9.4 shows this function graphed with the scatter plot.

The class agreed that this is a good model to show how the sampling standard deviation changes as the sample size increases. On the board, a student recorded this second important finding: *As the sample size increases, the standard deviation of the sampling distribution can be estimated using the population standard deviation divided by the square root of the sample size.* Next Murray invited the students who performed the simulations of population sizes 10 and 150 to transmit their 25 means to the view-screen calculator, using the calculator's linking cable. The class then viewed the histogram of each distribution. Murray asked the class to think of conjectures about the relative size of a sample and the resulting distribution. A student suggested, and the class agreed, that the pattern for the means from the 25 larger samples looked more like the normal distribution than the other pattern (from the 25 smaller samples) did. After a student recorded this last finding on the board, Murray told the class that their homework assignment was to produce further data to verify this conjecture. Murray then asked the class to summarize the outcome of their investigations. Referring to the board, they responded:

- ◆ As the sample size increases, the mean of the sampling distribution approaches the population mean.
- ◆ As the sample size increases, the standard deviation of the sampling distribution can be estimated using the population standard deviation divided by the square root of the sample size.
- ◆ As the sample size increases, the distribution of the sample means becomes more and more normal.

Murray asked students if they knew which important theorem these three rules constitute. When no one responded, he informed them that they had just shown justification for the central limit theorem for the distribution of sample means. The class was now conceptually prepared to understand inferential statistics and to use the calculator to help solve problems.

To assess his students' understanding, he assigned the six problems shown in Figure 9.5. (The answers are given in parentheses.)

Discussion between Colleagues

Describe students' reaction while engaging in this activity. Any surprise? Excitement?
Students are accustomed to performing simulations on the calculator, so I see no obvious reaction at first. However, their interest is sparked when we examine the graphs of the entire activity. That is when they become curious and express amazement that a trend seems to be emerging.

Many, if not most, AP students are quick to grasp and understand ideas. Why did you feel the need to engage them in this discovery approach?
The concepts embedded in inferential statistics are not easy to truly understand. I myself took many courses, including some at the highest level in graduate school, before I began to build an understanding of what I was doing. Actually, it was teaching the subject in high school and college that helped me develop a real understanding.

Figure 9.5 Assessment

1. We wish to take a sample to estimate the population mean. What does the central limit theorem tell us about selecting the sample and about the type of results we should expect?

   (The CLT would tell us to get a fairly large sample so that the sampling distribution would approach normality. Also, a large sample would reduce variability, so that our sample result should be relatively close to the population number we seek.)

2. The population of Sierra County, AZ, is thought to have a mean individual income of $24,750 with a standard deviation of $6,119. What is the probability that a random sample of 50 residents of this county will show a mean income that is

   a. Greater than $26,400?   b. Less than $25,000?

   (The samples of 50 are distributed normally with a standard deviation of 6,119 divided by the square root of 50, or 865.36. According to the standard normal (Z) table, the probability that a sample mean will exceed 26,400 is .028, and the probability that a sample mean will be less than 25,000 is .614.)

3. A sampling distribution of samples of 100 has a mean of 88 and a standard deviation of 2.09. What are the mean and variance of the population from which the samples are drawn?

   (The mean of the population is the same mean as the sampling distribution, which is 88. The standard deviation of the sampling distribution is the standard deviation of the population divided by 10 [the square root of 100]. By reversing the formula, population standard deviation is (10)(2.09) = 20.9. Variance is the square of standard deviation, 436.81.)

4. Seventy-five percent of city residents favor recycling garbage. If a sampling distribution of sample proportions drawn from this population has a standard deviation of .0475, what is the size of the samples in the sampling distribution?

   (The standard deviation of the sampling distribution =
   . The sample size = (.75)(.25)/.0475^2 = 83.)

5. Two samples of size 60 are randomly selected from a population. The proportion of left-handed people in the second sample is subtracted from the proportion in the first sample. If 11 percent of the population is left handed, what is the probability that the difference between the sample proportions is less than −.05?

   (According to the Z table, because the sampling distribution of the difference between sample proportions is theoretically normal, the probability is .1894 for the Z of −0.88.)

6. The mean age of listeners to KROK radio is 21.8 with a standard deviation of 3.51 years. On Monday, a random sample of 45 listeners is selected. A random sample of 65 listeners is selected on Friday. The mean age of Friday's sample is subtracted from the mean age of Monday's sample. What difference would there have to be so that the probability of having a greater difference was only one percent?

   (To have a probability of .01, the Z value would have to be 2.33. The theoretical standard deviation of the sampling distribution is .68. The difference would have to be (2.33)(.68) = 1.58.)

Share your general approach to the integration of calculators in your courses.

I see calculators as visual tools that have the capability to inspire students to think. They provide a picture that generates questions such as "What happens next?," "What caused this change?," "Why does this particular model fit the picture?" To me, the use of scatter diagrams to help students visualize functions is important. When we look at Figure 9.3, I ask, "What type of function that we studied in Algebra 2 do we see? If it is a decreasing function, what operations on the variables might we expect to see in the function?" This visual, or graph, is based on data they can relate to, so that the mathematical concept they are studying is no longer abstract.

Commentary

One of the principal research interests of J. Michael Shaughnessy, former NCTM president, has been the teaching and learning of statistics and probability. Results from his research recommend activity-based lessons that use small groups to help students confront their misconceptions, because getting students to use probability and statistics in their judgments and decisions, when appropriate, "is not easily remedied just by 'teaching them the right way'" (1992, 465). In his 2012 research with Noll, *Aspects of Students' Reasoning about Variation in Empirical Sampling Distribution,* there are additional recommendations:

> The findings in this study have implications for both practice and research. We believe that providing students with opportunities to create graphs from statistical experiments and to investigate their graphical displays for both nonstatistical and statistical forms of variability is a good starting place for facilitating robust statistical thinking about the various aspects of distributions of data (centers, variability, and shapes).

Murray's lesson adheres closely to this advice. His activity engages students in cooperative group learning requiring that they experiment with random values generated by the graphing calculator to help use samples and simulations to gather data, construct and compare representations of data in their graphs, correct each other's errors, and finally deduce the critical elements for the Central Limit Theorem (SMP1–SMP6, SMP8). Murray also applies recommendation from the American Statistical Association's report *Guidelines for Assessment and Instruction in Statistics Education (GAISE) Report* (Franklin et al., 2007), which delineates the four components of statistical problem solving and its principles that are applicable to all grade levels, K–12 (see Figure 9.6).

Figure 9.6 Steps in the statistical process and guiding principles for teaching statistics

---

Steps in the statistical problem-solving process

- Formulate questions
- Collect data
- Analyze data
- Interpret results

Guiding principles for teaching statistics

- Conceptual understanding takes precedence over procedural skill.
- Active learning is key to the development of conceptual understanding.
- Real-world data must be used wherever possible in statistics education.
- Appropriate technology is essential in order to emphasize concepts over calculations.
- All four steps of the investigative problem-solving process should be encountered at each grade level.
- The illustrative investigations should show situations in which the statistics is essential to answering a question, not just an add-on.
- Such investigations should be tied to the mathematics they illustrate, motivate, and emphasize.

Source: GAISE Report as demonstrated in Scheaffer and Tabor (2008).

Unit Overview

Discovering the Central Limit Theorem

Aim: What are the principles of the central limit theorem?

Objective: Students will cite and explain the principles of the central limit theorem based on data exploration.

Course: Statistics and Probability.

Source: Original, based on the work of Landy Godbold.

Grade Levels: Eleventh and twelfth.

Number of 50-Minute Periods: Two.

CCSSM Standards: Statistics: S.D1: Represent data with plots on the real number line (dot plots, histograms, and box plots); S.ID.2: Use statistics appropriate to the shape of the data distribution to compare center of two or more different data sets; S.ID.3: Interpret differences in shape, center, and spread in the context of the data sets; S.IC.1: Understand statistics as a process for making inferences; S.IC.5: Use data simulations to decide if differences between parameters are significant; Modeling: HSS-1D.A, HSS-MD.A.1, HSS-1C.A.1, HSS-1C.B.5.

NCTM Process Standards/Mathematical Practices: Mathematics as Problem Solving, Communication, Reasoning, and Connection/SMP1–SMP6, SMP8.

Mathematical Concepts: Students generate random data from a graphing calculator. They analyze calculator graph models of the sample means of the data to discover the three underlying principles of the central limit theorem.

Prerequisites: Exploratory data analysis; Probability; Functions; Simulation and sampling

Materials and Tools

- ◆ Graphing calculator for groups of students
- ◆ Graphing calculator view screen or Emulator
- ◆ Activity instruction sheet

Management Procedures

- ◆ Explain to students how the graphing calculator generates random numbers and calculates means and standard deviations.

- Group students, and have them complete the activity instruction sheet.
- As students discover a key principle, record it on the board. At the end of the activity, summarize the key findings.

Assessment
Students complete Figure 9.5. Collect and grade their work.

Resources

1. Chapter 5, this volume.
2. For K–12 teacher-made lessons that integrate the principles and guidelines discussed, visit the Statistic Education website: http://www.amstat.org/education/stew.
3. Read Murray's article with Madhuri Mulekar in *Mathematics Teacher* 103(1): "How Sample Size Affects a Sampling Distribution." The article includes a discussion of conducting this activity using statistical software.
4. NCTM: www.nctm.org. NCTM's Core Math Tools: www.nctm.org/standards/content.aspx?id=32706.

10

Susan Morere, Mary Ann Bates, Nezha Whitecotton, and Angela Guthrie: A Lesson Study on Real-World Applications of the Trigonometric Ratios

My beliefs about learning shape my teaching philosophy. I do not support the omission of parts of a concept that are being developed simply because a shortcut exists to reach a "correct answer." It is through conceptual development that students will create their own "shortcuts" and more efficient ways to solve a problem. Students need and should be provided time to process "how" as well as "what" they learned. Within my class, students make connections between their experiences and the larger concept and themes. The lesson study process helped my colleagues and me to develop a real-world application of mathematics that was both worthwhile and engaging for our students.

Susan Morere

Background

This chapter describes a lesson that was jointly developed by a small cohort of teachers participating in the lesson study process. Since Yvelyne's participation in and documentation of the first lesson study open house held in the U.S. (Germain-McCarthy, 2001, 2014), she has used every opportunity to engage preservice and inservice teachers in the process. The processes and documents described in this chapter for implementing lesson study were developed or significantly influenced by the work of Makoto Yoshida and Clea Fernandez of the Lesson Study Research Group at Teachers College, as well as by the work of Catherine Lewis from Mills College, Pennsylvania. In short, lesson study is a Japanese form of professional development that is teacher driven and focused on teachers collaboratively examining student data to improve student learning. Darling-Hammond (2014) values a collaborative process to teaching and learning because, she writes, "Perhaps the simplest way to break down professional isolation is for teachers to observe each other's teaching and to provide constructive feedback" (13). Since the first U.S. lesson study open house, much has happened for it to be viewed today as a viable form of professional development in the United States. We provide a brief update next.

Lesson Study

In the late 1990s, the examination of how Japanese teachers collaboratively crafted lessons was the source of the motivation to launch lesson study in the United States. (see chapter 1). Makoto Yoshida, whose 1999 dissertation focused on lesson study, was the first to coin the word "lesson study" from the Japanese *kenkyuu jugyou*, which means research lessons. Takahashi and Yoshida (2004) describe the characteristics for lesson study: Teachers begin with a focus on student learning to guide their discussions; they collaboratively plan and create a lesson based on student data; they implement and observe the lesson. A reflection of the process concludes a cycle of the process. Catherine Lewis (2000), elaborates on the characteristics:

1. *Research lessons are observed by other teachers.* The observing teachers may include just the faculty within the school or a wider group; some research lessons are open to teachers from all over Japan.
2. *Research lessons are planned for a long time, usually collaboratively.*
3. *Research lessons are designed to bring to life in a lesson a particular goal or vision of education.* The whole faculty chooses a research theme or focus. Typically, it is a broad goal or vision of education that goes beyond a specific subject matter and lesson.
4. *Research lessons are recorded.* Usually teachers record these lessons in multiple ways, including videotape, audiotape, observational notes, and copies of student work.
5. *Research lessons are discussed.* A colloquium follows the lesson. Typically, such a gathering begins with presentations by the teachers who taught and coplanned the lesson, followed by free or structured discussions; sometimes an outside educator or researcher also comments on the lesson.

(adapted from Lewis, 2000, 4–6)

This process is conducive to "high-quality mathematics instruction," which Peterson et al. (2013) describe as embodying six principles:

1. The Intellectual Engagement Principle that engages students with important mathematics;
2. The Goal Principle that guides student motivation, student performance, and student understanding;
3. The Flow Principle that stems from a worthwhile problem for students;

4. The Unit Principle that makes connections between grades and within mathematics;
5. The Adaptive Instruction Principle that engages students at a level appropriate to their current understanding of the content;
6. The Preparation Principle that guides the preparation of a well-thought-out, detailed plan that embodies the five principles.

(446–49)

The lesson study plan is one such "well-thought-out, detailed plan" in four columns that is very different from plans focusing on linear or procedural steps for conducting a lesson. Matthews, Hlas, and Finken (2009) describe the four-column lesson study format as one with columns for procedures, predicting student responses, preparing appropriate teacher responses, and assessing students' understanding.

University of New Orleans' Lesson Study Process

Susan and her colleagues were first introduced to the lesson study process through our UNO/LaSIP program. As one who has been recognized as a mathematics teacher of distinction (Louisiana Association of Mathematics Teachers, 2008) and as a "teacher who is making a difference" (Nicholls State University, 2010, 2012, 2013), Susan continually seeks to improve her teaching. For this reason, she decided to engage her colleagues in the lesson study process and to take charge of disseminating the work of the team by hosting a lesson study open house at her school, where the public could come and observe the lesson to provide further feedback to the team.

During the program, time was allowed to help teachers understand and begin the process of looking at student data to decide on a research topic for their lesson. Important to the process was having teachers complete Figure 10.1 to identify an overarching goal as well as a gap that is impeding advances toward that goal to focus their work. Teachers were also expected to work in their schools to continue the process with other colleagues and with the support of their principal, as well as to upload their lesson to the LaSIP website to share with others (http://mathed.math.uno.edu/viewforum.php?f=22).

Lesson Study across Content Areas and Schools

In one of the LaSIP workshops, Ivan Gill introduced a lesson on rockets, based on a demonstration by the Exploratorium staff out of San Francisco, which he crafted into a short project-based learning unit. He had the teachers building rockets out of colored paper and file cards, testing and selecting rockets for flight, brainstorming techniques for measuring rocket altitude, launching the rockets, and then measuring the altitude of rocket flight with simple, handmade inclinometers. The project continued with calculating rocket altitude, tabulating and graphing, then discussing and presenting results.

Ivan liked the lesson because it was academically rich; it utilized both math and science, could cross disciplines, and could be elaborated on in a number of academic directions. Even better, it could use math on different levels, from trigonometry to an elegant

Figure 10.1 Lesson study: Group goal selection

1. Think about the aspirations that you have for your students. What kind of students do you want to foster and help develop at your school? What qualities do you want your students to have by the time they leave your school?

2. What gaps do you see between these aspirations and how children are actually developing at your school?

3. Discuss these gaps with your group. As a group, select a "gap" that you would like to focus on with your lesson study. What "gap" have you selected?

4. Write a group goal that states the quality you would like to develop in your students, in order to address the gap that you have chosen.

Barbarina Ertle, Sonai Chokshi, & Clea Fernandez
2002 Lesson Study Research Group (lsrg@columbia.edu).

but simple graphical technique suitable for lower grade levels as well. Better still, if anything comes close to blowing stuff up to catch student interest, it's shooting rockets, and these rockets and their launchers can be made with simple classroom materials.

Susan and her team thought that Ivan's lesson, with some adaptation, could meet the goals of their lesson study. They adapted it to be taught in several different classes for the purpose of their project. The collaboration extended beyond one classroom to different schools: Angela was teaching Pre-Algebra and Algebra 1 at Patrick F. Taylor Science and Mathematics Academy, a selective public charter school in Jefferson Parish, not far from New Orleans; Susan taught Advanced Mathematics/Trigonometry/Pre-calculus; Mary Ann taught Geometry; and Nezha taught Algebra 1 at Archbishop Chapelle High School, an all-girls Catholic college preparatory school. They elected to adapt Ivan's lesson to be used at the different schools and at different math levels to address the following student conceptual gaps:

◆ Pre-algebra/algebra students sometimes do not adequately understand the necessity of using the relationship of the similar triangles to solve challenging tasks.
◆ Geometry students sometimes do not understand how to use the trigonometric ratios to solve triangles.
◆ Advanced math students may not adequately understand how to use the trigonometric ratios to find a measurement indirectly.

To address the gaps, they decided that:

◆ The tasks will provide direct experience with each gap in a concrete manner.
◆ Students will visualize the problem both in actuality and on paper.
◆ Students will analyze the actual outcomes.
◆ Students will then decide if their answers are possible and correct.

The team worked on each of the grade-level lessons and created a "knowledge package", which is a detailed mapping of the prerequisite concepts that students need to master in order to understand the research lesson. The concept of a knowledge package grows out of research by Liping Ma (1999) on how Japanese teachers prepare lessons. Each prerequisite skill has notes linking it to the grade-level skills necessary to understanding the lesson. The team's lesson used the school building and the security lights on top of the building to engage students in trigonometry. It was taught once and observed by the team and project staff, revised, and then taught again for the lesson study open house. Before the open house, students had constructed an inclinometer, and used it to measure the heights of various objects as shown in Figure 10.2. What follows is a documentation of the lesson study open house.

The Lesson Study Open House
Observers from the community included Bryan Jones from LaSIP, as well as teachers and coordinators from local parishes. The principal welcomed us, and then Yvelyne gave an introduction to the lesson study process. She followed this with an

Figure 10.2 Inclinometer

Height Site
Making Your Inclinometer

Here's how to make a tool that you can use to measure how tall something is—or how high a rocket or kite flies.

Copies of <u>Protractor for Inclinometer</u>
Scissors
Clear tape
A 3" x 5" card
A hole punch
50 cm of string
A washer or other small weight with a hole in it
A sheet of 8 1/2" x 11" paper (you can use paper from the recycling bin)

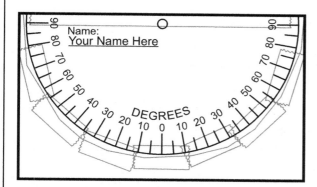

- Print out a protractor. Cut very carefully on the straight line on one edge of the protractor.
- Tape the protractor to the 3" x 5" card so that the straight side of the protractor matches up with the long side of the card.
- Use the hole punch to punch a hole through the circle on the protractor.
- Push one end of the string through the hole and through the washer. Tie the two ends of the string together making a loop on which the washer can slide freely.

- Roll a sheet of paper into a cylinder that's 8 1/2" long and about 1" across. Put tape on the seam so that the paper stays rolled, and then tape this cylinder to the card along the straight edge of the protractor. One end of the cylinder should line up with the edge of the paper.

Use the inclinometer to:

*Measure the height of the exit signs in the hallway outside of our classroom. Be sure to report data gathered, sketch a picture, and show all work.

*Explain how you can you use the inclinometer to determine the height of a tree.

Figure 10.3 Lesson evaluation

Grade Level _____   Lesson Study Site _____   Date_____

NOTE TO OBSERVERS: Please remember that you may ask students questions to understand their notes but not to guide or help them towards solution to problems.

QUESTION FOR OBSERVERS: In addition to the lesson's evaluation column, please complete and return this form to the lead teacher.

1. General impressions of the lesson?

2. What did students get from this lesson?

3. What was troublesome in this lesson?

4. How could this concept be made more accessible to students?

5. How could the context of the problem be made more interesting for this particular group of students?

6. How has the lesson affected performance for this particular concept? What evidence did you see?

7. Where do you see evidence of higher-level thinking in the students?

8. Has the lesson improved your content or pedagogical understanding? How?

9. Other comments?

---

explanation of the characteristics of its lesson plan and the evaluation column for observers. She instructed observers to keep notes in that column and also to complete the additional questions in Figure 10.3 to provide further feedback to the team. Craig Jensen, who is codirector of the grant, reviewed the protocol for observers, shown in Figure 10.4.

Figure 10.4 Lesson study protocol

The following protocol guidelines are meant to facilitate the lesson observation and debriefing process. Although these guidelines are meant to make these activities more constructive and efficiently organized, they are not meant to minimize the critical or reflective nature of the feedback session [1].

◆ <u>**Observing the lesson:**</u>

1. The obserrers, including the teachers who helped plan the lesson, should NOT interfere with the natural process of the lesson (e.g., by helping students with a problem). However, observers are permitted to circulate around the classroom during seat work, as well as communicate with students for clarifying purposes only (e.g., if they could not clearly hear what a student was saying). Otherwise, observers should stand to the back and sides of the classroom.

2. It is a good idea for observers to note their observations on the lesson plan itself. This procedure will not only help observers focus on the goals and activities of the lesson, but also help them organize their feedback for later.

3. It is also a good idea for observers to distribute observations among themselves. For example, a few clusters of observers could watch assigned groups of students, another observer (usually one of the planning teachers) could keep time, etc. The teacher should also prepare for this observation by distributing seating charts among the observers (if seating charts are not available, s/he could place nametags on each student), so that observers can conveniently refer to the children by name when discussing their observations and sharing their feedback.

◆ <u>**Preparing for the feedback session:**</u>

1. Instead of discussing the lesson immediately after it has been taught, the entire group should take a break to relax and gather their thoughts.

2. The group who planned the lesson should assign roles among themselves in order to help keep the discussion focused and on track. These roles include: moderator/facilitator (usually a member of the planning group besides the teacher who taught the lesson), timekeeper, and recorder(s).

3. The teachers who planned the lesson should sit together at the front of the room in panel formation during the feedback session. The purpose of this setup is to emphasize the idea that the entire group (not just the teacher who taught the lesson) is receiving the feedback.

[1] Sonai Chokshi, Barbarina Ertle, Clea Fernandez, & Makoto Yoshida. 2001 Lesson Study Research Group (lsrg@columbia.edu).

Susan and her team then distributed the lesson (Appendix 10.1), shared the lesson goals, and explained their knowledge package. They also reviewed their previous experiences teaching the lesson and the modifications they had made as a result of their reflection. Angela could not attend the open house, but her reflection on her adapted lesson is given in Appendix 10.2. The team also shared the student behaviors they wanted help observing during the lesson:

◆ Did students collaborate appropriately?
◆ What were some misconceptions or difficult areas for the students?

◆ Did students use the tools accurately to solve the problem?
◆ Did students understand and have enough time to complete the task?

Observers were next invited to Susan's classroom. The tools on students' desks included graphing calculators and iPads. Susan began the lesson with a PowerPoint on the tools used to create a map of India and determine the height of Mount Everest.

Susan:	*We're going to look at one from the 1800s from the British Geographical Society when they were mapping the country of India. How do you suppose they made maps in the 1800s? Did they use cell phones?*
Lauren:	They used stars. . . .
Brittany:	They used inclinometers. . . .
Susan:	*Inclinometers made with plastic straws? What kind of math did they use? Here's a bit of the map of India. Britain did a lot of mapping of her colonies. What do you notice?*
Lauren:	Triangles . . . there are a lot of triangles!
Susan:	*In the 1800s, using a method called triangulation, one of the inspector generals of the Society tackled Mount Everest using a "lightweight" tool, just under half a ton, called a theodolite. Here's a picture of the one they carted across India: Look at the eyepiece! This map is of Mount Everest in 1848, maybe 1849. They worked without GPS or airplanes to find the peak—yet their calculation was within a couple hundred feet of what we calculate it to be today. (Susan pauses, indicating a transition in the class.)*
Susan:	*OK, in our last class, you were asked to come up with a method to find the height of a tree without using an inclinometer. Did anyone come up with one?*
Kathy:	(laughing) you can use a ribbon. . . .
Susan:	*And how are you to measure the ribbon? You use a balloon tied to the ribbon and then measure the ribbon?*
Kathy:	You use a balloon tied to the ribbon and then measure the ribbon?
Lauren:	Use a long string. . . .
Susan:	*What about measuring Mt Everest? A **really** long string?*
Desiree:	Measuring tape? (laughter)
Susan:	*Brittany, want to show your idea?*

Brittany describes her method of comparing the shadows of the tree and that of a nearby person and shows her notebook drawing via the video projector. (see Figure 10.5)

Susan:	*OK, take out a sheet of paper: We're going to look at Brittany's idea a little closer.*
Desiree:	But does it matter where the sun is?
Susan:	*How will the sun affect this? Will it affect the length of the shadow? If so, where do you want to stand?*

Figure 10.5 Shadow method

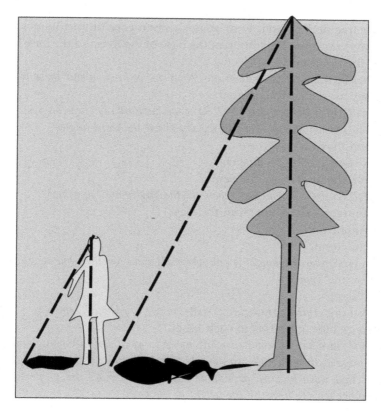

Brittany:	Next to the tree?
Susan:	*So the sun casts shadows of both yourself and the tree?*
Lauren:	Well, if I'm 5 feet then . . .
Susan:	*Can the shadow of someone be shorter than himself? Does that depend on the sun?*
Desiree:	But, what is the height of the tree?
Susan:	*Yes, how do we determine the height of the tree? You are using the shadow method: What part of your picture is making up the mathematical proportion?*
	(A student group puts up a sketch of a shadow technique for indirectly measuring height, similar to Brittany's Figure 10.6.)
Alyssa:	My shadow is here, the tree shadow is here. I'll set up the proportion: If the tree shadow = 42 feet, the height, which is *x*, is 35 feet.
	(On the video board, Alyssa, Faith, and Ruth place a hand sketch of a tree and a person casting shadows.)
Susan:	*Why do you think those ratios are equivalent?*
Faith:	I know—it's because of the sun—they have to be equivalent angles.
Susan:	*Who has some more parts drawn in your pictures? Let's look at this picture—why is it important to be next to or close to the tree? Is it because the angle from the sun is the same?*

Faith:	Is it because the angle from the sun is the same?
	(Susan puts up another drawing on the video board. This one shows both the tree and person, with angles drawn carefully to their shadows. She draws right-angle symbols at the base of the tree and the base of the person in the diagram.)
Susan:	*Sorry to draw on your diagram! What do we know about these base angles?*
Alyssa:	They are going to be equal. . . .
Susan:	*Equal? Like the right angles? So if we have two of three angles of the triangle equal to each other, what can we say about the third angle?*
Kathy:	Then they are *congruent.*
Susan:	*So why are the sides different?*
Kathy:	Well, the angles are the same. . . .
Susan:	*What do we call triangles where all the angles are the same?*
Desiree:	Geometry? (laughter from the class)
Kathy:	Equilibrium!
Joy:	Equilateral?
Susan:	*An **equilateral** triangle is one where all sides are the same length. Is that what these are? (pause)*
Kathy:	Similar?
Susan:	*What are **similar** triangles? What can we say about them?*
Lauren:	Their sides are ratios to each other.
Susan:	*Their sides have a common relationship to each other. One angle might be twice as large as the other one, so the sides might be twice as long. So that's where you get that ratio because in similar triangles the sides are proportional. Is there another way to measure the height of the tree?*
Desiree:	Climb it!
Susan:	*Climb it and drop the ribbon down? (laughter) But you can't leave the ground. Now, unless your name is Brittany, you need to come up with another method to get credit in your lab report. I suggest you look up the method that uses your thumb (holding her thumb up like a painter).*

Launching the Lesson

To launch the investigation, Susan shows a picture of a school building with the security lights on the roof.

Susan:	*What we need to do with our lab and inclinometer is a greater question. In order for the prom to go on, we need the outside yard, but there is a safety issue. On top of the building are security lights. The lights were just tested, and they are not working. In order to change the lights, we cannot leave the ground. In order to have Promfest, they have to be on all night. Maintenance needs to know what size ladder to bring.*
Desiree:	They can bring a bunch of ladders.
Susan:	*They can bring a bunch of them, but they won't; they are going to bring just one.*

Mirna:	They can bring one and climb it, and if it doesn't work. . . .
Susan:	*I don't believe that is going to happen! All right: How high are the lights on the building? You get one shot to get up there on a ladder and fix it. You need to get it right the first time. You need to stay on the ground in order to do this because there is a safety concern. You may use your inclinometers as a group. You need to discuss as a group how you are going to use the inclinometers. There are a couple of other tools you can use: One is a traffic cone, and a tape measure that is a little better than ribbon because, it does have inches marked! You are going to have to determine the height of the lights on the top of the building from the ground.*
Lauren:	Are we going to . . .?
Susan:	*You are going to have to meet as a group. It is overcast outside, so there will be no shadows.*
Desiree:	Do we know the height of the building?
Susan:	*No, you don't . . . how are you going to do this?*

Exploration

(Groups of students discuss their plans; there are murmuring and discussion from the class. Susan and classroom observers walk around between the groups checking on their discussion and their progress.)

Susan:	(to one group) *OK, that's the building; now you need the lights.* . . .
Desiree:	(in group): You can take the pencil and get the height of the tree. Here, read this. . . .
Andrea:	(reads from a website on iPad) You take a pencil in your hand and stretch your arm in front of you. . . .
Susan:	*Anyone need more time? I see a lot of solutions.* . . .
	(Groups continue to murmur and discuss.)
Susan:	*Jennifer's group says they are measuring the distance between the group and the building.*
Kathy:	We are going to measure an angle. . . .
Susan:	*An angle from where to where?*
Kathy:	From where we are, to the lights.
Susan:	*So here's the location to the lights.* . . .
	(Susan draws a diagram on board with profile view of building, with the security lights on top.)
Class:	(laughter)
Susan:	*. . . and with that, you are going to determine how high the lights are so we know what size ladder to bring. Megan's group mentioned what math we were going to use.* . . .
Desiree:	The *tangent.*
Susan:	*So the tangent of the angle (continuing to diagram on the board), Angle A, is going to help us determine the height of the light. How?*
Lauren:	It will give us the height of the building.

Susan:	*Over what Jennifer's group calls the height of the building, but where in this expression is the height of the light?*
	(The class gives a number of different responses.)
Susan:	*There, OK, nice. This is the height of the light, minus the height of the building. So to get the height of the light, I need to subtract the height of the building? How am I getting the height of the building?*
Lauren:	You measure it!
Susan:	*Measure it? How?*
Lauren:	You can do the same thing, but just go to the top of building. . . .
Susan:	*Please draw it.*
	(Lauren draws her idea and projects the drawings in her notebook [Figure 10.6]).
Susan:	*Jennifer says we need to measure again.*
Jennifer:	This height needs to be subtracted from this height.
Susan:	*Jennifer's sketch says we need to calculate the height to what part?*
Desiree:	To the top of the building.
Susan:	*To the top of the building—how will we get to the top of building? I am hearing from Desiree, how about someone else?*
Jennifer:	We need the height both to the top of the light and to the top of the building.
Brittany:	So if we subtract the height of the building from the top of the light, we'll have two pieces of information: a distance and an angle (shows sketch on Elmo, Figure 10.7).
Susan:	*Good, is that clearer? Megan? OK? So we will have two angles and two heights. In your groups, you will need someone to work the inclinometer. A second person will need to read the inclinometer. For the final project: Take your iPads outside so you can take video or camera shots.*
	(The groups discuss last-minute details; there is a buzz in the classroom as they confer. Then the students leave the building with tools and iPads. They start measuring the distance from the building with measuring tapes.)
Mirna:	(now outside the school building): We've got 35 degrees (reading inclinometer).
Jennifer:	Did you video something?
	(The students are involved in video recording, measuring distance using the cones and tape measures.)
Andrea:	It's 29.37 (feet). So then we need Tan(35), so height is 24.50.
Desiree:	Can we do lunch first before we do this? I'm starving. My hair needs . . .
Lauren:	My height is almost 5 feet.
Jennifer:	Ms. Morere, we have (a height of) almost 5 feet. Can we get lunch now?
Susan:	*You can stand in the shade, if you pick up your equipment.*
	(Back in the classroom, students start working with graph paper and pencils, recording data, making sketches.)
Lauren:	It's 4.9 feet (the height of the security lights on top of the building).
Brittany:	Then we're done!

Figure 10.6 Student sketch of building, angles to measure

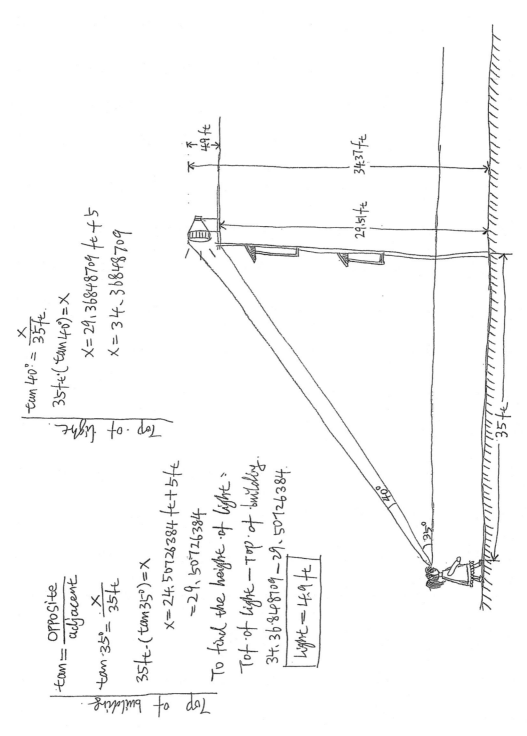

Top of building

$$tan = \frac{opposite}{adjacent}$$

$$tan\ 35° = \frac{x}{35ft}$$

$$35ft \cdot (tan\ 35°) = x$$

$$x = 24.50726384\ ft + 5ft$$

$$= 29.50726384$$

To find the height of light:

Top of light — Top of building:

$$34.36848709 - 29.50726384$$

Light = 4.9 ft

Top of light

$$tan\ 40° = \frac{x}{35ft}$$

$$35ft (tan\ 40°) = x$$

$$x = 29.36848709\ ft + 5$$

$$x = 34.36848709$$

Figure 10.7 Student sketch of measurement angles

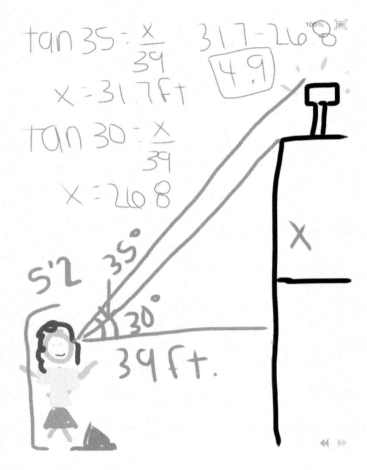

Susan: (working with a group) *My question to you is: Are you sure?*
                (Groups discuss results, murmuring and talking among themselves.)
Lauren and Brittany (discussing data):   This equals the height of the light. . . .
Susan (to group):   You've got to measure from your eye, not the top of your head. . . . (To
                class as a whole): I've got a question: Does it matter who measures?
Lauren: Yes, it does.
Susan: *If I'm measuring the height of the light and I'm five feet tall, doesn't it make the*
                height to the light different?
Desire: Yes, it does.
Susan: *To determine the height of the light, does your height matter?*
May: I can determine the . . .
Kathy: It'll change the . . .
Susan: *Draw me a picture, show me!*
Class: (excited chatter)

Figure 10.8 Student iPad-generated data table

Top of Building:

Person	Try 1	Try 2	Try 3	Average
Stacey	15	20	25	20

Top of Light:

Person	Try 1	Try 2	Try 3	Average
Stacey	20	30	25	25

Susan: (repeating) *Does the height of the person with the inclinometer matter when determining the height by this method?*

May: Let's measure again and take the average . . .? (see Figure 10.8)

(In the class, there is discussion, and sketching. Groups are busy calculating heights, angles. See Figure 10.7, previously cited.)

Summary

Susan (to a group): Test it to see if it matters, check the angles.

Susan (to the whole class): Try to summarize your results. Remember, your assessment is your report, your project.

(In the class, groups are in discussion, calculators are being used.)

Video narrator: What are you trying to determine at this point?

Desiree: The height of the light. Because you have to calculate them both, then subtract the building height.

Susan: *Are you sure you are answering one of the questions? Everyone else determined that her light was 9 feet tall. Is that correct?*

Desiree: No. I got 4.9!

Susan: *You didn't get 9 feet for those security lights on the top of the building?*

Desiree: No. What, did you go up there and measure it?

Susan: *No, but I think the contract from the installer says that they used an 8-foot ladder!* (To the rest of the class:) *For Friday, feel free to re-do your lab. Investigate why your measurements are off. Part of your class report is error analysis. Be sure to consult the rubric to guide you work* (see Figure 10.9, Figure 10.10)

(The class is filled with excited buzzing, comments. Note that Susan has deliberately introduced an element of doubt about calculations of the height of the light.)

Figure 10.9 Summary and rubric for task summary

The Problem: Maintenance needs to replace one of the bulbs and they want to know what size ladder to bring to the roof. How tall are the security lights posted on the main building?

(1) Analyzing the problem
What did your group discuss when trying to solve the problem?
What did you discover when we discussed the problem as a class?
Review the diagram of the situation.
What measurements did your group need to make?
Did your group repeat the measurements and use an average?

(2) Implementing a strategy
Redraw diagrams (if needed).
Calculate/recalculate height of the security lights if needed.
Did the height of the observer make a difference in solving this problem?
How did your group determine the height of the main building? How is this different from what you determined initially?

(3) Seeking and using connections
How does this task compare and contrast to the measurements you did yesterday with the inclinometer?

(4) Reflecting on a solution
Did your calculations provide a reasonable solution? If so, why? If not, why?
Could the problem have been solved another way?
Describe any possible errors in your data, calculations, and procedures.
How can the errors be reduced/eliminated next time?

(5) Extending the work
Using the method of triangulation, determine the distance to the water tower on the corner of David Drive and Veterans from our gym. Be sure to diagram, identify measurements, and show all work.

Group Report: Write a report that:
Diagrams the solution.
Includes all field measurements.
Shows all calculations.
Solves the problem.

Group Media Project:
Use Imovie or Keynote to make a media presentation of the group report.

Use the rubric on the next page to guide your work

Figure 10.10 Grading rubric

Student Name _____

	0	1	2	3	WT	Total
Title Page	Missing	Included				
Includes name of group	Missing	Included				
Lists group members and their roles	Missing	Included				
Identifies author of report	Missing	Included				
					X 1	
Pre-Lab						
Identify problem	Statement is missing	Statement is incomplete/ inaccurate	Statement is complete but is not identified	Statement is complete and accurate		
Group discussion outlined	Group discussion is missing	Notes from discussion are included but hard to understand and do not address either major point	Discussion notes are included, and address only 1 of 2 major points	Discussion notes are included, 2 major points are addressed		
Diagram	Missing	Included but missing labels and/or inaccurate	Included and accurate but labels are missing	Included, accurate, and labeled		
Identification of the measurements needed	Missing	Measurements are noted but identified incorrectly or some needed measurements missing	Measurements are noted and identified correctly, but units are incorrect	Correctly identified with correct units		
					X2	
Report						
Diagram of solution	Missing	Included but not labeled correctly	Included and labeled but errors apparent	Included, labeled, and correct		
Field measurements	Missing	Listed but not identified	Listed and identified	Listed, identified, and placed in a table		
Calculations	Missing	Included but inaccurate	Included but steps missing, incorrect units	Included, identified, and accurate		

Figure 10.10 (Continued)

Solution to the problem	Missing	Included but inaccurate conclusion	Included with errors	Included with accuracy		
					X2	
Critical thinking questions						
Could the problem have been solved another way?	Missing/ no attempt (includes "I don't know")	Attempt but major errors in reasoning	Attempt with some errors in logic	Attempt with accurate reasoning		
					X3	
Does the height of the observer make a difference in solving this problem?	Missing/ No attempt	Attempt without mathematical support (single answer response)	Attempt with diagrams to support mathematics, but inaccuracies	Attempt with diagram and accurate conclusion from mathematics		
Determine the height of the main building.	Missing/ No attempt	Used old diagram and lab data, missing height of observer	Redrew diagram, incomplete diagram, inaccurate conclusion	Redrew diagram, included height of observer		
How is this different than what you determined initially?	Missing/ No attempt	Inaccurate conclusion	Compared only numbers, did not identify reason for difference	Compared differences and identified cause		
					X2	
Data Analysis						
Corrections to Initial Calculations	Missing/ No attempt	If needed, incomplete and inaccurate	If needed, incomplete – missing diagram or calculations	None needed or diagrams redrawn, recalculations shown corrections accurate		
Describe any possible errors in your data, calculations, and procedures. How can they be reduced/ eliminated next time?	Missing/ No attempt	Listed only class discussion responses	Included Class Responses and offered suggestions for reducing / eliminating	Included class responses, offered suggestions, and included original idea		
					X3	

Figure 10.10 (Continued)

Literary Connection						
Write a short paragraph or two identifying what you learn from one of the selected readings about The Great Trigonometric Survey, Triangulation, or Mt. Everest.	Missing/ No attempt	Contained a summary without connection to the lab or connection was "a stretch", summary did not reflect reading the whole article	Identified what was learned from the reading, paragraph indicated the whole article was read	Identified what was learned from the reading, as well as a connection to the lab activity		
					X3	
Extras						
		Artwork on cover page	Typed – discussion questions/ tables (calculations and diagrams can be hand written)	Summary of more than one reading, or a third method of solving accurately presented		
					X1	
Turned in on time	Late -5/ day					

Susan: *I am interested in what you have to say in your summary reports. When you come back together as a group, you will have a final project where I want you to put all this together. You will have to do some outside reading for background material.*

Yvelyne: Thank you very much, class, for allowing us to observe. We very much appreciate your willingness to help us improve learning.

Observers return to the library for 30 minutes of reflection time to complete the lesson's evaluation column and the questions in Figure 10.4. They then have lunch, hosted by the school, followed by the colloquium.

Lesson Study Colloquium

Yvelyne (opening meeting): *We will now provide feedback on the lesson. We first start with reflections from Susan and her team and then go around the table but save Bryan for last since he is our invited commentator. Please do not interrupt speakers.*

Susan: In general, I thought the lesson did achieve the objectives but still needed additional time to allow students to complete the summary questions.

This group is very different from the seniors for the first trial of this lesson. They are easygoing and willing to do what you want. They are maybe too accepting that the light is 5 feet tall. I have no idea how tall the light really is, so the height I gave them is simply made up, because I felt they were just agreeing too much. They needed to look at their instrument a little more critically.

April: So you don't know that the light is 5 feet tall?

Susan: (laughter) I don't know what it is, it could be 5 feet tall, but I believe it is back away from the edge of the building a little bit. I think it is taller than 5 feet, but just the fact that they were so willing to accept that it was 5 feet tall means that I have some more work to do with them. I could see some of the questions throughout the year that will cause them to analyze their answers more deeply. They didn't like figuring out the height of the light because, you know, "they are not seniors." They're also not used to thinking first before delving into a problem. Consider the question of the height of the tree: Brittany was the only one really prepared to answer that question. The others were likely thinking, "When I get to class, the teacher's going to tell me how, so I don't need to do this." They will have to do the final project, which will force them to reflect, think deeper, and lead them to see that they really are capable of producing high-level product.

Finally, I liked participating in lesson study because I find that it improves not only the students' conceptual understanding but also the teachers', and thus the end result is a greater positive impact on students' learning.

April: How did you choose the groups for the class? Do you let them choose their own, or do you assign them?

Susan: The final project involves doing a video in iMovie or Keynote, so in a previous class I asked them if they had any experience using this software. I put an experienced student in each of the five groups, and then each of the remaining students put their names on the list. So the students did have a little input in the group decision. I was concerned about the technology; they were pretty evenly divided with the math.

Yvelyne: Thank you. And now we will have comments from team member Nezha.

Nehza: Overall the lesson went very well. I liked that it included a brief summary of the history of Geometry and how people use to measure elevation. This got the students' attention and created a curiosity about the lesson that kept them engaged and learning. They worked very well together using triangles and angle elevations. Students were exploring different ways of measuring the light on the top of the building and they were collaborating and exploring.

The only recommendation I have is, before going outside to measure the actual light, ask students if they have any questions. We need to be sure students know what they will be measuring. Several students were measuring the wrong angles or labeled their diagrams wrong so we need more work on that next time. (See Figure 10.7.)

Yvelyne: Thank you. Mary Ann is next.

Mary Ann: I enjoyed Susan's presentation of the material and have seen it both times she presented it. I felt that this second presentation was better received than the first because this second class was an honors class. They truly understand more, even though they are younger students.

My favorite aspect of the lesson was the "hands-on" work, letting the students go outside and actually complete the measurements. It is math in the "real world." Having the students go back and determine their mistakes is also an important part of math. This forces the student to be rigorous and persevere in solving problems. I thought the tie to history was also an important part of the lesson. I would recommend more time to make the measurements outside as the students were rushed to complete the work. A bit more time would allow for better accuracy.

This quarter, I will also be doing the activity. However, I will also let the students use a mirror to discover the answers with similar triangles to see which method is most accurate. We will be doing the height of the school flagpole instead of the double angles with the school roof.

Yvelyne: Thank you. Now we will hear from the observers. Let's go around the table and begin with April.

April: OK, let me see if I can read my writing. I was very impressed: You were very dynamic; the lesson addressed the student's critical thinking skills and kept them engaged the entire class. The lesson also integrated multiple levels of content and pedagogical practices: algebra, geometry, scientific method, and cooperative work. These are things the students are going to need in college. They need to learn to apply the strategies and methods they're learning. I like the use of technology in the class. There was evidence of higher-level thinking. I could hear them ask the questions: What formulas? What diagrams? The students would compare notes: "Why are you doing that?," "Look at mine."

Areas for improvement may be to consider calling on individual students rather than on letting students call out answers. I noticed that some students were lost and may have been embarrassed to say anything.

What I learned about pedagogy was how different this lesson is from many others. When I learned math I was told: "Here's the formula, and here's the textbook." My class was interactive only because we took turns reading the problems! I was really impressed at how students worked together to think out loud and make sense of the problem.

Yvelyne: Thank you. Next we hear from Craig, who is a Co-PI of the project.

Craig: Great job. I liked that the students, when challenged, would rise to the challenge to come up with a plan. I'm impressed with these students because others might have simply stood around. At around 11:05, you asked if height mattered, and one of the students near me said, "No, the height subtracts off," and another student said, "Well, if one person measures one angle and another measures the other, then there will be a difference." So they really were thinking through things. Overall I thought it was extremely good. In terms of what to flesh out more: When you talked about India, I wasn't sure if they were understanding the mathematics in the context. I don't know what they had before or what they already knew about that.

Susan: They have had four short readings, which gave them a little historical background, the application, and its use to the survey in India. The triangulation method is another reading that is on the school website. They are to tie in and summarize and make a connection for the final report. It's to expand their knowledge and get them to read.

Yvelyne: It also integrates the content with literacy, which is one of our LaSIP lesson requirements. Thank you. Now we go on to Ivan, who is co-PI of the project.

Ivan: I know what the original lesson was, so I was interested to see what you did with it. Given that the first one dealt with rockets, why did you decide to eliminate the rocket part and go with fixed structures like trees and buildings?

Susan: The main thing was time, and then, could I duplicate the rocket? I was uncomfortable with trying to duplicate the lab and the instrument for shooting the rocket. And then there was the problem with the other courses, pre-algebra, algebra, and geometry. We were trying to tie in similar exercises with the extension to the upper level material, and tying in indirect measurement. The trig course has application problems that involve using multiple parts of different triangles.

Ivan: So it tied in well with different grade levels. Yes, the construction of the rockets does consume a fair amount of time, but there is a fair amount of creative destruction and joy, and it's great fun.

I had the same question as Craig did regarding your preamble on surveying and Everest: I wasn't sure that the connection was being made. Consider the idea of taking the preamble and using that as an explanation or elaboration near the end of the lesson. Your problem is so clear and so engaging, why not just hit them with it? You can come back later and use the lesson on surveying to extend it and show how it can be used with different technology: Look how clear the results you could get using relatively simple tools.

I liked Craig's comment about their learning and discussion, but my worry was that someone's strong, facile answer was that of a strong, thoughtful student, and you might find there were others that would accept that answer quickly without thinking through it on their own. I didn't see evidence that all of the members of that group that I was harassing (laughter) really had come to that realization on their own.

Susan: Yes, there was a lot of piggybacking, and some of the students were just agreeing because she was saying it. That shows up in that report, as I commented earlier. In that first lesson, where I got the lab reports, I don't think a single person was able to show and explain their understanding. But when I gave it back to them with all the errors marked wrong and told them to put heads together and come up with an answer, it took them a couple more tries to get to where they could explain and show understanding.

April: That's why I asked the question. There were some faces that were completely lost, even when they were working in their groups. There would be one or two students writing everything down, but there would be others pretending to write but weren't really sure . . . so I was wondering how you incorporate the individualized attention? It sounds like the individual attention is through the homework and the comments in the lab reports.

Susan: Yes.

Ivan: Just a quick follow-up—I can't let go of those rockets (laughter). If you ever want to do the rockets, you can borrow the equipment from me. All of that stuff is actually very cheap, very simple, and costs less than ten dollars: a couple of recycled plastic bottles, electric tape, PVC pipe, tubing. These only cost a couple dollars.

Bryan: Yes, but sometimes it's important to minimize those variables that can screw up or distract children. Sometimes it's more about keeping it simple.

Leslie: I thought it was a great lesson, and I think you had the perfect class for it. I think a lower-level class wouldn't be able to do as much on their own. You would have had to push them a little more and do a little more in the classroom. But you were able to let them go with it, not telling them everything. It was really fun to watch. I agree that maybe the beginning stuff could have been at the end. I think that what was really good and interesting is that you are telling them not to trust what they get. Go back at it again. I loved their answers: "because it's a math rule, it has to be right." So getting them to think more about it—that is important.

The main problem is time and that is something we all have to deal with: It takes a lot of time. You can't do that for every topic. I tend to not let students explore very much on their own because of the time constraints. However, I must say that this observation has challenged me to be a little less afraid to let students go with minimal instructions.

Laura: Um, I think I have similar students. . . . I thought that one of the things that would have helped was writing some of the terms on the board that would be thrown out verbally: *proportion, similar triangles,* that sort of thing. While a lot of them knew those terms, it was clear that there were a few that were kind of like "hmmm."

I thought the lesson was a lot of fun, and the majority were enjoying what they were doing and were participating. One thing that I got out of it, that hopefully they got out of it as well, is that there are a variety of ways to answer those questions. I know that example about the tree, I have seen that diagram a million times, but there are other ways to do it, and you did require that they think about that too.

I really liked the way you encouraged the students coming up front, giving presentations to the whole group. Other students could see what they were doing. Another thing that they clearly got at the end was that careful measurement and careful use of the tool was important.

The question at the end really opened the door to curiosity to some and was a cause of disappointment to others. You could feel the energy in the room, with some of them saying, "Well, how could this be?" (laughter), which was great because that was exactly what you planned.

There was another thing that came to my mind: using miniatures and models; using them as a foundational activity. Perhaps it would be too easy for some, but that would at least give some people a framework for what they were supposed to do outside. Kind of like a "thought pump."

April: I just wanted to piggyback on what you were saying. I am a music teacher, and I work with a lot of students with disabilities. There's a lot in this lesson about inclusion and different learning styles. I actually thought that Susan's suggestion to "draw it, show me" was perfect. Yeah, they're thinking about it, but when they draw it they are showing what they are thinking, and you can see whether they are thinking the same thing you are. For the other students who are not as cognitively advanced, it really helps them to think about their process. When I was walking around, I could see the students getting very creative. They have trees with butterflies . . . even for the last time when we were going outside, one of them, instead of drawing a building, drew what she called a chipmunk. So it really allows students to use their own way of thinking and learning.

Norma: That was one of the things I wanted to say! I like the fact that they are so comfortable, that they ask questions. They don't mind blurting out whatever it is they are having trouble with. They don't feel threatened. They just want to share, and I thought that was really good, because then the atmosphere is one of learning. Maybe because there are no boys present! The lesson also went very well because of the way you launched it. That's the most important part of your lesson because it determines whether they want to do what you want them to do.

Cooperative groups: I wasn't sure how you put them together, but you did demand accountability, and you had individual accountability. That's one of the things you run into with parents, especially those that pay tuition. They want to make sure their student is getting more than a group grade. I like the way you kept refocusing on the math concepts; they can get lost, but you kept them focused.

The illustrations were very good, and they led to a deeper learning experience. The students didn't just get an answer: they had to tell you *why* they got an answer. One of the things, for those students who may be struggling, make sure at the end of the lesson you summarize all of the key points. So if they didn't get it during the lesson, they can get it at the end. At least you are focusing on the major points: "Even though I didn't tell you up front, here's what you should have gotten." One of the things Leslie and I noticed was the inclinometers—that's another lesson altogether—look at the precision of the instrument. How many of them were zeroed?

Leslie:	None of them.
Norma:	None of them. So that's another aspect you can play with: *precision*.
Ivan:	That's accuracy.
Norma:	Yes. Accuracy and precision.
Susan:	You don't distinguish between the two when you don't use them in the same sentence. That's where the error analysis comes in.
Norma:	Both, you need to look at both. What I gained from this observation is how student engagement can be supported through careful determination of the composition of group members, clear roles for each member to increase accountability, and the use of a rubric to guide the work and serve as an assessment.
Yvelyne:	Ok. So now it's my turn. My general impression? Definitely unrehearsed! Students were engaged, challenged, and asked to think critically, and, as a result, they were often baffled because of the kinds of probing questions that were being asked; they weren't sure of the answers; they had to think deeply because they were not solving the typical textbook problem of filing in the blanks in a drawing to determine how far a hypothetical boat is from shore. They weren't all sure how to proceed. There was confusion, but you have to have some of that productive struggle when wrestling with work that is unfamiliar.

I thought the context was interesting and relevant to the students. Here students had to go outside without a lot of instructions or any details about which tool to choose. I saw evidence of higher-level thinking when they had to determine the height of the tree because they didn't have a predetermined procedure to follow. They really had to think about it. I think what they got from the lesson was an appreciation for SohCahToa and similarity in helping to solve a problem meaningful to them.

About the pedagogical technique and what I learned: The kids were joking and laughing, and when I have seen kids act like that, they were intentionally trying to steer away from doing the work. That wasn't the case here. For these students, it was a way of thinking and preparing for the problem at hand. I enjoyed how the students enjoyed struggling with the task! Your classroom environment supported such interactions.

In terms of troublesome areas, one recommendation for next time is to consider discussing triangle similarity before launching the problem since it is a major concept for this lesson. Include problems on the preassessment where students decide which triangles are similar or congruent and why. To make that concept more accessible to students, you might have cardboard copies of congruent and similar triangles for them to quickly verify the characteristics or assign that for homework just to be sure students will be ready to apply those concepts for this lesson. And now we are ready for Bryan.

Bryan: Well, I liked it! It was thought provoking, engaging, well paced, and done well. I loved how the questions paced the whole lesson. It is one thing to ask questions; it's quite another to ask the right questions. There were a lot of best practices models here, and they all worked: the lesson itself was a real-world problem; the kids worked in groups and there was a leader; every group presented or asked questions which showed that, at least on some level, they were engaged. About the questions—in this case, instead of being thrown off by student questions or answers definitely intended to be ridiculous, you valued them and incorporated them as follow-up questions. The kids were bantering; you used it as brainstorming. That worked. My favorite question from the lesson was "Are you sure?" It forced students to think, whether right or wrong, and the error analysis was a wonderful way to end the lesson.

The technology also worked: Students not only had the technology, they used it. They used it inside as well as outside: It is one thing to have the technology in the classroom, but here it was actually being used appropriately to help solve the problem. I liked how the tools were integrated fairly and seamlessly to access directions for the class, record data during class, and then to turn in their analysis to summarize the data.

Assessment was well utilized. Informal assessment took place throughout the lesson. Individual groups asked questions and were expected to defend solutions and present to the class. More formal assessment will be the end report where students consolidate their understanding.

As for improvements, I did not get a strong connection between the map of India and the lesson itself, so I would try to include examples of a triangulation that was actually applied during that time or just assign the mapping as a reading. I also support Yvelyne's comment about bringing up prior knowledge. Making the connections to concepts they used in eighth or ninth grade is definitely useful and important to showing mathematics as a connected body of knowledge, so more emphasis in that area may help the lesson flow smoother.

Leslie: Just one comment about prior knowledge. They were having a hard time about conversion. One group converted 5 feet 6 inches into 56 inches. Another claimed 5 feet 2 inches was 5.2 feet. So this is something to be aware of for next time.

Susan: Thank you.

Yvelyne: Any other comments?

Ivan: I've one suggestion about the preamble dealing with triangles, triangulation, and surveying that you might want to share with students. In your example, one reason the British theodolite was so huge was not necessarily because their technology was primitive. It was probably because they were surveying on such an extraordinary scale. It had an immense azimuth ring (if that is what it would be called) because they were measuring over such long distances, and this could be brought into your discussion of precision and accuracy in measurement. Nowadays you'll see transits and theodolites that are quite compact, but I suspect they were normally not that much bigger back then when they were surveying their colonies (and everybody else's colonies). They would have used smaller instruments if they weren't trying to get halfway across India in a single sighting.

More to the point, when we introduced this lesson as the Rocket lesson, I was thinking about trigonometry, just as you used it in this class. But when I saw the graphical solution, I was taken aback by the elegance and simplicity of this approach. Using the graphical technique really drives home the concept of similar triangles, with one triangle being drawn to scale on graph paper yielding the solution to the problem.

Susan: And that's something: the idea of "to scale" that I would like to add. In that individual report, when they diagram their individual solutions, I'd like them to diagram "to scale" using grid paper. Then, even if they don't see that connection, they'll have it to scale already, and we can take rulers out to measure. They can see it.

Ivan: And if you supply them with graph paper, they will need to think about scale directly. Nothing against iPads, but if you only solve this problem with a computer graphics program, you might miss that entire mental process of actually having to draw something to scale. And you will miss understanding why each axis has to be drawn with exactly the same proportion in order to be useful.

Susan: Yes, that's a weakness. They don't realize that it makes a difference. I do have the final product assignment from the Fall class which I would like to show.

(Susan shows a PowerPoint and a video produced by the students that show and explain their roles, the problem they are trying to solve, the groups outside measuring distance, inclination, and the graphical representation of the measurements. The projects then show a discussion of the measurements, results, and methodology. The groups raise the question of whether the problem could be solved another way. This is followed by an analysis of error in the project and a summation of the India/Mount Everest survey.)

Yvelyne: Thank you very much, Susan, Mary, and Nezha. Special thanks also to the school leaders for making this day happen. Finally, we thank the observers for their work in helping to improve the lesson.

Susan: We too would like to thank everyone for the input which we will use to revise the lesson.

APPENDIX 10.1

Lesson Study Open House

Schools:

Patrick F. Taylor Science and Math Academy and Archbishop Chapelle High School

Team:
Lead Teacher: Susan Morere
Members: Mary Ann Bates, Angela Guthrie, Nezha Whitecotton

Aim: How tall are the lights on top of our main building?

I. Background Information

    A. Overarching Goal of the Lesson Study Group:
        The overarching goal is to produce students who are problem solvers and
        critical thinkers.
    B. Context for the research lesson

Teachers from Archbishop Chapelle High School and Patrick F. Taylor Science and Math Academy have collaboratively observed and revised mathematics lessons for the purpose of examining their teaching practices and student understanding by using the lesson study process. Through systematic examination of their practices, the teachers sought to improve the effectiveness of their students' classroom experiences. The lessons spanned several grade levels and were adapted to meet or exceed the Common Core Standards and expectations at each level.

The open house is being held at Archbishop Chapelle High School which is an archdiocesan, all-girls Catholic school serving approximately 750 middle- to upper-class families in East Jefferson and surrounding parishes. Although the student body has minimal ethnic diversity, the school promotes racial harmony through its ministry in the classroom and extracurricular clubs. The student body is 86 percent Caucasian, 7 percent Hispanic, 4 percent African American, and 3 percent Asian. Eighty-eight percent of the students are Catholic, and 12 percent are non-Catholic. Approximately 17 percent of the students receive financial assistance through academic scholarship, work-study, or faculty tuition reductions, and 14 percent of students receive free or reduced lunch.

The lesson was initially taught and revised twice. We taught it to two regular advanced math/trig classes and an Algebra 2 honors class. In general, we found that students had difficulty answering the higher-level questions on the rubric (e.g., could it be solved another way, or does the height of the observer make a difference?). We graded their individual summary and assigned students to groups to share and make corrections. We then had them create a group media presentation (PowerPoint or Imovie) as an assessment of the lesson. We modified the rubric to assess a group rather than individual project. Because students did not have enough time to process the information they gathered, we extended this lesson to three instead of two 90-minute lessons:

(a) Lesson 1 focuses on making and using the inclinometer.
(b) Lesson 2 focuses on using various tools to solve a real-life problem.
(c) Lesson 3 focuses on student sharing individual summary of lesson 2 to create a group media project.

The observation for the lessons study is of the second lesson with an Accelerated Algebra 2 class consisting of tenth- and eleventh-graders.

C. Prerequisite skills: Solving one- and two-step equations, proportions, equivalent fractions, similar figures

II. Unit Information

A. Name of unit from Guaranteed or Comprehensive Curriculum or CCSS:
Grade 7 (adv): Unit 2: Rates, Ratios, & Proportions; Unit 3: Geometry and Measurement
Grade 8 (adv), Grade 9: Chapter 10
Grade 9 (adv), Grade 10: Chapter 8
Grade 11 (adv); Grade 12: Right-Triangle Trigonometry
B. Goal of unit from current state curriculum:
Students are able to solve problems with similar triangles/lengths of corresponding sides and applications of the Pythagorean theorem and its converse.
C. Literacy connections

The following definition of mathematical literacy was developed by the Expert Group for Mathematics of the Programme for International Student Assessment (PISA) and incorporated during the development of this lesson. "Mathematical literacy is an individual's capacity to identify and understand the role that mathematics plays in the world, to make well founded judgments, and to engage in mathematics in ways that meet the needs of that individual's current and future life as a constructive, concerned and reflective citizen" (OECD, 2010).

Comprehension strategies for problem solving are also being used during the course of instruction, investigation, and classroom discussions. Some of the strategies employed are clarifying, comparing and contrasting, connecting to prior experiences, inferencing, predicting, questioning the text, summarizing, and visualizing.

In the area of mathematics, questioning techniques that promote concept development such as skimming questions and then probing deeper into the students thinking to get at misconceptions and alternative ideas are being incorporated. Additionally, the use of graphic organizers is included.

III. Lesson Information

A. Goal(s) of the research lesson:
Solve real world problems using proportional reasoning with right triangles. Write and solve algebraic and trigonometric equations that model real world situations.

B. CCSSM Standards: Similarity, Right Triangle and Trigonometry:
G. SRT.6,.7,.8
Mathematical Practices: MP1–MP6

C. How this lesson connects to overarching goal
Students who can complete these types of problems are using the following critical-thinking skills:
* Visualizing the problem both in actuality and on paper
* Comparing the actual event to the drawing on paper
* Using different representations to model a problem
* Connecting mathematics
* Making predictions

D. How this lesson connects to previous and next grade
On the Pre-Algebra level, students will use these problems to understand similar figures and proportional reasoning with right triangles.
On the Geometry level, students will revisit these problems and link them not only to proportional reasoning but also to the trigonometry of right triangles. On the geometry level, problems will include only one angle.
On the Pre-Calculus level, the trigonometry of the right triangles will also be covered. However, the problems will be of greater difficulty because the problems will include two angles.

E. Evaluation
Three to five questions to assess understanding a few days before to guide the lesson and after the lesson for its evaluation:

1. Trigonometric functions can be used to solve problems involving right triangles. The most common functions used are sine, cosine, and tangent.
Draw and label a right triangle; then state the relationship between the acute angles of the right triangle and the lengths of the sides of the triangles.

2. The escalator at St. Petersburg Metro in Russia has a vertical rise of 195.8 ft. If the angle of elevation of the escalator is, *10-21'36"*, find the length of the escalator.

3. Five-foot tall Sandra is standing on the ground 10 yards from the base of the school building. She measures the angle of elevation to the top of the building as 60°. Find the height of the building to the nearest foot.

4. When a 757 passenger jet begins its descent to Ronald Reagan Washington National Airport in Washington, D.C., it is 3,900 feet from the ground. Its angle of descent is 6°. To the nearest tenth of a foot:
   a. What is the plane's ground distance to the airport?
   b. How far must the plane fly to reach the runway?

F. Materials:
   Inclinometer, iPad
   Graphing calculator
   Paper and pencil
   Printed copies of protractor on cardstock paper
   Blank paper, tape, scissors, paper clips, string
   Mount Everest PowerPoint that shows the historical viewpoint.

G. Process of the study lesson—flow of the lesson

AIM for this lesson: How tall are the lights on top of our main building?

Steps of the Lesson: Learning Activities and Key Questions	Student Anticipated Questions or Responses	Teacher Things to Remember/ Teacher's Responses to Student Reactions	Evaluation
Intro Morning prayer Introduce guests Have students return to groups that created the inclinometer in previous lesson.		Have enough chairs ready for observers. Have lab materials for students available. Have students decide who will be the recorder, technician, videographer.	
LAUNCH: Part A Show PowerPoint of the mapping of India using triangulation and history of how early pioneers determined the height of Mount Everest. "Look at this map of India. What do you notice?" "Does that connect to yesterday's work?" "In the mapping they determined the height of Mount Everest, named after Sir George Everest, who was one of three involved in the mapping of India. To do so, he used a theodolite that weighs close to a ton. How can we measure the height of Mount Everest?" "By 1856, working without a GPS or planes to find the peak, they calculated the height to be about 29,000 feet, which is close to what we calculate today. They used a method called triangulation that involves measuring angles. If the distance between two locations is known and the angle from each of these locations to a third location is measured, then the rest of the distances and angles in the triangle can be calculated using trigonometry."	Most will say "triangles" "We solved problems with triangles yesterday." Responses will vary. Students have not worked with this topic, and the pretest results show that most did not put much thought in answering the pretest problems.	Materials: Survey of India PowerPoint that shows the historical viewpoint. Discuss methods students suggest and have them agree or disagree with the feasibility of the methods.	Are students interested? Are multiple students making suggestions?

Let's review the work from the last class. You were asked to find the height of a tree without using an inclinometer. Does any one have a plan?	"How about using shadows?"	Students may suggest shadows but be unclear about how to apply the method. Answers will vary and likely show that we will have to review this process. Probe further on the properties necessary to determine the height of the tree.	Are multiple students making suggestions?
"Are there connections between the information from the PowerPoint and the measurements needed to find the height of the tree?"	On the pretest, only Brittany came up with a plausible example.	If no ones comes up with an example, invite Brittany to share and require that other students find an alternative method.	Are students connecting the important ideas?
LAUNCH Part (B) "The school prom-fest is next month. The security lights on top of the main building are not working. You need to determine the height of the security lights on the top of the building so maintenance can know what size ladder to bring to the roof." Show students a picture of the building with the light.	"Can we get up on the roof?"	Students will want to measure the light directly. Emphasize that the height of the light needs to be determined form the ground. Only maintenance personnel are allowed on the roof.	Do students seem interested in the problem?

EXPLORE: "Your job is to devise a plan for using tools to determine the height of the light from the ground." You will need to think about how you will use the inclinometer and the other tools available. Sketch out your plan. "Select the tools you will use and proceed outside to do your measurements." Students proceed to the outside lawn to take the necessary measurements to determine the height of the security lights. Students work in groups, with each member taking on an assigned role (recorder, technician, videographer). After completing the measurements, the group should reconvene in the classroom. Students will be asked if the height of the technician (individual holding the inclinometer) made a difference in their result. They will be asked to support their decision. In groups, students should determine the height of the lights.	How do we diagram this? Which angles do we measure? Where should we stand to do the measurements? How many times should we measure? Some may measure or label the wrong angles. Some may/may not account for height of individual holding the inclinometer	Expect problems with diagramming the situation. Have a group discussion on a general approach to tackle the problem if necessary. Have students share their diagrams on the document camera. Students should take a cone, measuring tape, inclinometer, and their iPads Remind students to take good notes of their measurements and to take pictures of actions/process for their media project. Some may measure or label the wrong angles. Some may/may not account for height of individual holding the inclinometer. Students will be asked if the height of the technician (individual holding the inclinometer) made a difference in their result. They will be asked to support their decision.	Are students engaged? Are students applying problem solving skills? Are they taking responsibility for their roles? How well do students use the tools? What errors are evident? Are they taking responsibility for their roles? Are students listening to each other? Do they understand each other's ideas? What errors are evident?

SUMMARIZE		Are students working independently?
Individual students prepare a summary report, and within the report students answer the question "How tall is the light fixture?"	"I know one way but can't think of a different way."	Distribute the summary report and its rubric.
		Are they completing the work correctly?
After determining the height of the light on the basis of their data, students should conduct an error analysis. Is their answer reasonable? What could cause an error in their results?		Tell students to reflect on the class discussion and diagrams that were shared for other ideas.
		Higher-order thinking skills and problem-solving growth should be observed.
		How do students address the challenges?
EVALUATION		
Have students take the same four pretest questions for signs of greater understanding.		Tell students that they will work in groups the next day to share their results and to create a media project.
Tell students to "review the activities we did in class today. Do the best you can so that you can make media suggestions to your groups tomorrow."		Collect the posttest of the same four problems.
		Grade the summary sheets and posttest.

APPENDIX

Historical Connection

The country of India was mapped in the early 1800s as part of Great Britain's colonial authority. Great Britain's goal was to have a complete geographical knowledge of the country. In 1802, Colonel William Lambton led The Great Trigonometrical Survey of India. After Lambton's death, in 1823, George Everest led the quest to map the Indian subcontinent. Up until this time the only known method for locating a point on the Earth's surface was to make astronomical observations, which took months if not years to complete. Lambton used a surveying method called triangulation. By today's standards it took an extremely long time, but in 1800 it was faster than making astronomical observations. Today we use global positioning satellites (GPS) and aerial photographs to make maps.

Triangulation involves measuring angles. If the distance between two locations is known and the angle from each of these locations to a third location is measured, then the rest of the distances and angles in the triangle can be calculated using trigonometry.

The first Everest map (January 1858) shows the lines of sights from which measurements were taken for the Great Trigonometrical Survey. In 1856, Peak XV was calculated as rising 29,002 feet. The height of the mountain, as measured by GPS, is 29,035 feet.

References

Bluesci (Cambridge University Science Magazine), January 29, 2011, www.bluesci.
    org/?p=2028. Retrieved September 10, 2012.
Royal Geographical Society: learning resources for schools.

APPENDIX 10.2

Reflection on Lesson Study Implementation at Patrick Taylor

Angela Guthrie

I modified the original lesson to be taught without trigonometry because I was seeing a need in my classroom for a real-world connection. I noticed that the many theorems and practice problems were jading my students, so I moved the lesson up in my curriculum to provide them with a sense of how geometry can be used in the real world.

I modified the lesson to use geometric means to find missing side lengths instead of trigonometry. I had the students create the inclinometers, and we used them to help us calculate the height of our school's flagpole. Students needed to find the position to stand that would create a 90-degree angle from their line of sight to the top and bottom of the pole. Then, by measuring the line of sight to the flagpole as the geometric mean, students could calculate the height of the flagpole.

The first time I implemented it, many students had the misconception that they needed to find a position that was 45 degrees to the top of the flagpole, thinking that they just needed to split the 90-degree angle in half. They eventually realized their error after their calculations yielded unreasonable numbers. The next time I implemented it, in our discussions, before going outside, I emphasized more strongly that if they were to use the geometric mean, it needed to be within a right triangle, and I saw better results.

The students did enjoy the activity. I could see that they finally started to appreciate that geometry could be useful in the real world. I enjoyed being able to spend time on this kind of activity as well. It is very difficult with the time constraints of a single-semester course to take class time out for what for me, then, was a supplemental activity, but the positive benefits are clear. In the future, I will try to make adjustments so that more of these activities can be included in my curriculum.

Resources

A. Lesson Study Publications

Cooper, S., T. Wilkerson, C. Eddy, M. Kamen, S. Marble, D. Junk, and C. Sawyer. (2011). Lesson Study among Mathematics Educators: Professional Collaboration Enabled through a Virtual Community. *Learning Communities Journal* 3(1), http://celt.muohio.edu/lcj. Retrieved April 10, 2014.

Germain-McCarthy, Y. (2001). *Bringing the NCTM Standards to Life: Exemplary Practices from Middle School*. New City, NY: Eye on Education.

Germain-McCarthy, Y. (2014). *Bringing the Common Core Standards to Life: Exemplary Practices from Middle School*. New York, NY: Routledge.

Gorman, J., J. Mark, and J. Nikula. (2010). *Lesson Study in Practice: A Mathematics Staff Development Course*. Portsmouth, NH: Heinemann.

Hart, L., A. Alston, M. Yoshido, and A. Murata (eds.). (2011). *Lesson Study Research and Practice in Mathematics Education. Learning Together*. New York: Springer.

Hurd, J., and C. Lewis. (2011) *Lesson Study Step by Step: How Teacher Learning Communities Improve Instruction.* Heinemann.

Kamen, M., D. Junk, S. Marble, S. Cooper, C. Eddy, T. Wilkerson, and C. Sawyer (January 2011). Walking the Talk: Lessons Learned by University Mathematics Methods Instructors Implementing Lesson Study for Their Own Professional Development. In *Lesson-study Research and Practice: Learning Together,* edited by L. Hardt, A. Alston, M. Yoshido, and A. Murata. New York: Springer.

Lewis, C. (2000). The Core of Japanese Professional Development. Invited address to the Special Interest Group on Research in Mathematics Education, American Educational Research Association Meetings, New Orleans.

Ma, L. (1999). *Knowing and Teaching Elementary Mathematics: Teachers' Understanding of Fundamental Mathematics in China and the U.S.* Hillside, NJ: Lawrence Erlbaum and Associates.

Takahashi, A., and M. Yoshida (2004). Ideas for Establishing Lesson-Study Communities. *Teaching Children Mathematics* (May), 436–43.

Yoshida, M. (1999). "Lesson Study: A Case Study of a Japanese Approach to Improving Instruction through School-Based Teacher Development." Ph.D. diss., University of Chicago.

B. Lesson Study Web Resources

Global Education Resources: www.globaledresources.com/team.

Lesson Study Group at Mills College: www.lessonresearch.net/.

Lesson Study Network: To subscribe, visit https://mailman.depaul.edu/mailman/listinfo/lsnetwork.

Lesson Study Research Group at Teacher's College, Columbia University (no longer exists but resources are available): www.tc.columbia.edu/lessonstudy.

MATH: New Mexico, http://mc2.nmsu.edu/mathnm/lesson.html.

Lesson Study at the college level: Lesson Study Project Center for Advancing Teaching and Learning University of Wisconsin-La Crosse: www.uwlax.edu/sotl/lsp/guide/index.htm.

University of New Orleans for sample lesson study plans: http://mathed.math.uno.edu/viewforum.php?f=22.

William Patterson Center for lesson study directed by Makoto Yoshida: www.wpunj.edu/coe/lessonstudy/.

C. Resources on Rockets and SohCahToa

Germain-McCarthy, Y. (2005): *Mathematics and Multi-Ethnic Students: Exemplary Practices,* New City, NY: Eye on Education.

Mark Lonergan (chapter 4, this volume) has interesting resources:

SOHCAHTOA song: https://www.youtube.com/watch?v=ZsvWI0AHUpc&list=UL8Gkz2OzKyH4.

Video for launching paper rockets of the type Ivan used in LaSIP: https://sites.google.com/a/bostonartsacademy.org/baa-steam/math-initiatives/paper-rockets.

Exploratorium rocket website: www.exploratorium.edu/math_explorer/BBO_making Rockets.html.

NASA rockets website: www.nasa.gov/pdf/295791main_Rockets_Pop_Rockets.pdf.

Claudia Carter: How a Rumor Spreads—An Introduction to Logistic Curves

I chose this lesson for the whole-group video for my portfolio for National Board Certification. The national board standards encourage a variety of activities, teacher-student and student-student actions/reactions, and content that is relevant to real-world experiences. The lesson on logistic curves was perfect for my course objectives.

Claudia R. Carter, Columbus, Mississippi

One of the initiatives of the National Science Foundation is to fund projects to create reformed curricula. Claudia was invited to join a team of writers for a project called ARISE, written by COMAP (Consortium of Mathematics and Its Applications). COMAP structures projects so that the mathematics content "arises" out of problem situations. Claudia's lesson on investigating exponential and logarithmic functions was inspired by the work she did as part of this team.

"Suppose I told you that I know a really juicy rumor about our principal," she says to the students in her precalculus class. Students smile, and, having gotten their attention, Claudia distributes a handout that will guide the lesson (see Figure 11.1 with sample student response).

Part A requires that students write a description of their guesses about how a rumor might spread and to sketch a graph of the total number of people who have heard the rumor as a function of time. Claudia asks, "What do you think happens in the school over a short period of time, say in about a week?" As students work independently to answer this question, Claudia circulates around the room. She notes that, for the most part, students write a correct description, stating that the rate at which

Figure 11.1 Sample student response

This activity simulates the spreading of a rumor. You will participate in the class simulation.

PART A: Make a Prediction

Suppose there is a really good rumor about your principal.

1. Describe how this rumor might spread. A few people find out and then they tell more and more and pretty soon most people know some version of the rumor.

2. Sketch a graph representing what you described (the number of people who have heard the rumor, as a function of time).

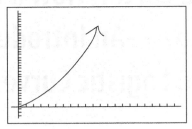

PART B: Class Simulation

3. Assume that each person repeats the rumor to one person at every turn. Predict how many turns it will take before everyone in your class has heard the rumor. 15 to 20 Turns

4. Keep track of the number of turns for the calculator simulation and the total number of people who have heard the rumor. Record the information in a three-column chart with the following headings:

TURN	Number of new people hearing the rumor	Total number who have heard the rumor
1	0	1
2	1	2
3	2	4
4	4	8
5	8	16
6	16	32 and so on

5. How does your prediction on the number of turns it would take for the rumor to spread to the entire class compare with the actual number of turns? I didn't take into account that you would run out of people to hear the rumor. I didn't think everyone would find out about it.

Figure 11.1 (Continued)

6. Graph the data the class collected on the grid below.

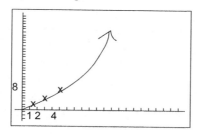

PART C: Computer Simulations

7. The one simulation by the entire class took a long time. Now look at the graph below, which shows a calculator program simulation for a class size 35 with five repetitions. Write a summary of similarities and differences between our single simulation and calculator simulation for five repetitions .

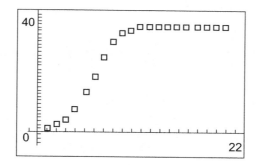

8. Which graph shows a clearer pattern? Why do you think this happens? They look very much alike; the five emulations have more points and the shape is clearer.

9. Describe the pattern.
   It is an S shape, where points start slow and increase fast and then level off

10. Write a comparison of what you answered to items #1 and #2 and the actual results from the simulation.
    I was off because I didn't count on running out of people.

11. List at least three other real-world situations that you would expect to show the pattern demonstrated by the function of spreading the rumor. Why do you expect the pattern to be the same?
    Just about anything that starts off with a few people and then finally reaches everybody, like a disease of popular tennis shoes.

the rumor spreads tends to slow down because there will be fewer and fewer people to tell. However, nearly all students incorrectly graph a curve that resembles an exponential function in which the number of people increases without bound. These formative assessments will guide Claudia's development of the lesson.

By means of a general discussion, she elicits from students the factors that affect how this rumor spreads. Students comment that some aspects of the rumor would probably change and that how fast it spreads depends on how many students each person tells. "Let's assume that each person tells one other person each day. We can use the random number generator of a graphing calculator to simulate the spread of a rumor," she tells them. Because the class has only 13 students, she assigns two different random numbers from 1 to 26 to each student and programs the calculator to randomly generate these numbers.

She tells students to begin Part B of the handout. They are asked to predict the number of turns it will take the calculator to spread the rumor to everyone in the class and then to keep a running tally of the total number of people who have heard the rumor. To help students understand the process, Claudia asks a series of questions (sample responses are shown in parentheses).

- ◆ If we start with turn 1 representing the person who starts the rumor, what can we enter in the chart? (The number of turns is 0, new people is 0, and total number is 1.)
- ◆ If we assume that each person tells one other person at every turn, how many random numbers should the calculator generate for the next three turns? (The second turn requires one random number, the third turn requires two, and the fourth requires four.)
- ◆ At the fifth turn, should we expect that a total of 16 people will have heard the rumor? Why? (No, because some numbers may be repeated—the person you choose to tell may have already heard the rumor.)

As Claudia calls out the numbers generated by the calculator to represent those who are told the rumor, she asks only those students whose number is called for the first time to raise their hands. "Student reactions vary at this point. Some are excited to be included. One student whose number was generated last pretended to look upset and commented that he was always the last to know!" Finally, she asks them to comment on how their predictions in Part A compare with the calculator's results. Students are generally surprised to see how far off were their predictions; most thought the rumor would have taken more time to spread.

Next they graph the table and compare the graph to their sketch in Part A. Many had graphed different curves, and Claudia asks them to describe their reasoning. Students' misconceptions become clear as they try to justify their graphs. A student who graphed a parabola explains that he assumed that the curve would continue to increase until it reached all students and then decrease. "Interesting," says Claudia. "Why did that not work?" The student correctly responds that he had forgotten that the y-axis represented the *total* number of people.

"What real-life situations *do* behave like parabolas?" she asks. Students' suggestions include a tennis player lobbing a ball and a plane taking off and landing. She asks students how a parabola could model the latter situation. Some students chuckle as they realize that the plane would reach the vertex of the parabola and then plummet toward the ground. "But a mechanical failure might cause something similar to that to happen," one suggests.

Returning to the calculator's simulation graph, Claudia asks students to describe how a graph that depicts the number of people who buy a hot new fad item might fit the graph and to indicate the part of this curve at which a store manager would want to have the greatest and smallest supply of the fad item. Once students' responses reflect a good understanding of the connection between the various parts of the curve and the real-life situation, Claudia asks them to describe the general shape of such a graph and to give its name. One student correctly identifies its shape as that of the letter S, and Claudia tells them that curves that level off in this S-shape are called logistic curves.

Too often, Claudia feels, students' only experiences with collecting data occur in science labs, where time constraints often reduce the opportunity to collect multiple sets of data. As a result, some students conclude that one set of data is enough to make an accurate prediction. To correct this misperception, in Part C of this lesson Claudia uses a second calculator to repeat the simulation five times. Before beginning work in this part, she asks students to distinguish between the data collected and analyzed in their own simulation and the result when the calculator is programmed to simulate the entire event. Students note that the calculator would be faster and that human errors that result when students forget their number or don't raise their hand when they should have would be eliminated. "Suppose I program the calculator to do five simulations for a class of 35 instead of just one simulation. Would that make a difference?" Claudia asks. One student responds that collecting a lot of data helps, because an average of the results might be a better indicator of the actual situation. "Hmm," Claudia responds. "Is an average always statistically better to work with?" Another student comments that a single large number or a small number may affect the mean, which would lead to misinterpretation of the data. Claudia takes this opportunity to talk about the law of large numbers and variability in data: "The more data we collect, the greater the chance of balancing the effects of observations that are not representative of the data as a whole." Having made the case for simulations that can run the experiment several times, Claudia has students complete Part C of the handout, which compares the calculator's graph of the simulation and the graph the class generated in Part B.

The final discussion centers on other real-life experiences that could be modeled by this curve. The students are quick to point out examples of the spread of disease. One student suggests population growth; another comments that this would be best modeled by an exponential function. Claudia brings the class into this debate. "What about population growth? Is it exponential, or does it follow the S-pattern of our logistic curve?" In answer to the last question, a student uses his hand to show the patterns of the curves as he explains. "The S graph starts growing slowly, increases sharply, and then tapers off. The exponential graph starts off the same way, but it doesn't level off. It keeps going through steeper increases."

Claudia shares the story of the economist Thomas Malthus, who wrote an essay in 1798 about factors, such as food availability, that stimulate or limit population growth. She invites students to comment and asks what other factors they think might affect population growth. Students suggest disease, pollution, death and birth rates, and natural resources. "Let's assume a group of people had all the items on this list but could not move out of the space of this classroom. What might happen?" she asks. The question launches a discussion about the impact of space on growth and about why it is sometimes necessary to transport animals to different locations.

Then Claudia asks students to think about why it can be difficult to recognize a logistic curve very early on. Students review the properties of the graphs they have drawn. They conclude that the initial slow growth rate is deceptive. Time must pass before the curve begins to rise sharply, and even more time must pass before it levels off.

"What is the population of the world today? Which curve best represents the world's population trend today?" Claudia's final questions have opened the door to further explorations of a rich topic. At the end of the lesson, Claudia collects Figure 11.1 and gives each student a grade. As they exit the class, several students comment, "This was the best class ever!" "Can we do this more often?" "The lesson relates to what I'm doing in genetics class!" "So, what was that juicy rumor?"

Discussion between Colleagues

Have you always taught from a problem-based perspective?
Mathematical applications and real-life problems have always played an important role in my teaching. I welcome the challenge of turning a mathematical lesson into an exciting learning experience by incorporating a variety of activities. It is gratifying to have students ask to do more of such activities—it indicates that they have a new appreciation for the power of mathematics.

Tell us a bit about your school and its students.
Our school is an eleventh- and twelfth-grade state-supported residential school that emphasizes mathematics and science, and our students come from all over the state of Mississippi.

Comment on students' reaction to this lesson.
The students react favorably because most are not familiar with the shape of the logistic curve. Because they learn quickly that their hypothesis may not be correct and that things are happening to cause this curve to behave differently, they are interested in learning more about the behavior of the graph and the situation it models.

Have you made any changes since the first edition of this book?

I continue to use this lesson with my students and have not really changed much because the students like the participation factor of simulating the rumor. I have shared the lesson with colleagues at my school and through presentations at local math conferences. The beginning of the lesson lends itself well to different grade levels. For example, even middle school students could understand the concept since the rumor, as a hook, is very appropriate, and the idea of graphing points of a different shaped curve is of interest to many students. I have used a similar version with my University Calculus 2 students because an introduction to differential equations uses similar applications.

What resources do you use to find engaging problems?

I am always searching for modeling type of problems or ways to figure out how modeling can play a role in problem solving, so I continue to use COMAP and NCTM publications as major resources for ideas.

Commentary

In her book *Smarter Than We Think*, Seeley (2014) describes what she calls the "Upside-Down Teaching" model:

> Teaching upside down involves choosing to first present to students a problem they are expected to mess around with for awhile, without first having taught them the particular rules or procedures they could use to solve the problem. Engaging students in this way helps them interact with the mathematics and sets them up to learn the mathematical content the teacher intends.
>
> (90)

This model is what Claudia and the team from COMAP utilize for lessons integrating mathematical models. Students will have many questions when using such a model, but it is important that the teacher be prepared not with the answers but with additional questions to guide students in answering their own questions. Claudia provides few answers, and her questions stimulate students' participation at a level that extends beyond the recall of facts so that students are reasoning and making sense of the situation through modeling with the help of technology (SMP4). She poses questions that require students to verify their thinking whether or not they are correct. Particularly notable is her use of students' incorrect responses to elicit further reasoning. For example, when a student incorrectly draws a parabola to represent the spread of the rumor, she not only asks him to explain his graph but also asks the class to think of real-life situations that *could* be modeled with parabolas. Through the use of probing questions, she elicits interesting examples from students of situations that do and do not fit the situations modeled by logistic and parabolic functions (SMP1, 2, 3). More important, the time spent on these discussions helps students see that incorrect responses are also opportunities for learning. This is a key factor that encourages students' thinking and participation.

The lesson is also a good example of classroom use of technology: As the class simulates the spread of a rumor, students compile and then analyze their own data; they appreciate the calculator's speed in handling multiple simulations, and its inclusion in the lesson provokes further thinking. NCTM's *Reasoning and Sense Making* document (2009) supports this process:

> Currently, many students have difficulty because they find mathematics meaningless. Without the connections that reasoning and sense making provide, a seemingly endless cycle of reteaching may result. With purposeful attention and planning, teachers can hold all students in every high school mathematics classroom accountable for personally engaging in reasoning and sense making, and thus lead students to experience reasoning for themselves rather than merely observe it. Moreover, technology should be used strategically throughout the high school curriculum to help reach this goal.
>
> (6)

Unit Overview

How a Rumor Spreads—An Introduction to Logistic Curves

Aim: What kinds of graphs best represent the spread of a rumor?

Objective: Students will use simulations of the spread of rumor to discuss properties of logistic curves and their applications to real-life situations.

Grade Levels: Advanced Algebra, Precalculus, Calculus.

Source: Project ARISE, written by the Consortium of Mathematics and its Applications (COMAP).

Number of 90-Minute Periods: One.

NCTM/CCSSM Standards: Algebra, Patterns and Functions; Modeling: F.L.E.3., F.IF.4.

NCTM Process/Mathematical Practices: Mathematics as Communication, Problem Solving, Reasoning; Models/SMP1–SMP4.

Mathematical Concepts: Students examine graphs of logistic curves to determine their properties. They compare and contrast them to those of exponential and quadratic functions.

Materials and Tools

- ◆ An overhead graphing calculator or graphing calculator Emulator
- ◆ Handout for recording and analyzing the data (see Figure 11.1)

Management Procedures

- ◆ Have students write a description of their guesses about how a rumor might spread and sketch a graph of the total number of people who have heard the rumor over time.
- ◆ Prepare for simulation exercise. Assign each student a number from 1 to 26. (If the class has fewer students, assign more than one number each.) Have students write down their numbers.
- ◆ To simulate the spread of a rumor, use a graphing calculator's random number generator to generate numbers from 1 to 26. Generate more numbers at each turn according to Figure 11.1.
- ◆ Have students raise their hands when their number is called for the first time. Have each student keep a record in Figure 11.1. Continue until all have heard the rumor.
- ◆ Discuss results with students and have them follow the instructions in Figure 11.1.
- ◆ Collect and grade Figure 11.1.

Assessment

Assess informally by observing students' participation during class. Collect Figure 11.1 and assign a grade.

Resources

1. Chapter 9, this volume.
2. COMAP: www.comap.com.
   COMAP creates learning environments where mathematics is used to investigate and model real issues in our world.
3. NCTM's Core Math Tools: www.nctm.org/standards/content.aspx?id=32706.

12

Teachers Adapting Tasks to Closely Align to CCSSM

In order for high school students to be engaged in reasoning and sense making in the classroom, the task—what students are asked to do—is critical.

NCTM's Reasoning and Sense Making Task Library, http://www.nctm.org/rsmtasks/

An excellent mathematics program requires impactful teaching that engages students in meaningful learning through individual and collaborative experiences that promote their ability to make sense of mathematics and reason mathematically.

NCTM's Principles to Actions (2014, 7)

One of the things Yvelyne does to continue growing in her understanding and application of the CCSSM is to attend CCSSM institutes. She participated in NCTM's K–8 institutes as well as in its online course for high school teachers that was facilitated by Kristin Keith. While the course, "Engaging Students in Learning: Mathematical Practices and Content Standards: Extended Online Professional Development—Grades 9–12," was a continuation of a summer face-to-face institute that she could not attend, the academic year follow-up topics included webinars, readings, or PowerPoints from the summer that were readily accessible. The extended sessions were also taped and available to participants during the term of the course. Kristin's ease with navigating Moodle and the Adobe Connect interfaces to present her work or that of other presenters helped teachers from across the United States to form a community of learners.

In addition to meeting teachers who care about teaching, she greatly enjoyed the opportunity to view or chat with presenters whose work she had read or seen applied many times in workshops. For example, rather than talk about the work of lead writers of CCSSM documents or of those who created CCSSM implementation tools, Kristin invited them as speakers or had participants view their recorded NCTM presentations. From the leaders Bill McCallum, Fred Dillon, Dan Meyers, Jonathan Wray, and Gary

Martin participants learned how to interpret and assess the mathematical practices as well as how to create and find those tasks that engage and challenge students.

Gary Martin's session focused on the qualities of effective tasks and how to get the most out of tasks that are designed to promote mathematical processes and practices. In his session, he referred to types of tasks to avoid:

> Selecting useful tasks is the first step in engaging students in the mathematical reasoning habits as described in the Common Core practices and NCTM Standards process standards. Too many times, we engage students in low levels of thinking but then expect them to shift into the higher levels. If all we do is engage students in closed ended problems, then that is what we will get back.

His and Dan Meyer's sessions showed how to create and adapt tasks to engage students at high cognitive levels. Dan demonstrated examples of tasks that do a disservice to students because they:

1. Reduce math to filling in the blanks and referring to worked problems as examples.
   In such problems, students are given all the information necessary to problem solve: the numbers, formula, a leading visual, etc. . . . and . . . if they get stuck, there are hints of where to find a sample worked-problem in the chapter.
2. Abstract the problem for the student.
   Textbook problems are typically decomposed into several parts that students have to process in order to answer the main question.
3. Hide the statement of the main problem from student until very end.
   This is a consequence of doing the abstractions for students. Because students are first guided with the important questions leading to the main problem, they do a lot of reading before coming to the statement of the problem.

Gary and Dan showed visuals and examples to illustrate and recommend engaging tasks that add abstraction and reasoning. These are recommendations from their sessions:

1. Start with an interesting problem rather than saving it until the end after students have learned the basics. Good news is that there may be no need to create one because it might already be at the end of the chapter in the text. Using such problems as a hook provides the context for having to learn the basics for the problems.
2. Don't hide the task from the student. Present the challenge question first, and allow students the opportunity to decompose the problem.
3. Have students abstract the problem. Don't do it for them.
4. Separate the tasks. Just as in real life, have conversations to help determine what should follow next, since in real life we often do not know ahead of time what to do.
5. Provide next steps *only* when students are ready for them.
6. Use visuals that are worth abstracting—that means the visual is interesting and has information that does not reduce students' opportunity to reason about which information is important or necessary to obtain.

7. Keep a camera or camera phone handy, and be ready to take interesting shots of the math that you may encounter unexpectedly.
8. Look for problems that already have the characteristics described or good visuals that you can easily transform.
9. Real-world problems are great, but do not overlook intriguing math questions that can be engaging if posed correctly to allow multiple entry points and strategies.

From NCTM's *Reasoning and Sense Making* (2009), which served as the text for Kristin's course, we find additional tips for helping students develop these habits of mind:

◆ Provide tasks that require students to figure things out for themselves.
◆ Ask students to restate the problem in their own words, including any assumptions they have made.
◆ Give students time to analyze a problem intuitively, explore the problem further by using models, and then proceed to a more formal approach.
◆ Resist the urge to tell students how to solve a problem when they become frustrated; find other ways to support students as they think and work.
◆ Ask students questions that will prompt their thinking—for example, "Why does this work?" or "How do you know?"
◆ Provide adequate wait time after a question for students to formulate their own reasoning.
◆ Encourage students to ask probing questions of themselves and one another.
◆ Expect students to communicate their reasoning to their classmates and the teacher, orally and in writing, using proper mathematical vocabulary.
◆ Highlight exemplary explanations, and have students reflect on what makes them effective.
◆ Establish a classroom climate in which students feel comfortable sharing their mathematical arguments and critiquing the arguments of others in a productive manner (2009, 11).

As an assignment, Kristin required the following:

Adapted Task and Written Summary:
1. Participants will adapt a task using sample textbook problems or problems that have been used previously. Participants will choose at least one NCTM process standard AND at least one Common Core mathematical practice to emphasize as they implement the task and reflect on the practice used.
2. Participants will implement the task in their classroom.
3. Participants will join and contribute in an e-Share reflecting on the process of modifying the task and implementing it in their classroom.
4. Participants will write a 1–2 page (double-spaced) summary on the implementation and reflection of the adapted task. The following must be included in the summary: Why you chose the task; which process standard and common core practice you have emphasized in the task; how you implemented the task; the overall outcome; and how you will change the task for next time.

5. Participants will submit their work on a forum in Moodle and post at least one substantive comment on the work of TWO other classmates. When posting their work, students must include: a.) a copy of the original task (including source information), b.) a copy of the adapted task, c.) the written summary.

For this chapter, Yvelyne received permission to include some of the tasks adapted by participants in the course. The tasks by Andy Winstead, Uriel Rodriguez, and Caroline Delaney are not from teachers from the course but from teachers participating in a professional development grant supported by the Louisiana Systemic Initiative Project.

Carol Lavery: Constructing an Equilateral Triangle, Fairfax High School, Virginia

Figure 12.1

Original Task

Given a set of instructions, students construct an equilateral triangle. Students are expected to memorize the steps in order to perform various constructions throughout the school year.

These instructions were taken from a web site called Math Open Reference available at the following web page address: www.mathopenref.com/constequilateral.html

After doing this	Your work should look like this
Start with the line segment AB which is the length of the sides of the desired equilateral triangle.	
1. Pick a point P that will be one vertex of the finished triangle.	
2. Place the point of the compass on point A and set drawing end to point B. The compass is now set to the length of the sides of the finished triangle. Do not change from now on.	

Figure 12.1 (Continued)

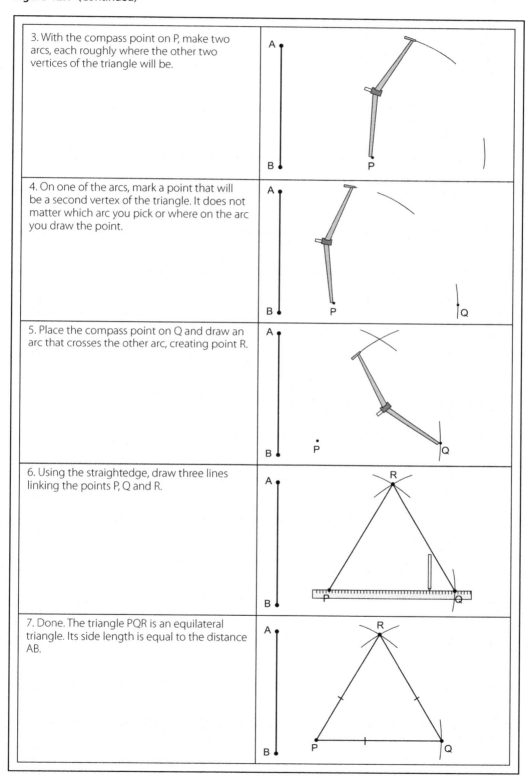

3. With the compass point on P, make two arcs, each roughly where the other two vertices of the triangle will be.	
4. On one of the arcs, mark a point that will be a second vertex of the triangle. It does not matter which arc you pick or where on the arc you draw the point.	
5. Place the compass point on Q and draw an arc that crosses the other arc, creating point R.	
6. Using the straightedge, draw three lines linking the points P, Q and R.	
7. Done. The triangle PQR is an equilateral triangle. Its side length is equal to the distance AB.	

Figure 12.1 (Continued)

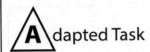dapted Task

Students are tasked with developing and communicating the steps for constructing an equilateral triangle.

<u>**NCTM Process Standards**</u>

Connections – recognize and use connections among mathematical ideas.

While tasked with developing a construction for an equilateral triangle, students will make connections between:

- A standard construction for copying a segment and the radius of circle,
- A standard construction for bisecting a segment and the intersection of two congruent circles, and
- A construction of an equilateral triangle and the intersection of two congruent circles.
- A construction for the perpendicular bisector of a segment and a construction of an equilateral triangle.

Communication – communicate mathematical thinking coherently and clearly to peers and teachers.

Students will practice communicating their ideas with clarity and precision while describing the steps of their construction in either verbal or written form.

<u>**Common Core Standards (High School Geometry)**</u>

G-CO.13   Construct an equilateral triangle.
G-CO.12   Make formal constructions . . .
             Copy a segment and bisect a segment.
             Students use these constructions in this activity to discover G-CO.13.

G-CO.9   Prove Theorems about . . .
             Points on a perpendicular bisector of a line segment are exactly those equidistant from the segments endpoints.
             This is a possible extension of the activity through investigation and inductive reasoning. A technology tool such as Geometer's Sketchpad could be used.

<u>**Background Knowledge**</u>

Students will already be familiar with two basic constructions: (1) copy a segment, and (2) bisect a segment. Students likely have previous knowledge of equilateral triangles from middle school.

<u>**Supplies**</u>

Compass, straight edge, paper and student handout (attached).

<u>**Teacher Notes**</u>

Assign the following task to your students. Designate a set amount of time to complete the task and share results with a partner (5–10 minutes).

Task: Construct an equilateral triangle (triangle with 3 congruent sides). Remember that you should only use a compass and straight edge in formal constructions.

Figure 12.1 (Continued)

Display examples of equilateral triangles if needed. Do **not** provide the student handout until students have time to come up with ideas and have a chance to share with a partner and/or present to the class.

Although rulers should not be used in formal constructions, do not correct students using them during this initial phase of the task. This allows for multiple points of entry for this task. Some students are not yet comfortable with the use of a compass. Some students will struggle while using only a ruler. It hopefully will increase their awareness of the compass as a useful tool.

After 5-10 minutes, have students present their constructions or sketches. This component of the activity is critical for developing communication of mathematical ideas. Students who may not normally be comfortable presenting may enjoy presenting their sketches or constructions. During student discourse, try to remain neutral as various approaches are presented. When presentations are completed, differentiate between sketching and constructing. Some students will be able to sketch triangles remarkably close to equilateral triangles. They can be praised for their artistic ability or spatial awareness, but point out that they still need to know how to construct an equilateral triangle as well. Anticipate that many students will need more direct instruction to construct an equilateral triangle. The following activity is designed to assist with this instruction. Use the student handout for this activity.

Activity

Students will be provided segment, $\overline{AB}$. They will be asked to construct Circle A with radius $\overline{AB}$. Figure 1 is the desired result of this step. Do not provide a visual until students have attempted this first step.

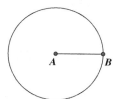

Figure 1

After they have done this step of the activity, they will be asked to construct segments that are two times and three times the length of AB. They will be asked to justify their construction. Anticipate and look for different approaches and have students present their constructions. If needed use clarifying questions that lead students to a discourse on the connection between the radius of a circle being the segment that is being duplicated when "copying segments."

Next students will be asked to construct Circles A and B with radius $\overline{AB}$ and to label the points of intersection of the two circles as C and D. Again, do not provide a visual while students are completing this step. Check for understanding of vocabulary and naming conventions by having students display their work on a document camera (if available).

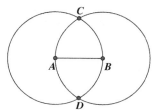

Figure 2

Ask students to verbalize (in writing or with a partner) any constructions they already know that are similar to this construction. Hopefully some will notice that line CD is the segment bisector

Figure 12.1 (Continued)

(perpendicular bisector) of $\overline{AB}$. Display visuals of this construction and a more traditional construction of a perpendicular bisector of a segment after student presentations are completed.

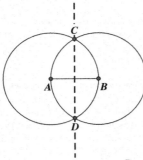 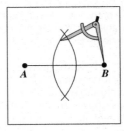

Figure 3

Ask students to compare the lengths of AB, BC and AC. Leaving this open ended will allow for multiple points of entry for this task. Some students may choose to use a ruler to measure the lengths. Some may use a compass to compare or justify that they are congruent. Hopefully some will recognize that these segments are congruent since they are radii of congruent circles. Have students discuss their findings with their partners and present to the class.

If no one has recognized that an equilateral triangle can be constructed, ask students to draw AC and BC.

After students have completed this activity, ask them to write the steps for constructing an equilateral triangle. Permit students to work with partners and have them verbalize the steps with their partners to check for correct vocabulary and precise mathematical language. Consider developing a "class" description of steps to constructing an equilateral triangle.

The student activity sheet used for this task follows on the next page.

Student Activity Sheet: Develop the Construction for an Equilateral Triangle

Task 1: Given $\overline{AB}$ below, construct Circle A with radius $\overline{AB}$.

A   **B**

Compare/contrast this circle construction to the construction you learned for copying a segment. Discuss with your shoulder partner and summarize your thoughts below.

At the bottom of the page, construct a line segment three (3) times the length of $\overline{AB}$.

Figure 12.1 (Continued)

Task 2: Given $\overline{AB}$ below, construct Circles A & B with radius $\overline{AB}$.

There will be two congruent circles that intersect when you have completed this task. Raise your hand when you have completed this step so a teacher or helper can review your work. Be ready to describe your circles in precise geometric terms.

A   B

Label the points of intersection of the two circles as C and D. Compare/contrast this circle construction to the construction you learned for bisecting a segment. Discuss with your shoulder partner and be prepared to share your thoughts with the class.

Using a straight edge, draw $\overline{AC}$ and $\overline{BC}$. Measure AC and BC. Make a conjecture about the triangle created. Find a way to justify your conjecture mathematically.

Summary

I used this adapted task in one of my inclusive, general education classes where I coteach with a general education teacher very early in the school year. The class consisted of freshmen, sophomores, juniors, and seniors. There was a very wide range of background knowledge and educational needs in the class. The task was for students to construct an equilateral triangle without a set of instructions. The students had already learned to copy a segment and to find the midpoint of a segment using a compass. They had not learned a construction for an equilateral triangle yet. A decision was made to simply task the students with constructing an equilateral triangle and to see if some could develop a construction on their own. Only a few minutes were allotted for this initial task; then students were asked to present their work. Following the presentations, an activity sheet was provided.

Anecdotal Findings

Several students attempted to sketch an equilateral triangle rather than construct one. This was permitted to allow for multiple points of entry on the task. Students were reluctant to present their work at first. After someone presented an exemplary construction and after someone presented a sketch, students who did not normally participate were asking permission to present. The student activity that followed was designed to lead students to a discovery of an equilateral triangle construction. During the activity, one of my students with an autism spectrum disorder diagnosis who is usually off task called out to me and said, "I constructed an equilateral triangle!" Overall, I was pleased about the participation of the class and pleasantly surprised at the progress some of my students at risk were making.

At the end of the activity I wanted students to justify that our construction was definitely an equilateral triangle and that it would be for all cases. My students and I struggled here. I think that perhaps it would have been more successful if students had more experience with formal proofs. I may use this in future years after we have worked on proofs. Refer to my adapted task document for more teacher-related notes and ideas.

Later in the school year, my coteacher and I noticed some positive results of this activity. Another one of our students with an autism spectrum disorder would often complain if he finished a task before other students. We started to task him with various constructions. We didn't provide directions for them. He was able to construct a rhombus by starting with the activity we had used for the equilateral triangle. We hadn't even discussed polygons in our class at that point. He used his construction for a rhombus as an alternative method to construct a line parallel to a given line through a point. We taught our class the method that involves copying an angle (using corresponding angles), but we encouraged our students to use other methods if they worked. In another one of our cotaught classes, a student with a learning disability developed an alternative construction for parallel lines as well (he copied the alternate interior angle rather than the corresponding angle). We praised him for demonstrating his understanding of angle relationships by using a construction different from the one we had presented. This student often did not demonstrate very high levels of mastery on standard assessments. He really appreciated the spotlight on his learning in this situation.

Note to Readers

When we e-mailed the profile to Carol for any edits, she wrote:

> in the anecdotal part, I changed all the sentences to past tense. When I wrote this for the NCTM class, some were in the present tense. My co-teacher and I have since seen some positive results later in the year from this activity that we did so early this school year. I am attaching some student artifacts that I shared with other math teachers during an in-service this month because I referred to students developing different versions of constructions on their own in my anecdotal section. (Readers: see Figure 12.2 for an example.)

We think Carol's comment demonstrates the litmus test of a good professional development program: What teachers learn is transformed into classroom teaching, is shared with colleagues, and continues to evolve *after* the program is over.

Figure 12.2 Students' Versions of Constructions

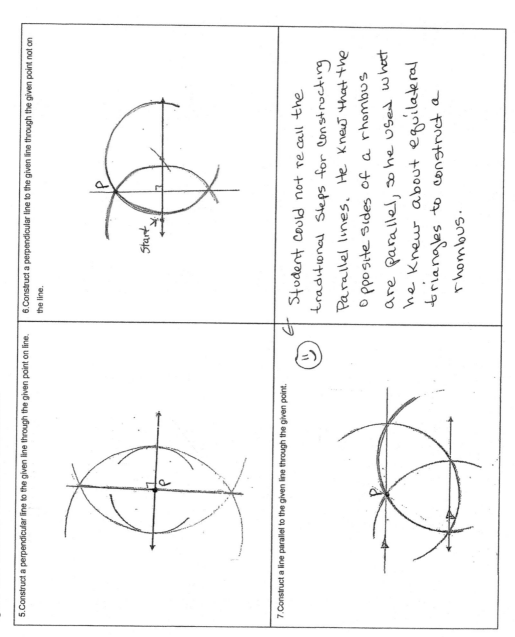

5. Construct a perpendicular line to the given line through the given point on line.

6. Construct a perpendicular line to the given line through the given point not on the line.

Start

P

7. Construct a line parallel to the given line through the given point.

P

:-)

← Student could not recall the traditional steps for constructing parallel lines. He knew that the opposite sides of a rhombus are parallel, so he used what he knew about equilateral triangles to construct a rhombus.

Rick Barlow: Composition of Functions, Fremont High School, Sunnyvale, California

Source of Original Task: Pearson Algebra 2 Common Core Edition 2012, 403, #60.
CCSS Standards: FBF.1: Compose functions.
CCSSM Math Practice: SMP2: Students can reason quantitatively and abstractly.

I chose a task on composition of functions because I feel that composition of functions is one of those very abstract concepts in math that can easily be distilled to a procedure.

NCTM Process Standard: Problem Solving

Original Task

Suppose your teacher offers to give the whole class a bonus if everyone passes the next math test. The teacher says she will give everyone a 10-point bonus and increase everyone's grade by 9 percent of his or her score.

    a.   You earned a 75 on the test. Would you rather have the 10-point bonus first and then the 9 percent increase or the 9 percent increase first and then the 10-point bonus?
    b.   Is this the best plan for all students?

Adapted Task

We will consider the following question today: Can the output of one function be the input of another function? In other words, can the range of one function be the domain for another function?

    Directions: Work with your team to answer all questions below. Answer the questions posed in this task **in your notes**. This task will launch into the learning objective for today. Therefore, all questions are important to the discussion we will be having as well as to your understanding of the learning objective.

    Mr. Barlow is considering the following proposal: If everyone passes the test, he will give the whole class a bonus. Mr. Barlow will give everyone a 10-point bonus **and then** increase everyone's grade by 9 percent of his or her score.

    1.   First, consider adding 10 points to your score. Why is this a function (we'll call it the **add 10 function**)? What is the input and what is the output of the **add 10 function**? Draw a diagram or table in your notes to represent this situation.
    2.   Misty, a student in another class, correctly described the domain for the **add 10 function** as "all the students' original test scores." What is the range?
    3.   Misty wrote this in her notes: "The input for the second function (increasing the grade by 9 percent) is the output from the first function (the **add**

10 function)." What does Misty mean? What are the input and output for the second function (we'll call it the **increase by 9%** function)?

4. Ms. Helft is considering offering a different proposal to her Algebra 2 students. If everyone passes the test, she will increase the scores by 9 percent **and then** add 10 points. Ms. Helft is using the same two functions as Mr. Barlow, but in a different order.

   a. What is Ms. Helft's first function?

   b. What are the domain and range for this function?

   c. What is Ms. Helft's second function? What are the domain and range for this function?

   d. Remi thinks Ms. Helft's proposal is like Mr. Barlow's proposal where the range of one function becomes the domain of another function. Is Remi correct?

      I. If you think he is correct, what range is becoming a domain? The domain of which function?

      II. If you think he is wrong, how would you describe the relationship between the **add 10 function** and the **increase by 9%** function?

   e. You got a 72 on the test. Would you rather have Mr. Barlow's proposal of a 10-point bonus first and then the 9 percent increase, or Ms. Helft's proposal of a 9 percent increase and then the 10-point bonus?

Procedure

I introduced the task by saying something like this to the students:

> Sometimes the domain and range for a function are described in words rather than numbers. For example, for the function "students to their age," "all the students" is the domain and "the students' ages" would be the range. This idea is important to the task you will be working on today—not in numbers but using a verbal description.

Then students should work on the first scenario for about seven minutes. Circulate to listen for students describing the domain and range of the functions and using the range of one function and the domain of another. Stop students after about seven minutes for a class discussion about domain and range and the idea that the range of one function (original score +10) could be the domain of the second function (score times 9%). Ideally, the teacher can share student work or specific things the teacher heard students say to make the connection about composing functions (I would not recommend using the phrase "composition of functions" yet). After this discussion students will start on the second scenario. Let students work for about 10 minutes. The answer to the question about which teachers' proposal is better is important mostly to emphasize that the order in which you compose functions matters. Conclude the task by debriefing the two main points: You can use the range of one function as the domain for another, **and** the order of composition matters.

My next step would be more formal notes on composition and then procedural practice on composing functions.

Summary

I started my lesson on composition of functions with this task. Students walked in and took a seat, we said hello/greeting/housekeeping, and then they got to work. I ran the task in two blocks, and this "cold open" approach worked great in one block and failed miserably in the other block (more on that later).

Students worked in groups for about 10 minutes on reading the task, getting started, and discussing the first scenario. I then stopped the class to discuss the answers to the questions for the first scenario. At this time, I also shared strategies that I saw students use to get started on the problem.

After a whole-class discussion, students moved on to the second scenario and worked on it with their groups. Again, after about 10 minutes, I stopped groups to discuss the answers to their questions. This then led to formal notes on composing functions and then a different activity to practice the procedure of composition. A very flipped lesson!

The Overall Outcome

The first time I ran the task, the overall outcome was confusion. Part of it was the timing: My first block class (7:30 A.M.) on a Monday was *not* the day to introduce this concept. Also, the number of students who had trouble understanding increasing by percents caught me off guard. I had a coworker look over my task before I gave it to the class, and that was my colleague's feedback: The increase by percents will be an issue. Boy, was it an issue. My first block class really got stuck on that idea, and it impeded their ability to access the task.

I briefly considered not doing it in my fifth block class, but a coworker suggested that doing a task once is not enough to get a feel for it. So I *had* to do it again! I'm glad I did. I started the conversation by warning students not to get caught up in changes by percents and to just consider it *an increase*—leave it at that. They did, and the task did a better job of addressing the conceptual understanding I was hoping for.

What I Would Change for Next Time

Next time, I will remember the change by percent thing. I think the problem was a little too confusing, also. There were too many questions for students to process, and I used too much ambiguous language (I need to use input/output or domain/range, but I can't switch back and forth). I think a leaner, meaner, more focused version of this task would still address the conceptual understanding. This really is to introduce composition as an abstract concept, then to build to the procedural part of compositions.

Cheryl Tokarski: Exploring Absolute Value, Chase Collegiate School, Waterbury, Connecticut

Figure 12.3

Exploring Absolute Value

I chose to implement a task that would help students better understand absolute value equations and their solutions. Students have struggled with absolute value equations and inequalities in the past. In addition, I saw this as a good way to introduce the concepts of translation on a number line rather than students seeing it for the first time in two dimensions with functions.

Original Task

In previous years, I have given a lesson that talked about:

- Absolute value as a distance
- The Algebraic definition of absolute value
- How you solve absolute value equations by isolating the absolute value, applying the absolute value principle, and then solving the two resulting equations for the values of the variable that make the equation true.
- And, of course, that you must check for extraneous solutions

Students were then assigned practice problems for homework which instructed them to:
Solve each equation and check your answers   For example:

1. $2|3x - 2| = 14$
2. $|x + 4| + 3 = 17$
3. $|3x + 5| = 5x + 2$

Adapted Task

1. Solve and graph the solutions for each of the following equations on the number lines provided.

 $|x| = 5$

$|x - 3| = 5$

$|x2 - 3| = 5$

What do you notice when you compare the solutions of these three equations?
Can you connect what you are seeing in the graphs with the form of the equations?

2. Based upon what you learned in #1, can you give the solutions of the following equations without actually going through the process to solve the equation?

$|x| = 15$
$|x - 1| = 15$
$|3x - 1| = 15$

What I wanted the students to see was the fact that the constant term inside the absolute value causes the graph to shift on the number line and that as a result we were actually looking at the absolute

Figure 12.3 (Continued)

value as a distance from a point other than 0. In addition, the coefficient of the variable inside of the absolute value has a scaling effect on the graph and thus the solution.

Standards Applied
This task allowed students to employ the Process Standards and Common Core Practices listed in the table below:

Process Standards	Common Core Practices
Reasoning and Proof	Reasoning abstractly and quantitatively
Communications	Look for and make use of structure
Connections	

Task Implementation
I implemented this task as part of a 40-minute class session in two College Prep-level Algebra 2 classes. We had already discussed the basic definitions of absolute value—both as a distance and the algebraic definition of $|x| = \begin{cases} x, \text{ if } x \geq 0 \\ -x, \text{ if } x < 0 \end{cases}$

I posed the first question on the board and gave students the chance to work together in groups to solve and graph the equations and see if they could make sense as to how the graphs were changing from one to the next. Student discussion in the first class was outstanding and the students were able to get to the fact that from the first to the second equation, the solutions were shifted to the right three units on the number line. They were able to make sense of why this would happen and also to extend this idea on their own with discussion of what happens if $x + 3$ were inside the absolute value rather than $x - 3$ in the second equation.

Students needed a little help understanding what happened when we moved to the third equation. There was a lot of good discussion, and I used questioning (What do you notice about the distance between the solutions on the graph? How does the form of the equation relate to this change? Can you find the center of the graph? Where might that come from?). The students did make the connections after a few minutes, and there was a lot of good discussion in the room.
I then presented the second set of equations and asked the students to use what they had learned from the first set to determine the solution to the equations without actually going through the algebraic process to isolate the variable. All groups were able to quickly get to the solutions of the first two equations (the first one of course being trivial), and with a little discussion, they were also able to get to the solutions for the third one. I loved that there were a few students in the room who expressed some confusion and their peers stepped up to explain what was going on—it didn't have to come through me.

For some reason, and I am still trying to figure out why, the second group did not take to the activity nearly as well as the first group. They needed a lot of prodding and support through the process. I had to resort to questioning on the second equation of the first set; they did not reason their way through it as the first group did. I also tried the same line of questioning with regard to the third equation as I had used with the first group, but it took a lot more to get them there. I am still not 100 percent sure that all of the students in that group actually do understand the concept in full and am revisiting it in other ways as we go forward.

When I use this task again in the future, I will likely add an extension to it to include some discussion about extraneous solutions and the fact that you do not have to go through a full evaluation of your solutions to reason that your solution does not work. While this is a bit unrelated to the task outline here, there was some natural discussion as we looked at additional problems that the kids brought forward in the first class. I liked how the discussion went so much that I want to revisit it and see if there is a way to broaden the task and include it as well.

Holly Erwin-Harding: Calculating Areas of Irregular Figures, Blacksburg New School, Blacksburg, Virginia

Source of Original Task: This is a standard textbook question for finding area of a track and was retrieved from http://toolboxes.flexiblelearning.net.au on September 10, 2013.

Mathematical Content: G.MG.1: Use geometric shapes, their measures, and their properties to describe objects.

Mathematical Practice: SMP2.

NCTM Process Standards: Reasoning and Proof, Communication, Connections.

Figure 12.4 Original task

Calculating Area of Irregular Figures

Find the area of the figure.

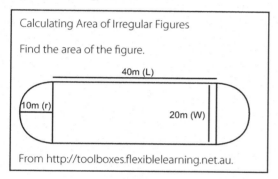

From http://toolboxes.flexiblelearning.net.au.

Figure 12.5 Adapted task

This task consists of six different levels of problem, and may be utilized in two different ways. One way to use this task is for students to start at level 1 and work through each level in turn up to level 6. Each level completed helps propel the student to the next level. A second way to use this task is for students to enter the task at the level where they feel comfortable. This will allow for students of different levels to work together on the same problem.

CALCULATING THE AREA OF IRREGULAR FIGURES

Level 1. Calculate the area of the following figures:

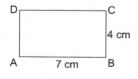

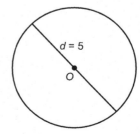

Area of ABC = —————

Figure 12.5 (Continued)

Level 2.

The kindergarten teacher wants to purchase two rugs to put in the reading center of her classroom. She found two rugs; one is 5' x 8' and the other is round with a diameter of 4'. What is the total floor area she can cover with these two rugs?

Level 3. Find the area of this figure.

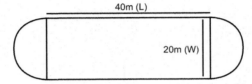

Level 4.

The ice skating rink needs to be refinished, and the Zamboni operator charges a price to do this based on the square footage of the rink. If the rink is shaped like a 20' x 30' rectangle with a half-circle attached at each short end, what is the area of the rink to be refinished?

Level 5.

Find the area of this figure.

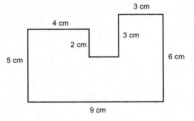

Level 6.

As our school continues to get bigger, we are starting to get cramped in the middle school. It has been suggested that one solution to the problem might be to build a new extension to the school. This addition could be either just an enlargement of the middle school or could also include a multipurpose room. Look at the attached satellite photo of the school property. Determine where an addition could go.

a. Determine the largest possible addition if we limited it to just an expansion of the middle school. It should be located within 15 feet of the current middle school and not require the removal of existing structures or trees. The minimum size of this expansion is two-thirds the size of the current middle school. Determine the dimensions of the new building and calculate the area. To maximize area, use composite or other than rectangular shapes.

Figure 12.5 (Continued)

b. Determine where the addition could go it we built a multipurpose building. The multipurpose building should be 25 percent larger than the current middle school and can be located on any side of the school, so long as no existing structures must be moved. Determine the dimensions of the new building and calculate the area.

Summary

My adapted task covered the topic of finding area in irregular figures. There were several factors that contributed to choosing my task. The actual topic is one that my students had trouble with when we first covered it in the first weeks of class. There are several steps that go into understanding how to solve these kind of problems, so I found this problem conducive to scaffolding and allowing students to use what they learned in one level problem to lead them into the next level.

I teach Geometry, and my overarching goal for the entire course is to emphasize problem solving, logic, and the "why" we do things. As such, I emphasized all of the "Problem Solving" process standards as I developed and implemented this task. I also emphasized the principles "communicate their mathematical thinking coherently and clearly to peers, teachers, and others" and "analyze and evaluate the mathematical thinking and strategies of others" as the students discussed their problem solving strategies with each other. The Common Core mathematical practice emphasized in this task was "4. Model with mathematics"; students used basic problems to design an addition to our school.

I implemented the task by giving the students a packet that presented all six levels of the problem and explained that they could choose where to start. I have two students who are both bright but in different ways. They chose to start at the beginning and work through all six levels. They discussed each problem, then worked together and compared answers. When they disagreed about solutions, they explained their process to each other and came to a consensus on the correct answer. I stayed out of the discussions except to encourage the students to become more precise in their explanations and to draw them out when they sounded weak in their explanations. The students were strong in levels 1–4, and the emphasis in precision became important when we got to levels 5 and 6, where the students were weaker and had challenges determining how to solve the problems. I made the students explain their process in detail and in this way helped the students to understand where they were weak in their understanding.

Overall, this task was very successful, especially in levels 1–5. It was especially effective in identifying and resolving a weakness for one student while solving the level 5 problem. I was pleased to hear the students observe that they could use previously completed problems to help them with later problems. One student even commented that he enjoyed the task, but found level 6 hard. The level 6 problem did not go as well as I had hoped. It took a few minutes of discussion for the students to agree on what had to be done. The biggest problem was that the students got caught up in trying to calculate the area of the existing building using the map legend and scale and wasted a lot of time. Then, they had a hard time figuring out how to come up with a new building of a given area with an irregular shape. When developing this task, I envisioned that they would choose to create the new building in what I thought was an obvious location and with a particular shape, which would have a fairly simple area to calculate, especially given the problems we had previously completed. They did not go in that direction and came up with much more complicated shapes with areas they couldn't figure out how to calculate.

To use this problem again, I must revise level 6 to remove distractions so that the students can focus on the learning objective. First, I need to use a map for which the scale is not such an issue. As much as I liked the idea of having the problem reflect reality, I think this map needed some "creative editing" of trees and such to make it easier for the students to identify potential locations for the new building. The task should be more obvious in specifying that the new building must be a composite or irregular figure. Additionally, I need to make sure that the students have the appropriate basic skills to solve the problems.

Andrew Winstead and Uriel Rodriguez: Quadratic Models for Real-Life Data from Hurricane Katrina, New Orleans Math and Science Charter School

Source of Original Task: Original.
Mathematical Content: N.CN.7; A.REI.4 ; IFIF.4.
Mathematical Practices: SMP1- SMP4, SMP6.
NCTM Process Standards: Problem Solving, Connections, Communication, Representation.

Original Task

Rather than use the textbook models for having students practice solving quadratic equations, we created some models for students to determine how closely they represented real-life situations.

Adapted Tasks

Figure 12.6 Summary of the PowerPoint on trends in New Orleans pre- and post-Katrina

While watching the video, students are to take notes and answer the guiding questions.
Essential Question: Is New Orleans making a comeback after 2005?

I.   Catalyst/Hook
II. Essential Question
III. Population Trends: Integrates Math/Reading
IV. Local Businesses: Math/Reading
V.   New Housing: Math/Reading
VI. Crime Rates: Math/Reading

How do you measure if a city is doing well?

   Population: More people entering the city because they choose to.
   Local Business: More business staying in the city and putting money back into the city.
   Housing: More buildings and houses built in the city to support the growing population.
   Crime Rates: Lower, which shows strength in the community/government/officials.
   Population Trends

New Orleans population fluctuated until it reached its peak around the 1960s.
Soon after the introduction of urbanization (suburbs), many people left the city.
After Katrina, a sharp decline in population occurred in which areas?

   Local Businesses
   Housing
   Crime Rates

New Orleans has consistently experienced a high homicide rate during the previous two to three decades.
Its average annual per-capita homicide rate (59 per 100,000) was the highest among large cities in the
   country from 1990 to 2010, based on Bureau of Justice statistics from FBI Uniform Crime Reports.
In 1994, 421 people were killed (85.8 per 100,000 people), a homicide rate that has not been matched
   by any major city to date.
The homicide rate rose and fell year to year throughout the late 1990s, but the overall trend from 1994
   to 1999 was a steady reduction in homicides.

Figure 12.7 Progress of New Orleans's recovery—video catalyst

Name: _____ Period: _____ Date: _____

Answer the following questions as you watch the video.

1. According to the video, what percentage of the city was estimated to be under water?
    _____

2. Seven years after Hurricane Katrina, there are _____ dollars of construction projects
    being completed in New Orleans.
3. Rod Miller, President and CEO of New Orleans Business Alliance, believes that "the creativity you see
    walking down the street . . . translates into creativity in _____."
4. Since Hurricane Katrina, how much money has been invested in hurricane protection?
    _____

Answer the following questions after you watch the video and think about what was said.
Considering all New Orleans has to offer, what do you feel was impacted the most by the devastation
of Hurricane Katrina?

_____
_____
_____

Figure 12.7 (Continued)

Do you feel that New Orleans has recovered or not recovered or is still recovering from Hurricane Katrina? Why do you feel this way?

_____

_____

_____

Another hurricane will strike New Orleans in the future. Do you feel that New Orleans will be adequately prepared for the hurricane and are you concerned about the city's recovery?

_____

_____

_____

Video credit: Thread NOLA: Progress of New Orleans' Recovery, http://www.youtube.com/watch?v=EBKP2hz4t-I

Figure 12.8 Quadratic New Orleans

Name: _____ Period: _____ Date: _____

Population

The following equation models the population of New Orleans over time. The function p(t) represents the number of people in 10,000s, and t represents years, with $t = 5$ being the year 2005.

$$P(t) = 10t^2 - 60t + 80$$

Estimate when you would expect the population to grow to 2.4 million people.

Local Business

The following equation models the percentage of locally owned business over time. The function $B(t)$ represents the percentage of New Orleans businesses that are local and t is time in years, with $t = 0$ being the year 2000.

$$B(t) = 5t^2 - 30t + 25$$

In what year were there no locally owned businesses?

New Construction

The following equation models the number of new construction projects over time. The function $N(t)$ represents the number of new construction projects in 100s, and t is time in years, with $t = 10$ being the year 2010.

$$N(t) = 2t^2 + 4t - 70$$

In what year did the number of construction projects in New Orleans drop to zero?

Crime Rate

The following equation models the crime rate in New Orleans. The function $C(t)$ represents the crime rate as a percent, and t is time in years, with $t = 0$ being the year 2000.

$$C(t) = -2t^3 + 16t^2 + 40t$$

In what year did the crime rate reach a maximum?

Figure 12.9 Has New Orleans recovered?

Blog post by Kenny Klein

As a musician I travel often. People that I meet and speak to know that I live in New Orleans, and I am constantly asked the same question: "How is the recovery from Katrina going?" It seems like a simple question. Katrina was a highly publicized event, and people are genuinely concerned.

But the truth is, it's a very complicated question with a complicated set of answers. While the term Mardi Gras is certainly still synonymous with New Orleans, and we are certainly still known for music and indulgence, Hurricane Katrina may be the most defining event of our city in this century. We live every day with reminders of the hurricane, from the wreckage of buildings, to the continued presence of FEMA markings, to the fact that eight years later, we are only now beginning to rebuild our public schools. We got the message that the nation's government did not officially desire to help us (although the people of the nation certainly did), and this as much as anything has coalesced us as a city. Yet we still struggle to rebuild our properties, and in many cases, our lives.

For anyone unfamiliar with the particulars of Katrina, here is the inscription from the New Orleans Hurricane Katrina Memorial:

"On August 29, 2005, Hurricane Katrina made landfall upon the Louisiana and Mississippi Gulf coast, bringing devastation to many communities. In New Orleans, storm surge and the failure

of the levee system caused flooding in over eighty percent of the city, trapping thousands. In the chaotic aftermath New Orleanians faced desperate circumstances in homes, hospitals, the Superdome and other makeshift shelters. Despite the heroic efforts of first responders, medical personnel, volunteers and the military, over 1,100 citizens lost their lives in the disaster."

Perhaps you can see why nearly a decade later, Katrina and its aftermath still haunt this city. It is in our surroundings, and in our thoughts and prayers, constantly.

Two years ago I took a trip down to the Lower Ninth Ward, the area hit hardest by Katrina, to see what the neighborhood looked like six years later. I took a series of photographs and posted them on a blog site I maintained at the time. Today I took the same trip, to see what has changed two years later, now eight years after the event.

DESTRUCTION
In many areas of the Ninth Ward and elsewhere, the devastation of Katrina is still evident. In some places, houses still lay in ruin. In others, only stones or cement remain of what was once someone's home.

REMINDERS
A few years ago a good friend moved to New Orleans to finish a project with me. When she arrived, I told her I'd take her for a drive around the better parts of the city to look for apartments. As we drove, she became incredulous. "This is a good part of the city?" she asked. "One of the best," I told her.

"But, what about the graffiti?" she challenged.

"What graffiti?"

She pointed to the face of a building.

"Oh," I said. "That . . ."

Many buildings in New Orleans still bear the markings painted on them eight years ago by rescue workers. The marks usually take the form of an X, with indications of which agency inspected the building, the date of the inspection, hazards, and number of bodies found. Some home owners maintain the markings on their home as a sign of pride. Local artists create the symbol in brass, to hang on doors. In the example at the top of this section, the house was inspected by E troop of the 82nd Calvary, Oregon National Guard (E/8) on September 16, nearly three weeks after Katrina struck. The team could not enter the building (NE). In the example below, the building was inspected twice, as there was no entry in the first inspection: no bodies were found. The agency that inspected the building is obscured.

Figure 12.9 (Continued)

REBIRTH

Thanks to the efforts of celebrities, builders, countless volunteers, and the New Orleans population, New Orleans is being rebuilt. The television show *Extreme Makeover: Home Edition* built Musician's Village in the Upper Ninth, four blocks of houses where musicians who lost their homes and their instruments could buy new homes at amazingly affordable prices.

Everywhere I wandered today in the Lower Ninth I saw building. Most of it is thanks to an organization founded by actor Brad Pitt, and run largely by volunteers, called Make It Right NOLA. Make It Right is building ninety new, green homes in the Lower Ninth. The styles of these homes are amazing, and all are built with the latest green technology.

There is no easy answer to the question "is New Orleans recovering?" For some, amazing new opportunities have sprung Phoenix-like from the tragedy of Katrina. Others still remain in exile, having made lives for themselves in other places, but longing for the life they had here. Still others mourn the 1,100 dead. Organizations like Make It Right, Teach for America, and Habitat for Humanity show us every day that the nation has not forgotten.

Figure 12.10 Open response

Name:_____ Period: _____ Date: _____

Directions: Now that we have worked out several math problems relating to the resurgence of New Orleans, you will write a paragraph responding to the Essential Question for today.

Is New Orleans facing a comeback after 2005?

RUBRIC

Y/N	Assertion: Does the writer restate the question and provide his/her own opinion?
Y/N	Evidence: Does the author cite at **least two sources** (math related, from the problems we worked out in class)?
Y/N	Commentary: Does the writer explain how each source proves that his/her assertion is correct?

Procedures

1. We began with introducing the lesson objective. We told students that they would be watching a video and a PowerPoint on New Orleans's recovery after Katrina and that information from both sources would be needed to solve their math problems for this class.

2. We had students read the video questions in Figure 12.6 to direct their attention to the important details and then showed the video on New Orleans's recovery at http://www.youtube.com/watch?v=EBKP2hz4t-I.

3. After the video, we allowed students a short amount of time to formulate answers to the video questions and then discussed them.

4. We then showed a PowerPoint (summary of ideas is in Figure 12.7) to introduce each problem they would consider for the remainder of the class (Figure 12.8). We then allowed students time to try and solve each math problem as we circulated to help when necessary.

5. After students solved each problem, we reviewed the problem as an entire class and encouraged students to draw conclusions about their calculations as they relate the mathematics back to the original context of the problem.

6. After performing all the calculations, students were to read the accompanying article about the recovery of New Orleans (see Figure 12.9).

7. After reading the article, students were to complete an essay assignment summarizing the lesson as in Figure 12.10.

Summary

Overall, we thought that the lesson went well. The students were interested in the video at the beginning of the lesson and participated throughout the remaining period. We always emphasize to students that it is important for them to have an opinion *and* to be able to support that opinion with sound reasoning. Thus, we were glad to see that most, if not all, students formed some sort of opinion about the devastation brought by Hurricane Katrina. If we were to teach this again, we would have students get into groups and discuss questions about the opening video. They would discuss each in their groups and then present their answers to the class so that they all could have a voice.

For the actual content of the lesson, we were satisfied with the results but not with the means because it was near impossible for us to create many equations that closely modeled the real-life data in the lesson. In the future, we would rather have this lesson taught near the end of our solving-quadratic-equations section because we would want the students to be familiar with graphs and to be able to solve with the quadratic formula. This would allow us opportunities to create more relevant questions because we would not have the concern of making sure that the equations were factorable. We would also want the students to look at real graphs and data about the information presented and have the students draw conclusions about each other's calculations. More important, we want them to be able to explain how their equation models the data and what they could do to have the equations fit the data better.

We also need to allow for more time on this lesson because, even with an hour and a half, we still did not get to teach everything that we wanted. For example, because we believe that literacy is just as important in the STEM classes as it is in English class, we were going to have the students read the article on the recovery of New Orleans. With the video information, our calculations, and this article, the students were to formulate a short essay to answer the question "Has New Orleans recovered from Hurricane Katrina?" The students would need to support their reasoning using data from the video, the calculations/predictions, and the article to support their answer.

Caroline Delaney: What Would Struggling Students Like to Know about Linear Equations? Warren Easton Charter High School

Source of Original Task: Original.
Mathematical Content: HSA.SSE.A.1, B.3; HSA. REI.A.1.
Mathematical Practices: SMP6, SMP8.
NCTM Process Standards: Problem Solving, Connections, Communication, Representation.

Original Task

I give pretests to my Algebra students to help determine what they remember from eighth-grade algebra. The pretest includes graphing different types of linear equations and their applications. Because students typically scored poorly, I decided to adapt the pretest to include "I Wonder" questions that would help me determine the students' problem areas.

Figure 12.11 Adapted task

Name_____ Date_____

Directions:

1. Make a statement on "What I am Noticing" about the eight equations below. Do not write eight different notice statements. Analyze the table as a whole.
2. Translate each equation to the y = form and graph it on the calculator.
3. Complete the "What I Wonder" side by stating at least 2 different questions you would like answered.

What I am Noticing . . .	What I Wonder . . .
$4x + 5y = 20$	
$3x + 4y = 36$	
$5x + 3y = 15$	
$7x - 4y = 28$	
$4x - 3y = 9$	
$10x + 30y = 90$	
$y2 = x2 + 4$	

Summary

Below is a collection of what students wondered about. I keep those questions on a poster board, and, as I teach the unit, I have students answer each of the questions at the appropriate time.

I WONDER:

1. Why do we have to solve for y = ?
2. If you can solve a linear equation without moving the y to one side.
3. Will there always be an x on the other side of the equal sign?
4. Why not solve for x instead of y?
5. How the equation will look as a graph.
6. How does the graph help?
7. Where do all of the negatives come from?

Figure 12.11 (Continued)

8. Why every x has a fraction in front of it?
9. If the fraction in front of the x can be simplified.
10. If the fraction in front of the x can be written as a decimal.
11. If you can have an answer without a fraction.
12. How you get rid of fractions.
13. Why, at the end, you put y over everything.
14. If you can change the variable—does it have to be x and y?
15. If $3x+4y = 6$ is the same as $4x+3y = 6$?
16. If this is used in real life.
17. Why this is important to do.

Multiple-Choice Assessment with Challenging Tasks

The multiple-choice questions were created or selected from multiple sources by Kristin Keith and teachers at Battlefield High School, Haymarket, Virginia.

Figure 12.12 Sample multiple-choice assessment

Created by:

1. Which of the following equations will have exactly 1 real root?

    A) $f(x) = 9x^2 + 12x - 4$ **B)** $f(x) = 2x^2 + 5x - 16$
    C) $f(x) = x^2 - 6x - 9$ **D)** $f(x) = 4x^2 - 8x + 4$

2. Identify the properties that justify the work between Step 3 and Step 4 and between Step 5 and Step 6.

Write the letter of the property in the blank provided after the step.

Step 1: $2(2x + 3) = (3)(4 + x)$
Step 2: $4x + 6 = 12 + 3x$ A. Associative Property of Addition
Step 3: $4x + 6 - 3x = 12 + 3x - 3x$ B. Commutative Property of Addition
Step 4: $4x - 3x + 6 = 12 + 3x - 3x$ } ———— C. Distributive Property
Step 5: $x + 6 = 12$ D. Identity Property of Addition
Step 6: $x + 6 - 6 = 12 - 6$ } ————   E. Subtraction Property of Equality
Step 7: $x = 6$ F. Multiplication Property of Equality

3. Circle each quadratic equation and graph that has a solution at 4. You must circle all that apply.

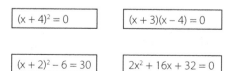

$(x + 4)^2 = 0$ $(x + 3)(x - 4) = 0$

$(x + 2)^2 - 6 = 30$ $2x^2 + 16x + 32 = 0$

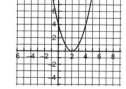
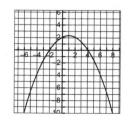

Figure 12.12 (Continued)

> **4. Use the given numbers to create an ordered pair representing a solution to** $y < x - 4$
>
> **ANSWER: (_____ , _____)**
>
> $\boxed{-6}$ $\boxed{-2}$ $\boxed{-1}$ $\boxed{0}$ $\boxed{4}$
>
> **Directions: You may use a number twice. Be sure to write your answer in the space provided.**

Resources

1. NCTM's Reasoning and Sense Making Task Library: www.nctm.org/rsmtasks/.
2. NCSM **Great Tasks** publication: www.ncsm.org.
3. A list and examples of engaging videos produced by Dan that include alignment to CCSSM are at the site given here, or readers can just Google *three acts by dan meyer* for his work: https://docs.google.com/spreadsheet/pub?key=0AjlqyKM9d7ZYdEhtR3BJMmdBWnM2YWxWYVM1UWowTEE&output=html.
4. Illustrative Mathematics Program: http://illustrativemathematics.org.
5. Other resources at the end of chapter 3, this volume.
6. These are the readings on tasks assigned in Kristin's course:

   Chamberlin, M., and J. Zawjewski. (2006). A Worthwhile Mathematical Task for Students and Their Teachers. *Mathematics Teacher* 12(3).

   Cory, B. (2010), Bouncing Balls and Graphing Derivatives. *Mathematics Teacher* 104(3).

   Gonzalez, G., and A. DeJarnette. (2013). Geometric Reasoning about a Circle. *Mathematics Teacher* 106(8).

   Sanchez, W. (2013). Open ended questions and the process standards, *Mathematics Teacher* 104(3).

   Wong, B., and L. Bukalov. (2013). Improving Students' Reasoning Geometry. *Mathematics Teacher* 107(1).

13

Don Crossfield: Marching from Algebra to Trigonometry and Beyond

Nothing provides as concrete a model as using the students themselves for points on a plane. My students no longer ask why calculators don't draw the expected graphs. After anticipating and then observing where one equation and then another will send their classmates, they can visualize clearly what certain operations do to graphs. Later, when we use the calculator, they can envision people marching around inside their calculator at their command. One of the biggest payoffs for me and for students is that we encounter the idea of analytic geometric transformations early in the year. Using graphing calculators later just flavors the pot. Our analogies carry on for years of future math classes.

Don Crossfield, Roseburg, Oregon

Before students arrive at Roseburg High School, in Roseburg, Oregon, on the day Don Crossfield has designated as "Marching Day," he prepares a Cartesian coordinate system on the pavement outside a tall building on his school's campus. The building's outdoor stairways serve as natural balconies from which to observe the human graphs that his students will soon be forming.

As Don's Algebra 2 students enter class, he escorts them to the Cartesian plane area and instructs them to stand somewhere on the grid at a point whose coordinates are integers. The stage is set, and the lesson is ready to proceed in phases. Phase One involves giving all students the experience of moving to their new location when Don calls out instructions:

Add 1 to your second coordinate.
Subtract 2 from your first coordinate.

Triple the value of your second coordinate.

Divide the value of your first coordinate by two.

Create a good instruction to make the group spread apart horizontally, and at the same time squish together vertically.

Make your second coordinate the negative of its original value.

Make your second coordinate the absolute value of its original value.

Make your second coordinate the reciprocal of its original value.

Make your second coordinate the reciprocal of 4.

Make your second coordinate the absolute value of 11.

To plant the seed of the idea that inverse functions reflect points about the line $y = x$, Don positions himself at (15,15), looks toward the origin, and instructs everyone to exchange the values of the first and second coordinates and move to the new spot. Once they have moved, he then says, "Cool . . . from here it looks like everyone on my left moved to my right and vice versa. When have we seen this happen?" His hope is that students will say the line $y = x$ acts as a line of reflection. "Sometimes students don't express this idea very clearly," he says, "but at least we get a glimmer of the idea, and when we encounter it later, students are better prepared to explain the situation mathematically."

Once Don sees that students understand how changing the values of the coordinates affects the overall graphs, he initiates Phase Two. He hands each student one playing card—ace through eight of any suit or a black queen. Red cards stand for negative numbers, blacks for positives, and queens for zero. All the integers from –8 to 8 are thus represented twice. The card each student receives will be his or her x coordinate. He sends half the students (for example, those holding diamonds and clubs) up to the balcony and instructs the other students to position themselves along the x axis, each standing on his or her assigned first coordinate. Each student on the balcony will observe a partner below.

Now the fun begins. Don holds up a series of poster-size sheets. Each sheet shows an equation that defines the second coordinate in terms of the first. At this juncture, even with Algebra 2 students, Don sometimes needs to teach or review the procedures for interpreting an equation to determine the y coordinate from the x coordinate. He instructs each student to move to the location (x, y) defined by his or her playing card and the equation. Meanwhile, their partners on the balcony see the same equations, predict the outcome, and provide support and guidance from above. Don says:

> I do show the balcony group the upcoming sheets before the marchers see them, so that they can predict first and then *ooh* and *aah* . . . it has a good effect on the group on the plane to see the previous marchers get all excited about the predictions. I caution them all the while to be quiet, not to give the new kids on the block any advantages.

Each set of equations begins with students positioned at what Don calls the "at-ease graph" or the "default equation," which is $x = y$. Holding up the posters, Don calls out the equations, pausing to give the "points" time to maneuver. Figure 13.1 has examples of typical equation sets with Don's comments to teachers in parentheses.

Figure 13.1 Equation sets for marching

Set 1:	(a) $y = x$	(b) $y = x + 2$	(c) $y = x + 3$	
Set 2:	(a) $y = x$	(b) $y = x - 3$		
Set 3:	(a) $y = x$	(b) $y = 2x$		
(For (b), have students hold hands first so that they feel and notice a stretch rather than any rotating effect. Ask students to describe this change to make sure that they declare it to be a stretch and not a rotation.)				
Set 4:	(a) $y = x$	(b) $y = -2$	(c) $y = .5x$	(d) $y = .5x + 1$
(I rarely use fractions other than ½.)				
Set 5:	(a) $y = x$	(b) $y = 3x - 2$		
(Cover up the -2 term. After they move to the $3x$ term, say, "Oh. I forgot to show the rest of this example!")				
Set 6:	(a) $y = x$	(b) $y = 12x + 4$ (Cover the $+ 4$ term.)		
Set 7:	(a) $y = x$	(b) $y = 1x$	(c) $y = (-x)(-1)$	
(For (c), covering the (-1) really emphasizes how multiplication flips the graph about the x axis. Sometimes I pretend to be covering yet another factor and thus goad them to guess that it's another factor of -1. Enjoy and have fun with the students!)				
Set 8:	(a) $y = x$	(b) $y = 2x + 1$	(c) $y = 2(x + 1)$	(d) $y = -2x - 1$
(For (c), have them note the distributive property, but don't stress that the line appears to have been moved horizontally by one. Time enough for them to observe that later.)				
Set 9:	(a) $y = x$	(b) $y = \text{abs}(x)$	(c) $y = x + 2$ (Cover the $+ 2$)	(d) $y = \text{abs}(x + 2)$
Set 10:	(a) $y = x$	(b) $y = x - 3$ (Cover $- 3$.)	(c) $y = \text{abs}(x - 3)$	(d) $y = \text{abs}(3 - x)$
(For (c) and (d), cover the absolute value symbols first. A quick discussion occurs here about the differences between the binomials $(a - b)$ and $(b - a)$.)				
Set 11: (a) $y = x$		(b) $y = \text{abs}(x) - 2$		
(Cover the $- 2$.)				
Set 12: $y = \text{abs}$ (where you are now) $- 2$				
(Cover the $- 2$.)				
Set 13: (Simply show the card for Set 12 to them again for a nice introduction to recursiveness. I keep the card $y = \text{abs}(\text{abs}(x) - 2) - 2$ to show them what the original instructions would look like, *after* they've already moved there.)				
Set 14:	(a) $y = \text{abs}(x + 2) - 3$		(b) $y = \text{abs}(\text{abs}(x + 2) - 3)$	
Set 15:	(a) $y = x$	(b) $y = x^2$	(c) $y = x^2 - 4$	(d) $y = \text{abs}(x^2 - 4) - 2$
(Cover $- 2$)				
Set 16:	(a) $y = x$	(b) $y = x^2$	(c) $y = (-x)^2$	
(For (c), students note that nothing changes, but ask them: "Why? What happens if parentheses are removed, as in $y = -x^2$?")				
Set 17:	(a) $y = .5x^2$	(b) $y = .5x^2 + 3$	(c) $y = \text{abs}(.5x^2 + 3)$	(d) $y = \text{abs}(.5x^2 - 3)$
Set 18:	(a) $y = 6/x$	(b) $xy = 6$	(c) $xy = 0$	(d) $x = \text{abs}(y)$

About halfway through the equations in Figure 13.1, just before the absolute value equations appear, Don tells the groups to trade roles, but he uses his assessment of the process to determine how to proceed. For this particular class, he comments, "I could see that all the multiplication by negative 1 wore out my first group, and I can say that I assigned the new group stuff that I was worried the first group would not be able to handle." Don now tells the new balcony students to play two roles: "One is to determine where your clone will move, to make sure they don't foul up our pretty designs, and the second is to try to guess or predict what overall picture will be formed." While students are examining the equations, they begin to anticipate the following graphical effects:

Horizontal and vertical translations;
Horizontal and vertical stretching and shrinking;
Reflections around the axes (and mildly around $y = x$);
The absolute value "broken graph" effect; and
Any asymptotes (poor $x = 0$).

Having students do human graphs of $y = \text{abs}(\text{abs}(x + 2) - 3)$ as in Set 14 seems likely to cause total chaos! Surprisingly, Don thinks that the concept of absolute value is one of these general principles that really comes across well on Marching Day. When students first see it, they are standing in $y = x$ formation, and he orders them to move to $y = \text{abs}(x)$. After only some of them move, he "chastises" the others about being slow to move to their new locations and then discusses why some people move and some don't. Students run into it again a couple of graphs later, when they are standing in $y = x + 2$ formation, and he asks them to move to $y = \text{abs}(x + 2)$ instead. He asks the students on the balcony if they could have predicted the movement, and they again restate the idea that absolute value simply reflects the negative values up over the x axis. Don says:

The neat thing about graphing like this is that each "point" on the plane only has to figure out its own value and not worry about anyone else's. This means that the person who is numbered –1 only has to plug that value in and move to the new location. Continuity of functions pretty much assures that they will be "peer pressured" into the correct spot, and their partner on the balcony is also doing the calculation, so we catch errors pretty quickly.

Before inserting a second absolute value symbol, Don has students observe that, in changing from $\text{abs}(x + 2)$ to $\text{abs}(x + 2) - 3$, some students are again moved to positions below the x axis. His question about how to "flip" those students up with the rest of the crowd generally gets students to volunteer the exact equation: $y = \text{abs}(\text{abs}(x + 2) - 3)$, which he has them do next.

Finally, students return to the classroom to debrief. On subsequent days, Don shows the sheets again, and students describe the graphs in terms of stepping forward, flipping, bending, squishing—all natural terms to describe their own physical movements on Marching Day. He provides or asks students to generate additional functions to graph.

In later weeks, students learn to check their graphs with graphing calculators.

Don notes that students' processing of all they learned from the Marching Day graphs may be curtailed if calculators are brought in sooner. He fears that students may not internalize as much if they view the calculator as simply "a gadget that makes me not have to remember all that stretching and twisting and flipping." Memories of those movements very easily extend to applications of graphs studied in trigonometry and beyond. In some of his comments in the next section, Don explains how.

Discussion between Colleagues

There is no doubt that Marching Day catches the attention of your students as soon as they enter class. On other days, how do you typically start a lesson?

My goal (which sometimes is realized!) is to have the students start the class with their own mathematical observations from the past 24 hours. To get them started, I typically bring up something from my experience—a problem or a comment or something humorous and mathematical. For example, during the first couple of weeks on relations and functions, I began each day by saying something humorous like, "You know, I was driving to the gym for the volleyball tournament this weekend, and I thought to myself, 'Gee, if I drive faster, I'll get there sooner,' and then I thought, 'Hey, speed of trip, length of time of trip—you know, I think we have a function!'" Or "Sunday before church we put a pot roast in the oven to eat for lunch, and the thought of that roast really distracted me during church . . . not the good taste or smell but just wondering how close it was getting to done, getting warmer and warmer each minute, and then I thought, 'Hey, length of time in oven, temperature of roast, you know, we have a function.'" We might also comment about last night's sports event (scores at five-minute intervals constitute a relation) or facts concerning hunting season . . . there is *always* something. Students begin to generate their own humorous "Hey, I think we have a function" stories so that it gradually gets them to start recognizing functions and mathematical relationships everywhere.

Where did you get the idea for this lesson?

I invented it. Although virtually all of my best ideas are "stolen" from others, this particular one is my own doing. I needed a peppy lesson one dismal October day, and so I put all the desks outside the room and locked the door. I let students come into the room only after the bell rang, passing out the cards outside before they entered. It worked so well that I've just gradually altered and refined it but kept the basic premises.

How do you prepare for rain?

I do have a fallback procedure ready. I watch the weather patterns and have everything ready for whichever day in a certain five- to six-day span seems to be the most amenable to standing outside for 30 minutes. However, a couple of years ago I was facing some rainy weather, so I reserved one of the gymnasiums. Kids standing on bleachers get almost as good a view of the nature of the graphs. (Care should be taken to not deface the gym floor with tape, or it might be hard to gain access to that stage in future years.) On another rainy day, I moved my coordinate plane into the cafeteria area. Fortunately my two algebra classes were first and second periods, so that I could set things up before school. I was worried that the observing students wouldn't get quite the same effect, but they stood or sat at roughly the line $y = -15$ and things worked well. In fact, because they were closer to me, I was able to keep them more actively involved in the guessing—I could sneak over and show them the new equation card before my marchers saw it, and they could talk over their predictions. If other indoor facilities are not available, I can always use my classroom.

Describe your students' interactions and reactions as human graphs.

My students have a blast. At the start of the lesson, there is some timidity, especially because the marching group knows that their every movement is on public display before the balcony group. But that goes away as they gain confidence in their ability to correctly position themselves. There is always some good-natured bantering when a person makes a miscalculation and ends up a significant distance from the "neighbors," but a genuine camaraderie grows as they try to develop appropriate pictures for the graphs. Some of them have even tried to imitate an army (all take three steps forward at the same time on a given student command).

The entire lesson is one of communication, from people above shouting correction at people below to neighbors of people below explaining why they should get closer. The idea of continuity occurs simply because people don't like to stand out and away from their peers. In essence, they are peer pressured into graphing continuous functions. In subsequent weeks and months, every time that I am able to clear up a misunderstanding by reference to something from that lesson, I hear happy sighs and an occasional "Can we do that again?"

How do you assess student understanding of the lesson?

That's an easy one to answer. My primary feedback is immediate, not just from their correct movement but from their entire body language. I get primary feedback from students in the balcony group who offer corrective comments to their clones or to the group as a whole. I can see from the movements of students who are on the grid not only the accuracy of their reasoning but also, by how fast they move, their sense of confidence or insecurity. I have more than enough sheets of equations, and I am sure to keep a marking pen with me, so that I can create variations of it on the spot for the additional practice students may need.

I get secondary feedback when we go upstairs and debrief. The following day I get a considerable amount of feedback when I essentially march through two-thirds of the cards again on the overhead and listen to their conceptions and misconceptions. I get further feedback when I watch them making drawings later that period. The calculator provides me with still more opportunity for assessment—students inundate me in the following days with questions concerning why it didn't draw what they thought it would. As I listen to their questions, I am frequently able to adjust their thinking a little.

Oftentimes, teachers will bypass a good engaging activity because they think it will take too much class time. How would you convince a teacher to give it a try?

The additional time we take to do the graphs is *well* worth it. My students learn a remarkable amount of material in a short time. Problems distinguishing domain and range are dispelled because it's not just a matter of confusing the first and second coordinate but of confusing your card with your location on the plane. One year we made a reference to a "house of cards," and that phrase stuck with the kids, because the idea of a house corresponds to the idea of a domain. So, we distinguish between domain and range ("What does your card say?" vs. "Where do you march?"). We also introduce the concepts of inverse functions and rational functions, rigid transformations, stretching and flip transformations, and the basic idea behind absolute value.

Finally, nothing is as concrete a model as using the students themselves for points on a plane. I have done it now five times and have modified it each time. What goes particularly well is that every student has to buy into it. Nobody can hide—even if they get by the first few graphs by just being "neighborly." It's also more interesting for us to talk about the moves that students make in given situations rather than the moves a calculator makes. For example, adding 9 to the function will make everyone take nine steps forward. Absolute value makes the quadrant 3 and 4 students literally jump the axis. When we graph $xy = 18$, we have all kinds of analogies and stories to explain what happens to the person whose card is $x = 0$, and it makes for an easy transition to rational functions at the appropriate stage of the course.

Comment on the extensions of this process to trigonometry and beyond.

One of the biggest payoffs for me and for students is that we encounter the idea of analytic geometry transformations early in the year. We haven't really even discussed linear or quadratic functions at this point. I really believe that the human graphs they constructed enhanced their understanding of concepts such as the ideas that adding a constant to a function raises it, multiplying a function by a constant stretches or squishes it (with a possible flip when the factor is negative), and taking the absolute value of a function bends the function at the x intercepts.

When I hit quadratic functions, I begin with the function $y = x^2$, and then leap to $(y - 2) = (x - 3)^2$. We discuss how the vertex seems to have been moved, and we tie it to $y = (x - 3)^2 + 2$. By the time we get to conics, the idea of translating the center doesn't even need to be brought up. Likewise, the idea of replacing the variables in $x^2 + y^2 = 25$ with $x/2$ and $y/3$ is an obvious one for them. Exponential functions have the property that $y = 2\sin5(x - 7) + 2$ gives the same graph as $y = (2^x)(2^3)$, or $y = 8(2^x)$, so students are quick to see that a horizontal shift of an exponential function gives the same result as a vertical stretch. We explore the properties of logarithms by graphing $y = \log(4x)$ and noticing that there is an apparent vertical shift.

Someone will always note that $\log(4x) = \log4 + \log x$, so the graph is an obvious one, and the nice idea about logarithms (the inverse of exponential functions) is that a horizontal stretch/squish is equivalent to a vertical shift. In fact, the entire inverse-function concept occurs when I ask them to graph $x = \text{abs}(y)$. Invariably, students come up to me the next day having thought about what it looks like, and we generalize that when you trade the variables, you trade the axes the variables are controlled by. That's all it takes—for a first visit.

By the time these kids get to the trig and circular functions and we look at the basic types of graphs, it takes very little time to get them to graph variations like $y = 2\sin5(x - 7)+2$. I have much better results with long-term ability to mentally picture graphs, and we are able to use our graphing calculators as a tool for verification instead of as the all-knowing mechanical genie.

Any extension ideas?

Each year more ideas for extending this process come to mind. Currently, each student has an invisible coordinate plane with them at all times. It sits three inches out from their face, with the origin at nose level (similar to facing the plane from an overhead projector). When I need a change of pace in classroom routine, I tell them to put some points out on their coordinate plane using their fingers. Then I tell them to add 3 to their second coordinates, and I check to see if all hands levitate appropriately. We double the first coordinates, take the absolute value of the second coordinates, all those things we did at the beginning of Marching Day. It's a nice, quick review. A good set of test questions is to give them the one-dimensional analogous situation, like playing the piano, and have them describe movements.

Also, we have ventured into three-variable equations. For this lesson, I put the x and y axes on the classroom floor and string a paper tape that represents the positive z-axis from the ceiling. We discuss plotting points, midpoints, distance between points, and the ways that three variable "linear" equations now produce planes. Students soon see why we need an algebraic plan to solve a three-dimensional system—graphing three planes in space to see their point of intersection usually makes their heads spin! The next day I ask students to imagine a three-dimensional coordinate set of axes in front of them, oriented just like the classroom—x and y axes on a plane parallel to the floor, with the z axis vertical. Then we play the same game—pick points at random with your fingers, add 4 to the z coordinate, and reflect the points through the origin. This is great fun! And you get a lot of information quickly as you watch the students who need to be watched.

My analysis class marched in previous years and is now exploring functions in a more general sense. We've discovered quite easily that replacing the x variable in an equation by $x + 3$ forces the x coordinate to become 3 *less*, and their background with Marching Day makes the jump to the graph an easy one. We have developed a *law of compensation*, which basically says that whatever you do to the *variable* creates the opposite effect on the *coordinate*, and, because we know how changing the coordinates affects the graph, we can graph stuff such as $y = \text{abs }(4x)^3 + (4x)^2) - 3$ pretty quickly by simply thinking about the graph of $y = x^3 + x^2$ *as*, $y = x^2(x + 1)$. We "sew" the graph through the appropriate x intercepts (twice through the origin, because there are three factors, so that the graph comes out the same side it went in), then we squish it toward the y axis, flip up quadrants 3 and 4, and slide the graph down 3.

Any other tips for readers who wish to try Marching Day?

Replacing a second coordinate with its reciprocal is a difficult idea for students but really handy the next year when we graph all sorts of equations of the form $y = 1/f(x)$, including the secant, cosecant, and cotangent functions in trigonometry.

For graphs similar to $y = 6/x$, I've palmed the queen (zero) cards beforehand and dealt them on purpose to people who I thought could use the teasing. A student who is overconfident beyond his or her skill level is a natural here (someone who needs to be gently teased into place), because when we get to $y = 6/x$, he or she will be frequently confused about where to stand and often will wander to the origin—only to have me tell him or her that, instead, I have "poofed" him or her into temporary nonexistence and would he or she please explain why.

This student is one of the "special" students that we talk about when we review locations of those who "just disappeared" or were "lazy" because they didn't want to move when everyone else did or whom we could trust to remember the entire graph ($y = x^2$ or $y = abs(x)$) because they had a "special location." Initially, it is also best not to give equations that are better viewed from a horizontal shift perspective, such as $y = (x - 3)^2$. Although students can graph it just by point plotting, I prefer that they think of it as a sideways shift of the graph of $y = x^2$. If the students were to actually slide left or right on Marching Day, they might feel the need to exchange their cards, because it indicates their first coordinate. That would be very confusing, so I suggest waiting until the study of point-slope form for lines to introduce the idea of horizontal shifts in equations.

A way to introduce the point-slope form of a line that forges later links to higher-order equations is to just take an equation such as $y = 2x$ and then have Mr. $x = 0$ migrate somewhere, taking the rest of the class with him. If he wanders to the point (2,3), then we get the equation $(y - 3) = 2(x - 2)$. Similarly, when studying quadratic equations, start with $y = 2x^2$, have Mr. $x = 0$ migrate again, to get the analogous equation $(y - 3) = 2(x - 2)^2$. If students are prepared for the idea of points migrating, they don't have any trouble with the effects on the resulting equations.

How else do you use the Marching Day experience?

Need an opening activity? Most any day, ask students to pull out their invisible coordinate line/plane/space and plot 10 imaginary points, then call out transformations for them to demonstrate. I tease students who put all fingers out in a single quadrant and also query a few kids with thoughts like, "Brieana, is your little finger above or below the x axis?" or "No fair, Julian, making all 10 finger points collinear." This is a way to get them to think about the locations of the points. In the near future, having students call out the transformation for me to observe should be fun. Imagine having a student say, "Multiply the x coordinate by a negative 3," and then exclaim, "Oh wait, let me turn around so you can see it from my direction." I think I have the germ of even functions/odd functions lurking in that idea somewhere.

Commentary

In their review of the research on students' understanding of graphing, Wagner and Parker (1993) report that little more than half of the students who have completed an algebra course are able to complete work beyond point plotting. In addition, those who progress to graphing simple equations have difficulty translating information from the graph to its equation. Other researchers cite the concepts of variables and functions as troublesome for many students to understand (Chazan and Yerushalmy, 2003; Schoenfeld and Arcavi, 1988). Even after completing high school and a college freshman course, Oehrtman, Carlson, and Thompson (2008) report, students' understanding of functions remains poor.

To remediate some of these gaps is considered crucial to the understanding of higher mathematics. Steketee and Scher (2012) draw from research to recommend that teachers provide students "ample opportunities to directly and continuously manipulate variables as they observe and analyze the resulting behavior of functions. Such experiences could include a variety of visually effective representations that highlight different aspects of the concept of function and encourage students to develop a fuller concept image" (262).

Don's *human graph* activity provides such experiences for students. His requirement that students simultaneously use different ways of looking at classes of functions as they think through and connect the tabular, symbolic, and graphical forms of representations is important to *what* and *how much* students learn. How does the human graph experience promote such learning? Students first predict what the graph might look like, begin with the equation (symbolic) to perform mental calculations (tabular), and then physically move to a point on the plane to complete the graph (graphical). In so doing, the model fulfills some of the CCSSM standards on building new functions from existing functions and analyzing functions using different representations. What is particularly strong and significant about Don's human graphs is that they serve as a unifying, coherent, yet concrete model for the progression of the graphing of functions from algebra to trigonometry while incorporating SMP4.

Don's decision to go beyond his classroom walls was an excellent investment of class time not only because the activity focuses on important mathematics but also because of its positive impact on students' dispositions: "Students enjoyed the idea of a coordinate plane on the concrete where everyone walks. Taking them outside automatically aroused their curiosity, which in turn produced a positive frame of mind." Once, when Don did the lesson again, the yearbook staff came and took pictures. "They were seniors who remembered it from their young and innocent days and wanted to record it."

I asked Don if he had any published works and was reminded that he had written a wonderful article, "The Power of One" (*The Mathematics Teacher*, October 1993). When I expressed my appreciation for the article, he e-mailed me back to say:

> Thanks for the ego boost. You must have known how my calculus class went today . . . 3D vector projections, dot products, and a *warm* afternoon *right after* lunch. . . . I tried having people holding my Tinkertoy coordinate system, other people holding my vectors and shining flashlights to help us see the shadows cast on other vectors, but I think pulling teeth would have been easier . . . ahh well . . . tomorrow's another day.

Unit Overview

Marching from Algebra to Trigonometry and Beyond

Aim: How can we easily graph the effects of constants on some functions?

Objectives: To have students create human graphs to deduce the effects of transformations on the coordinate plane.

Course: Algebra/Algebra 2/Trigonometry/Precalculus.

Source: Original.

Number of 50-Minute Periods: Two to three.

NCTM/CCSS Standards: Geometry: Congruence 2 (G-CO.2); • Functions: Interpreting Functions: IF.A.1, 2; IF.C.7b, 7e, 9; Functions: Building Functions: BF.3, 4; Analyze Functions: F.IF.7a, 7b, 7e, 8a, 8b, 9.

NCTM Processes/Mathematical Practices: Mathematics as Problem Solving, Communication, Representation/SMP1, SMP4, SMP7, SMP8.

Mathematical Content: Students begin with basic graphs of the form $y = x$ and $y = abs(x)$ to determine the effects of various transformations on the graphs. Extensions to trigonometry and analysis are included.

Prerequisites: Experience graphing $y = mx + b$, $y = x^2$, and $y = abs(x)$.

Materials and Tools

◆ Large space to draw a coordinate grid on the floor or pavement.
◆ Adding-machine paper for axis. The length varies with room available. Typically an x axis of 30 feet long, numbered from -10 to 10 at about 1.5-foot intervals, and a y axis about 45 feet long, numbered from -10 to 20 at about 1.5-foot intervals, works well.
◆ Sets of equations written on 8" x 10" sheet, one function to a sheet.
◆ Graphing calculator for pairs of students.
◆ Playing cards, ace through eight of any suit, plus the black queens.

Management Procedures

◆ Before class, draw or tape the axes on the ground.
◆ Have each student stand on a point.
◆ Call out simple commands and have students move about the grid to graph them.

- Call out sets of functions and have students graph them.
- Give each student a playing card and send him or her to stand on the grid at a point whose first coordinate matches his or her card.
- Divide students into groups. Have one group continue graphing while the others observe and assess the graphs produced.
- Reverse roles.
- Discuss the process with students and have them determine the effects of the variable on the graphs.
- Present new graphs or ask students to create new ones to sketch by hand. Have them check their results with each other and the graphing calculator.

Assessment

Observe and make note of the confidence levels of students as they march to form new graphs, participate in the follow-up discussion, and hand-sketch new functions.

Resources

1. For a direct application of Don's human graph to inequalities while keeping the students in the classroom, see activity three in the NCTM article by Wallace-Gomez:

   Wallace-Gomez, P. (2014). "Algebraic Activities Aid Discovery Lessons." *Mathematics Teacher* 107(5), 354–58.

2. To make the explicit connection between transformations of ordered pairs and transformations of functions, see this article by Hall and Giacin:

   Hall, B., and R. Giacin. (2013). Exploring Function Transformation Using the Common Core. *Mathematics Teacher* 107(2), 132–37.

14

The CCSSM: Making It Happen

The profiles in this book show how teachers who are correctly implementing the vision of the NCTM/CCSSM standards provide multiple opportunities for their students to engage in solving worthwhile problems for which there are no fixed rules. As with real-life challenging problems, no hints are given that say, "Use this very quick way to solve it!" The students have to read, research, and analyze the problem; decide on some plausible pathways for a solution; do the work to solve it; and then present and defend the work. Throughout this process, students quickly apply their basic skills and use technology when appropriate. As students struggle to find solutions, the teacher or friends help by facilitating when necessary. Equally important, small groups work in teams to solve the problems, thus building students' capacity to listen and appreciate different ideas as they try to communicate their own. It is through such processes that students develop the awareness and persistence to try a multistep approach to solving problems, not just in mathematics but also in all areas of life—school, work, family, and community. Such productive engagement with problems provides the tools for productive thinkers to engage in society as productive citizens.

CCSSM: New Way for Teaching Math?

Most commentaries on the CCSSM refer to it as a "new" way of teaching math. For example, in the article by Motoko (2014) in the *New York Times*, he writes, "The new instructional approach in math seeks to help children understand and use it as a problem-solving tool instead of teaching them merely to repeat formulas over and over. They are also being asked to apply concepts to real-life situations and explain their reasoning."

As the profiles in this book show, teachers who have adhered to the principles in NCTM's *Curriculum Standards* and its revisions from 1989 to 2001 have taught and continue to teach math in this "new" way. They would likely express feelings similar to those of former NCTM president Linda Gojak in her interview with Motoko:

> I taught math very much like the Common Core for many years. . . . When parents would question it, my response was "Just hang in there with me," and at the end of the year they would come and say this was the best year their kids had in math."
>
> (*New York Times*, July 29, 2014)

That CCSSM is seen as a new way for doing math is a sad commentary on how long it takes for meaningful educational change—that is not mandated—to be implemented in the classroom. Would it be easier if such a change were mandated for a nation? Motoko writes: "In Louisiana, John White, state superintendent of education, said that politics aside, applying the Common Core math standards would take time. 'This is a shift for an entire society,' he said. 'No one should be under any illusion that it's going to take just a year or two to rethink the way that we teach mathematics, because it is really challenging'" (*New York Times,* July 29, 2014).

Guidelines and Recommendations for Implementing CCSSM

In the first edition of this book, the final chapter raised issues and concerns that educators and the community needed to address to educate our children for their future, and it also provided some recommendations. Three books already accomplish those tasks very well, so it is not necessary for this edition to do so. For additional advice, guidelines, and recommendations on how to realize NCTM's and CCSSM's vision for students, we recommend these resources:

1. *Principles to Actions: Ensuring Mathematical Success for All* (NCTM, 2014)
2. *It's Time: Themes and Imperatives for Mathematics Education* (NCSM, 2014)
3. *Smarter Than We Think* (Seeley, 2014)

We wish our readers joy and success in their productive struggles for providing the best education for our children.

References

Boaler, J. (2002). Learning from Teaching: Exploring the Relationship between Reform Curriculum and Equity. *Journal for Research in Mathematics Education* 33(4), 239–58.

Burrill, G. (1996). President's Message Column. *National Council of Teachers of Mathematics News Bulletin* (July/August), 3.

Carpenter, T. P., and E. Fennema. (1992). Cognitively Guided Instruction: Building on the Knowledge of Students and Teachers. In *Researching Educational Reform: The Case of School Mathematics in the United States,* edited by W. Secada (special issue of *International Journal of Educational Research*), 457–70.

Chapin, S. (1997). *The Partners in Change Handbook: A Professional Development Curriculum in Mathematics.* Boston: Boston University Press.

Chazan, D., and M. Yerushalmy. (2003). On Appreciating the Cognitive Complexity of School Algebra: Research on Algebra Learning and Directions of Curricular Change. In *A Research Companion to the Principles and Standards for School Mathematics*, edited by J. Kilpatrick, D. Schifter, and G. Martin, 123–135. Reston, VA: NCTM.

Cirillo, M. (2013). What Are Some Strategies for Facilitating Productive Classroom Discussions? NCTM Research Brief Discussion. www.nctm.org/uploadedFiles/Research_News_and_Advocacy/Research/Clips_and_Briefs/research%20brief%2020%20%20strategies%20of%20discussion.pdf. Retrieved March 28, 2014.

Clark, L., J. DePiper, T. Frank, M. Nishio, P. Campbell, T. Smith, et al. (2014). Teacher Characteristics Associated with Mathematics Teachers' Beliefs and Awareness of Their Students' Mathematical Dispositions. *Journal for Research in Mathematics Education* 45(2), 246–84.

Confrey, J. (1990). What constructivism implies for teaching. In *Constructivist views on the teaching and learning of mathematics*, edited by R.B. Davis, C.A. Maher, and N. Noddings, 107–22. Reston, VA: National Council of Teachers of Mathematics.

Council of Chief State School Officers. (2013, April). Interstate Teacher Assessment and Support Consortium. In *TASC Model Core Teaching Standards and Learning Progressions for Teachers 1.0: A Resource for Ongoing Teacher Development.* Washington, DC: Author. www.ccsso.org/Documents/2013/2013_INTASC_Learning_Progressions_for_Teachers.pdf. Retrieved March 24, 2014.

———. (2011). Interstate Teacher Assessment and Support Consortium (InTASC) Model Core Teaching Standards: A Resource for State Dialogue. www.ccsso.org/Resources/Programs/Interstate_Teacher_Assessment_Consortium_%28InTASC%29.html. Retrieved March 24, 2013.

Council of Chief State School Officers and the National Governors Association. (2010). *The Common Core State Standards.* www.corestandards.org/terms-of-use. Retrieved March 24, 2014.

Crowley, A. (2013). Teaching the Common Standards in Math: Getting Rid of the GPS. *Education Week*, March 13, 2013. Retrieved October 20, 2013 from www.edweek.org/tm/articles/2013/03/13/ccio_crowley_math.html

Cuoco, A., P. Goldenberg, and J. Mark. (2010). Organizing a Curriculum around Mathematical Habits of Mind. *Mathematics Teacher* 103(9), 682–89. http://www2.edc.org/cme/showcase/HabitsOfMind.pdf

———. (1996). Habits of Mind: An Organizing Principle for a Mathematics Curriculum. *Journal of Mathematical Behavior* 15(4), 375–402. www2.edc.org/cme/showcase/HabitsOfMind.pdf. Retrieved April 27, 2014.

Curtis, J. (2011). Project-Based Learning: Real-World Issues Motivate Students. *Edutopia, What Works in Education, April 5, 2014*. www.edutopia.org/project-based-learning-student-motivation. Retrieved April 5, 2014.

Darling-Hammond, L. (2014). One Piece of the Whole: Teacher Evaluation as Part of a Comprehensive System for Teaching and Learning. *American Educator* (Spring). www.aft.org/pdfs/americaneducator/spring2014/Darling-Hammond.pdf. Retrieved April 14.

Davis, B. (1996). *Teaching Mathematics: Toward a Sound Alternative*. New York: Garland.

DeJarnette, A., J. Dao, and G. González. (2014). Promoting Small-Group Discussions. *Mathematics Teacher* 19(7): 415–19.

Dewey, J. (1929). *The Quest for Certainty*. New York: Minton, Balch.

Fowler, B., and R. Swift. (1999). Relabeling Dice. *College Mathematics Journal* 30(3), 204–8.

Franklin, C., G. Kader, D. Mewborn, J. Moreno, R. Peck, M. Perry, et al. (2007). *Guidelines for Assessment and Instruction in Statistics Education (GAISE) Report*. Alexandria, VA: American Statistical Association. www.amstat.org/Education/gaise/GAISECollege.htm. Retrieved March 20, 2014.

Gallian, J. (2013). *Contemporary Abstract Algebra*, 8th edition. Boston: Brooks/Cole Cengage Learning.

Gardner, Martin. (1978). Mathematical Games. *Scientific American* 238, 19–32.

Germain-McCarthy, Y. (2001). *Bringing the NCTM to Life: Exemplary Practices from Middle Schools*. New City, NY: Eye on Education.

Germain-McCarthy, Y. (2014). *Bringing the Common Core Standards to Life: Exemplary Practices from Middle Schools*. New City, NY: Tyler and Taylor Group.

Gojak, L. (2014). A Reflection of 25 Years in Mathematics Education. *NCTM Summing Up*, April 1, 2014 (2012–2014). National Council of Teachers of Mathematics. www.nctm.org/about/content.aspx?id=35990. Retrieved April 1, 2014 from www.nctm.org/about/content.aspx?id=41883.

———. (2013a). Common Core State Standards for Mathematics: An Uncommon Opportunity. *NCTM Summing Up*, April 4, 2013 (2012–2014). National Council of Teachers of Mathematics. www.nctm.org/about/content.aspx?id=35990. Retrieved March 24, 2014.

———. (2013b). Are We Obsessed with Assessment? *NCTM Summing Up*, November 4, 2013 (2012–2014). National Council of Teachers of Mathematics. www.nctm.org/about/content.aspx?id=35990. Retrieved March 24, 2014.

Haberman, M. (1991). The Pedagogy of Poverty versus Good Teaching. *Phi Delta Kappan* 73(4), 290–94. www.habermanfoundation.org. Retrieved March 24, 2014.

Hall, B., and R. Giacin. (2013). Exploring Function Transformation Using the Common Core. *Mathematics Teacher* 107(2), 132–37.

Hiebert, J. (2003). Signposts for Teaching Mathematics through Problem Solving. Teaching Mathematics through Problem Solving: Prekindergarten–Grade 6, edited by F. K. Lester Jr., 53–61. Reston, VA: National Council of Teachers of Mathematics.

Hiebert, J., T. P. Carpenter, E. Fennema, K. Fuson, P. Human, H. Murray, A. Olivier, and D. Wearne. (1996). Problem Solving as a Basis for Reform in Curriculum and Instruction: The Case of Mathematics. *Educational Researcher* 25(4), 12–21.

Hiebert, J., R. Gallimore, H. Garnier, K. B. Givvin, H. Hollingsworth, J. Jacobs, et al. (2003). *Teaching Mathematics in Seven Countries: Results from the TIMSS 1999 Video Study*. (NCES 2003–013). Washington, DC: U.S. Department of Education, National Center for Education Statistics.

Hiebert, J., and D. Grouws. (2007). The Effect of Classroom Mathematics Teaching on Students' Learning. In *Second Handbook of Research on Mathematics Teaching and Learning*, edited by F. Lester, 371–404. Charlotte, NC: Information Age.

Kaput, J. J. (1993). Technology and Mathematics Education. In *Handbook of Research On Mathematics Teaching and Learning*, edited by D. A. Grouws, 515–55. New York: Macmillan.

Kelly, D., H. Xie, C. W. Nord, F. Jenkins, F., J. Y. Chan, and D. Kastberg. (2013). Performance of U.S. 15-Year-Old Students in Mathematics, Science, and Reading Literacy in an International

Context: First Look at PISA 2012 (NCES 2014–024). U.S. Department of Education. Washington, DC: National Center for Education Statistics. http://nces.ed.gov/pubsearch. Retrieved April 1, 2014.

Kimball, M., and N. Smith. (2014). The Myth of "I'm Bad at Math." *Atlantic Monthly Group*, www.theatlantic.com/education/archive/2013/10/the-myth-of-im-bad-at-math/280914/. Retrieved March 18, 2014.

Knuth, D. (1992). Two Notes on Notation. *American Mathematical Monthly* 99(5), 403–22.

Lappan, Glenda, James Fey, William Fitzgerald, Susan Friel, and Elizabeth Phillips. (2002). *Connected Mathematics*. Glenview, IL: Prentice Hall.

Lewis, C. (2000). Lesson Study: The Core of Japanese Development. Paper presented at to the Special Group on Research in Mathematics Education, American Educational Research Association Meetings, New Orleans, April 2000.

Ma, L. (1999). *Knowing and Teaching Elementary Mathematics: Teachers' Understanding of Fundamental Mathematics in China and the U.S.* Hillside, New Jersey: Lawrence Erlbaum.

Matthews, M., C. Hlas, and T. M. Finken. (2009). Using Lesson Study and Four-Column Lesson Planning with Preservice Teachers C. *Mathematics Teacher* 102(7), 504–9.

Mokoto, R. (2014). Math under Common Core Has Even Parents Stumbling. *New York Times*, Sunday, June 29, 2014. www.nytimes.com/2014/06/30/us/math-under-common-core-has-even-parents-stumbling.html?_r=1. Retrieved July 1, 2014.

Mullis, I. V. S., M. O. Martin, P. Foy, and A. Arora. (2012). Chestnut Hill, MA: TIMSS & PIRLS International Study Center, Boston College. http://timssandpirls.bc.edu/timsspirls2011/downloads/TP11_UserGuide.pdf. Retrieved July 23, 2014

National Council of Supervisors of Mathematics. (2014). *It's Time: Themes and Imperatives for Mathematics Education (NCSM, 2014)*. Bloomington, IN: Solution Tree Press.

National Council of Teachers of Mathematics. (1989). *Curriculum and Evaluation Standards for Learning Mathematics*. Reston, VA: National Council of Teachers of Mathematics.

———. (1991). *Professional Standards for Teaching Mathematics*. Reston, VA: National Council of Teachers of Mathematics.

———. (2000). *The Principles and Standards for School Mathematics*. Reston, VA: National Council of Teachers of Mathematics.

———. (2006). *Curriculum Focal Points for Prekindergarten through Grade 8 Mathematics*. Reston, VA: National Council of Teachers of Mathematics.

———. (2009). *Focus in High School Mathematics: Reasoning and Sense Making*. Reston, VA: National Council of Teachers of Mathematics.

———. (2010). *Developing Essential Understanding of Functions in Grades 9–12*. Reston, VA: National Council of Teachers of Mathematics.

———. (2014). *Principles to Actions: Ensuring Mathematical Success for All*. Reston, VA: National Council of Teachers of Mathematics.

———. (n.d.). *An Administrator's Guide to High School Mathematic*. www.nctm.org/uploaded-Files/Math_Standards/FHSM_AdminGuide.pdf. Retrieved April 1, 2014.

National Governors Association Center for Best Practices and Council of Chief State School Officers. (2010). Common Core State Standards for Mathematics. Washington, DC: NGA Center for Best Practices and CCSSO. www.corestandards.org. Retrieved October 20, 2013.

———. (2013). High School Publishers' Criteria for the Common Core State Standards for Mathematics. www.corestandards.org/assets/Math_Publishers_Criteria_HS_Spring%2020 13_FINAL.pdf. Retrieved April 1, 2014.

National Research Council. (2001). *Adding It Up: Helping Children Learn Mathematics*, edited by J. Kilpatrick, J. Swafford, and B. Findell. Mathematics Learning Study Committee, Center for Education, Division of Behavioral and Social Sciences and Education. Washington, DC: National Academy Press.

Noll, J., and J. Shaughnessy. (2012). Aspects of Students' Reasoning About Variation in Empirical Sampling Distributions. *Journal for Research in Mathematics Education*, 43(5), 509–556.

Oehrtman, M., M. Carlson, and P. W. Thompson. (2008). Foundational Reasoning Abilities That Promote Coherence in Students' Understandings of Function. In *Making the Connection: Research and Practice in Undergraduate Mathematics,* edited by Marilyn P. Carlson and Chris Rasmussen, 27–42. Washington, DC: Mathematical Association of America.

Organization for Economic Cooperation and Development. (2010). PISA 2009 Results: Executive Summary, p. 41. www.oecd.org/edu/school/programmeforinternationalstudentassessment pisa/33693997.pdf. Retrieved April 2, 2014.

Organization for Economic Cooperation and Development. (2013). PISA 2012 Results: What Makes Schools Successful? Resources, Policies and Practices (Volume 4), PISA, OECD Publishing. http://dx.doi.org/10.1787/9789264201156-en. Retrieved April 2014.

———. (2014). Do Students Have the Drive to Succeed? InFocus March Newsletter. www.oecd. org/pisa/pisaproducts/pisainfocus/pisa-in-focus-n37-%28eng%29-final.pdf. Retrieved April 1, 2014.

Partnership for Assessment of Readiness for College Careers. (2014). Model Content Framework— Mathematics. www.parcconline.org/mcf/mathematics/parcc-model-content-frameworks-browser. Retrieved April 1, 2014.

Peterson, B., D. Corey, B. Lewis, and J. Bukarau. (2013). Intellectual and Other Engagement Principles of Mathematic Instruction. *Mathematics Teacher* 106(5), 447–50.

Piaget, J. (1973). *To Understand Is to Invent.* New York: Grossman.

Reardon, S. (2013). No Rich Child Left Behind. *New York Times.* Opinion Page. http://opinionator. blogs.nytimes.com/2013/04/27/no-rich-child-left-behind/. Retrieved March 26, 2014.

Rogers, C. (2013). The Potential of Participatory Culture & the Pedagogy of Poverty. National Writing Project. http://digitalis.nwp.org/site-blog/potential-participatory-culture-pedagogy/4649. Retrieved July 25, 2014.

Scheaffer, R., & J. Tabor. (2008). Statistics in the High School Mathematics Curriculum: Building Sound Reasoning Under Uncertainty. *Mathematics Teacher* 102(1), 56.

Schmidt, William H., Curtis C. McKnight, and Senta A. Raizen. (1996). *A Splintered Vision: An Investigation of U.S. Science and Mathematics Education.* Dordrecht: Kluwer Academic Publishers, 1996.

Schoenfeld, A., and A. Arcavi. (1988). "On the Meaning of Variable." *Mathematics Teacher* 81(6): 420–27.

Seeley, L. C. (2014). *Smarter Than We Think.* Sausalito, CA: Math Solutions.

Shaughnessy, J. M. (1992). Research in Probability and Statistics: Reflections and Directions. In *Handbook of Research on Mathematics Teaching and Learning,* edited by D. A. Grouws, 465–94. Reston, VA: National Council of Teachers of Mathematics.

Simon, M. A. (1995). Reconstructing Mathematics Pedagogy from a Constructivist Perspective. *Journal for Research in Mathematics Education* 26(2), 114–45.

Slavin, R. E. (1990). *Cooperative Learning: Theory, Research, and Practice.* Englewood Cliffs, NJ: Prentice Hall.

Smith, M., E. Hughes, R. Engle, and M. K. Stein. (2009). Orchestrating Classroom Discussions. *Mathematics Teaching in the Middle School* 14 (9), 548–556.

Smith, T. (2014). Does Teaching Kids to Get 'Gritty' Help Them Get Ahead? National Public Radio interview with Angela Duckworth. March 17, 2014. www.npr.org/2014/03/17/290089998/does-teaching-kids-to-get-gritty-help-them-get-ahead. Retrieved March 28, 2014.

Stein, C.C. (2007). Let's Talk. Promoting Mathematical Discourse in the Classroom. *Mathematics Teacher* 101 (4), 285–89.

Steketee, S., and D. Scher. (2012). Using Multiple Representations to Teach Composition of Functions. *Mathematics Teacher* 106 (4), 261–68.

Stiff, L. V. (2001). President's Message Column. *National Council of Teachers of Mathematics News Bulletin* (December), 3.

Stiff, L. V., J. L. Johnson, and M. R. Johnson. (1993). Cognitive Issues in Mathematics Education. In *Research Ideas for the Classroom: High School Mathematics,* edited by S. P. Wilson, 3–20. Reston, VA: National Council of Teachers of Mathematics.

Stiggins, R., and J. Chappuis. (2006). What a Difference a Word Makes: Assessment FOR Learning Rather Than Assessment OF learning. *National Staff Development Council* 27(1) (Winter). http://cusd.capousd.org/edusupport/Articles/What%20a%20Difference%20a%20 Word%20Makes.pdf. Retrieved April 2, 2014.

Sturman, L., B. Burge, R. Cook, and H. Weaving. (2012). *TIMSS 2011: Mathematics and Science Achievement in England.* Slough: NFER.

Takahashi, A., and M. Yoshida. (2004). Ideas for Establishing Lesson-Study Communities. Teaching Children Mathematics (May), 436–43. Reston, VA: National Council of Teachers of Mathematics.

Tennessee Department of Education. (2013). Common Core State Standards: Fluency in Mathematics. http://tncore.org/sites/www/Uploads/2.25.13Additions/fluency%20documents%20 final.pdf form. Retrieved April 1, 2014.

U.S. Department of Education. (2014). Teacher Shortage Area Nationwide List. www2.ed.gov/ about/offices/list/ope/pol/tsa.doc. Retrieved July 23, 2014.

Vygotsky, L. S. (1978). *Mind in Society: The Development of Higher Psychological Processes,* edited by M. Cole, V. John-Steiner, S. Scribner, and E. Souberman. Cambridge, MA: Harvard University Press.

Wagner, S. and S. Parker. (1993). Advancing Algebra. In P. S. Wilson (Ed), *Research Ideas for the Classroom: High School Mathematics.* New York, NY: Macmillan.

Wallace-Gomez, P. (2014). Algebraic Activities Aid Discovery Lessons. *Mathematics Teacher* 107(5), 354–58.

Wheatley, G. H. (1991). Constructivist Perspectives on Science and Mathematics Learning. *Science Education* 75(1), 9–21.

Wilson, L. D. (2007). High-Stakes Testing in Mathematics. In *Second Handbook of Research on Mathematics Teaching and Learning,* edited by F. Lester, 1099–1110. Charlotte, NC: Information Age.

Wood, R. (1987). *Measurement and Assessment in Education and Psychology.* London: Falmer Press.

Yoshida, M. (1999). "Lesson Study: A Case Study of a Japanese Approach to Improving Instruction through School-Based Teacher Development." Ph.D. diss., University of Chicago.

$$3(x^2+y)+2(3y+4B)$$

$$=3x^2+3y+6y+8B$$

$$=3x^2+9y+8B$$

ALSO OF INTEREST

Bringing the Common Core Math Standards to Life

Exemplary Practices from Middle Schools

Yvelyne Germain-McCarthy

As middle schools shift to the Common Core State Standards for Mathematics, many math teachers are left wondering what the new standards should actually look like in the classroom. By taking a look at real Common Core math classrooms across the country, this book shows how effective middle school teachers are meeting the new requirements and covering topics such as proportional reasoning, the Pythagorean theorem, measurements, and more.

978-0-415-73341-0 • 232 pages

SPECIAL FEATURES:

- Real examples of how exemplary teachers are meeting the CCSS in engaging ways
- Commentary sections to show how you can implement the exemplary lessons in your own classroom
- Practical, ready-to-use tools, including unit plans and classroom handouts

---

Routledge
Taylor & Francis Group

Routledge... think about it
www.routledge.com/eyeoneducation